TWO CENTURIES OF RUSSIAN VERSE

two centuries of russian verse

An Anthology

FROM LOMONOSOV TO VOZNESENSKY
EDITED, WITH AN INTRODUCTION
AND NOTES, BY

AVRAHM YARMOLINSKY

TRANSLATIONS FROM THE RUSSIAN BY

BABETTE DEUTSCH

RANDOM HOUSE   NEW YORK

First Printing
© Copyright, 1949, 1962, 1965, 1966, by Avrahm Yarmolinsky
All rights reserved under International
and Pan-American Copyright Conventions.
Published in New York by Random House, Inc.,
and simultaneously in Toronto, Canada,
by Random House of Canada Limited.
Manufactured in the United States of America
by The Haddon Craftsmen, Inc., Scranton, Pennsylvania
Designed by Betty Anderson
Library of Congress catalog card number: 66-10992

ACKNOWLEDGMENTS

The editor herewith thanks:

Max Eastman—for permission to reprint his translation of "Message to Siberia" by Pushkin.

Faber and Faber Ltd.—for permission to reprint the following translations by Frances Cornford and Esther Polianowsky Salaman: "I Come Again" by Fet, "The Hay Harvest" by Maikov, "The Hawk" by Blok, from *Poems from the Russian*, chosen and translated by Frances Cornford and Esther Polianowsky Salaman, Faber and Faber Ltd., London, 1943.

Harold Furth—for permission to reprint his translation of "Second Canzone" by Gumilyov.

Roman N. Grynberg—for permission to translate Mandelshtam's "Lady Past Mistress You," and "For the Sake of the Thundrous Valor" from *Aerial Ways*, a Russian-language miscellany, edited and published by Roman N. Grynberg, New York, 1961, Volume 2.

Vladimir Markov—for permission to reprint his translation of "Incantation by Laughter" by Khlebnikov.

Victor Erlich and Jack Hirschman—for permission to reprint their translation of "Moonlit Night" by Mayakovsky.

Holt, Rinehart and Winston, Inc.—for permission to reprint Richard Wilbur's translation of "Anti-Worlds" by Voznesensky, from *Half-Way to the Moon*, edited by Patricia Blake and Max Hayward. Copyright © 1963 by Encounter Ltd.

Random House, Inc.—for permission to reprint the following poems from *The Poems, Prose and Plays of Alexander Pushkin*, edited by Avrahm Yarmolinsky, Copyright 1936 by Random House, Inc.: "Though Soporific," "Winter Evening," "On the Translation of the *Iliad*," "Elegy," "From *Eugene Onegin*, Tatyana's Letter."

FOREWORD

Beginning with verse by a writer of the mid-eighteenth century, when modern Russian letters took their rise, this anthology concludes with works by men and women who are responding with the freshness and energy of youth to their world in our own day. The arrangement is roughly chronological. By and large poets belonging to the same group are placed together. The volume is made up largely of shorter poems and in some instances part of a sequence finds a place. Included also are several passages, sufficiently integrated to be excerpted, from compositions too long to be presented in full. Such are the excerpts from Pushkin's *Eugene Onegin*, "Poltava," "The Bronze Horseman," from Lermontov's "The Demon," from Mayakovsky's "Going Home!" Room was made for two unabridged long verse narratives: Blok's celebrated poem of the Revolution, "The Twelve," and Pushkin's delightful *Tale of the Golden Cockerel*, based on a story in Washington Irving's *Alhambra* and source of the libretto for Rimsky-Korsakov's *Coq d'Or*.

Poems were chosen primarily for their intrinsic qualities, in the hope that these would show through the veil of translation. Naturally, limitations of space played a part in the selection, as did the resistance of some texts to Englishing. Certain pages were allotted to verse that, being eloquent of the period and the circumstances in which it was written, has a documentary value. Here belong such diverse pieces as Ryleyev's "Citizen," Nekrasov's "Freedom," Marienhof's "October," Mayakovsky's "Tale of How Fadey Learned of the Law Protecting Workingmen," made to order for the Moscow local of the Printers' Union. The poems from Akhmatova's "Requiem" cycle, composed in the late thirties and still on the Index in the Soviet Union, are an example of work that is of both topical and literary interest.

A large part of the book is devoted to poems written since the Revolution. It is not, however, fully representative of the work published in the Soviet Union during the past half century: too much of that was propagandist, thick with what Yeats called "impurities." Some of it has been admitted here, for reasons stated above. There are not a few lyrics composed in the past dozen years, during which verse has been flourishing with new vigor. Among the authors of this period are Yevtushenko and Voznesensky, already known outside of Russia. In most cases one cannot predict whether a young writer will develop into a poet of stature, but it seemed well to include pieces by novices which are of good workmanship and expressive not of mandatory optimism but of a genuinely sanguine temper, of delight in and sensitivity to the natural world, of honest personal feeling.

Strict faithfulness to the form and texture of the originals was naturally not feasible, nor even always desirable, since the prosodic practices and resources of the two languages, while similar, are by no means identical. Nevertheless, in not a few instances it was possible to adhere to the metre and the rhyme scheme of the Russian work. Thus the unexpected changes of metre in Tyutchev's "Silentium" have been reproduced in the English version. Again, off-rhyme, so widely used in twentieth-century Russian verse and not unfamiliar to readers of poetry in English, was employed in translating a number of lyrics, notably those by Pasternak. The method followed throughout was the antithesis of two diverse styles of translation now practiced: one is the bald literal version, or "pony," in a frame of explication; the other uses the original text as a springboard for leaping into an almost totally different poem, representative of the translator rather than of the author. As distinguished from versions in these modes, the translations in this book are the result of an attempt to give, as fully as the exigencies of the task and the skill of the translator allowed, equivalents of the original poems. Offering as it does a glimpse of two hundred years of verse-making, this anthology presents work that of course varies enormously in theme, form, texture, and tone.

Most of the poems were rendered into English verse by

Babette Deutsch, on the basis of prose drafts, formal schemes, and revisions by Avrahm Yarmolinsky, and sometimes after a solution arrived at after an agreement to disagree. In the case of the few versions by other hands, the names of the translators are given on the Contents page. The year under the poem indicates the date of first publication or, if bracketed, the date of composition. Petersburg (St. Petersburg), the former Russian capital, was renamed Petrograd after the outbreak of World War I and Leningrad after Lenin's death in 1924. To avoid anachronism, all three designations are used. The footnotes are by the editor.

The present volume is a thoroughly revised and much expanded edition of *An Anthology of Russian Verse, 1812–1960*, published in 1962. Changes have been made in the text of many poems, a number have been omitted, and about a hundred have been added. The Introduction, which is in the nature of an historical sketch of Russian poetry, has been revised and brought up to date, as have the bio-bibliographical notes at the end of the volume. *An Anthology of Russian Verse, 1812–1960*, is a revised and augmented edition of *A Treasury of Russian Verse*, published in 1949, itself a completely revised and expanded edition of a book that had been reissued in an enlarged form in 1927, after having been first brought out in 1921.

B.D.

A.Y.

CONTENTS

ALEXANDER PUSHKIN (*continued*)

ALEXANDER BLOK

VLADISLAV KHODASEVICH

IVAN BUNIN

NIKOLAY GUMILYOV

BORIS PASTERNAK

MARINA TSVETAYEVA

INTRODUCTION

Russia's Middle Ages may be said to have lasted until the end of the seventeenth century. During that period Church Slavic, formed on a South Slav tongue, was the literary medium. It was first used in a translation of the Bible and of liturgical texts made by two Greek missionaries to Moravia in the ninth century. On Russian soil this language was modified under the influence of the vernacular. Both translations and original writings took their rise shortly after the Christianization of the country toward the close of the first millennium. The works produced during the next seven centuries were for the most part of a devotional or edifying nature. Bookmen, mostly monks, also composed chronicles and made versions of Byzantine secular compilations, such as histories, cosmographies, a bestiary.

A single work of a high literary order relieves the aridity of the scene: *The Lay of Igor's Campaign*. A short epic couched in rhythmic prose, it is an account by an unknown bard of a disastrous campaign led by several Russian princes against hostile nomads. Descriptions of valor in battle are followed by passages of patriotic oratory and there is also a moving lament for the captured Prince Igor; the tale ends on a note of rejoicing at Igor's escape from captivity. There may well have been other such gests, set down for the entertainment and exhortation of the princes and their retinues, but if there were any, none has survived. Thus, to the haunting quality of the *Lay*, its uniqueness adds a touch of mystery. Certainly there was a large body of tales and songs, as well as ballads that mingled fantasy and traces of myth with faint echoes of history. The language of all that was told or sung was close to folk speech. Passed on by word of mouth from generation to generation, this material was not recorded until recent times.

The modern era, inaugurated in the reign of Peter the Great (1689–1725), meant an abrupt break with the past. For the land of the czars, which knew nothing in the nature of a Renaissance or an Age of Enlightenment, the eighteenth century was a period of apprenticeship to Western masters, in literature as in other skills. The meager medieval heritage had pitifully little to offer by way of form or substance. Russians translated, and imitated, the authors of classical antiquity and the French neoclassicists as well. Verse evolved before prose, though this was eventually to become the country's chief glory. The unbroken tradition of modern Russian literature, specifically poetry, goes back no farther than the middle years of the century.

There had been versifiers before that time, but no poets, and they used an imported prosody unsuited to the native speech. It prescribed a set number of syllables in the line, with no fixed pattern of stresses, although accent is so prominent a feature of Russian as to make this desirable. There was no swing to the poetasters' productions: heavy-handed, often crudely didactic pieces, abounding in archaisms. In spite of the obligatory feminine rhyme, they were indistinguishable from lame prose. By mid-century, syllabic versification was abandoned in favor of another system based on the regular alternation of stressed and unstressed syllables. This accentual-syllabic prosody, also apparently taken from the West, became the mold in which Russian verse was to be cast. Succeeding generations were merely to refine upon it, until in our own time it found rivals in freer arrangements.

The prosodic reform was launched by Mikhail Lomonosov. Perhaps again taking a hint from foreigners, who since the days of the Elizabethans had emphasized literary decorum, he sought to bring order into the prevailing stylistic chaos by formulating standards. Works of a "high" rank, *i.e.*, dealing with serious or solemn matters, demanded, he taught, a style abounding in elements derived from the language of the Church books and a syntax patterned on that of Latin periods. In other works he permitted an admixture of the vernacular. In addition to being a preceptor regarding style, Lomonosov was a practitioner of verse. He wrote chiefly odes, often to order, on court occasions (two of these compositions were dedicated to Emperor Ivan VI, age one, who was deposed after "reigning" for thirteen months). The demand for panegyrics was also met by several of Lomonosov's contemporaries and immediate successors. Other classical genres—such as epistle, satire, song, and fable— were also cultivated in accordance with definite rules. These works, though not without literary merit, are chiefly of historic interest.

A genuine, though intermittent, poet, indeed perhaps the first to whom Russia may lay claim, was Lomonosov's follower, Gavriil Derzhavin. This courtier of Catherine II possessed great verve and a keen eye for movement and color, to judge from some of his descriptions, be it of a waterfall or a festive board, unfortunately too lengthy to be anthologized. He dealt with the commonplaces of poetry such as nature, God, death, in personal if stiff accents. Sometimes he made bold to deviate from conventional metrics and from other canons of classical rhetoric as set forth by Lomonosov. The prolix poems in which, tempering flattery with mild irony, he celebrates the virtues of his empress or the triumphs of her armies, or, again, attacks injustice in high places, contain passages of unusual effectiveness. The old sybarite's Anacreontic pieces occasionally achieve a homely charm, when he avoids didactic emphasis, the blight of the age. That verse with an explicit moral can, however, be delightful is proved by the shrewd and racy fables of Ivan Krylov (1769–1844), the Russian La Fontaine.

Derzhavin lived to witness Russia's victory over Napoleon. The venerable poet bequeathed what he called his "outworn lyre" to Vasily Zhukovsky. It was a generous gesture on the part of a writer who, if he had sometimes disregarded Lomonosov's precepts, was nevertheless a pillar of classicism. Young Zhukovsky, on the other hand, was one of the writers who preached, and practiced, "the new style." This faction, which originated at the turn of the century and was violently opposed by the diehards, championed a medium close to the speech of the educated gentry, a language purged of uncouth archaisms, modernized, simplified, emulating the elegance and precision of French and the mellifluousness of Italian.

Zhukovsky himself steered clear of heroics, solemnity, grandil-

oquence, indulging rather in reverie and lachrymose sentiment
and speaking for the claims of the heart. There was little in the
Russian temperament and the Russian scene to favor this early
variety of romanticism, tender-minded and pietistic. The trend
was short-lived and sterile. In any event, Zhukovsky—the author
of elegies and ballads—was less a poet in his own right than a
translator, sometimes at second-hand, of verse, ancient and
modern, from both East and West. As such, he performed a
signal service to the native culture. Literarily speaking, Russia
had long been a debtor nation, and it is notable that virtually
every poet applied himself to making foreign verse accessible
to his compatriots. Whatever defects Russian poetry may have,
they are not the fault of inbreeding.

Not Zhukovsky but a younger and incomparably more gifted
writer was responsible for the emergence of Russian literature
from the awkward age. Alexander Pushkin's adolescence coin-
cided with the second decade of the new century. Those were
exhilarating years. The victory of 1812 enhanced national self-
consciousness; fresh winds were blowing from widened horizons,
liberal influences were in the air. The time was ripe for the rise
of a literature rooted in native soil and nourished by what had
been absorbed from the West. Pushkin was foremost in shaping
that literature and, by the same token, modern literary Russian.
He completed the work of the promoters of the "new style" by
drawing on all the resources of the language, including the
speech of the untutored folk that Krylov, for one, had used
earlier. The very indigenous quality of his work gave Russian
letters for the first time a more than local significance and
allowed them to transcend the national boundaries.

Pushkin's genius was manifold, but he was above all a poet,
by the concensus of his compatriots an unequaled master of
the language. He never lost the taste for classic sobriety and
for what he called "the charm of naked simplicity," which
made Mérimée declare him "an Athenian among the Scythians." His passionate nature knew the discipline of a keen
intelligence, of a capacity for detachment, of a sense of measure. The Anacreontic strain in his youthful verse, which did not
stop at blasphemy and cheerful ribaldry, was of brief duration,

as was the Byronic unrest that marks the long narrative poems of his early manhood. The writings of his maturity, notably *Eugene Onegin*, which gives the fullest measure of his powers, have an objective, realistic quality that implies an acceptance of life on its own terms. Not that he remained unaware of the tragic predicaments inherent in the human condition. Although he hated bigotry, sycophancy, oppression, injustice, he was no rebel against either Church or State. A man of the world, he lived to the full in his works and days alike. Those who must depend on translation may agree with Flaubert that the Russian master is "flat." To the native, sensible not only of Pushkin's sanity and balance but of his generous humanity and, above all, the unobtrusive felicity, the superb artistry of his style (which, for Tchaikovsky, had the effect of music), his verse is a source of pure joy. The Revolution, which has caused so many revaluations, has only enhanced his luster. Ranked with the greatest figures in literature, he is the object and to some degree the victim of mountainous exegesis and of a veneration that in the Soviet era has acquired a quasi-official tinge.

There were a number of lyricists among Pushkin's contemporaries, some younger, some older men. They admired him, without paying him the tribute of imitation, each having a character of his own. Their work, while of a minor order, is that of skilled, style-conscious craftsmen who took their vocation seriously. It wants the tone of self-assured serenity that poetry had in Derzhavin's age. There is no lack of light and witty pieces, such, for example, as those of Prince Vyazemsky, but the elegiac mood prevails. Melancholy is characteristic of the melodious verse of Konstantin Batyushkov (1787–1855), the last half of whose life was darkened by insanity. Baratynsky's verse, often falteringly cerebral, is marked by a persistently gloomy outlook. In one of his poems he projects an apocalyptic vision of mankind passing from a brilliant era of industrial progress to one of complete prostration and ending with extinction, whereupon "imperial nature," rid of the human species, returns to its primeval majesty. While the language of poetry abounds in classical clichés like the Muses, the Graces, nymphs and naiads, traces of realism and even of naturalism are discernible in the verse. Thus, Baron Delvig (1790–1831), Pushkin's schoolmate and lifelong friend, invites his Muse to don now the chiton and now the sarafan. In some of the pieces by his fellows patriotism goes hand in hand with conservatism; elsewhere, notably in the clumsy performance of Kondraty Ryleyev, it has a radical orientation. Alexey Koltsov, a man of the people, who found congenial the style of the folksong, does not belong to this group of writers, all of them scions of the privileged class.

Tyutchev was another contemporary of Pushkin, surviving him by many years. Of the men, aside from the masters, who made the first four decades of the nineteenth century an age of poetry, Tyutchev is perhaps the most likely to elicit a sympathetic response from today's reader. His diction has a slightly archaic complexion, his sensibility and mentality are poles removed from those of the eighteenth century. He is indebted to German romanticism, with its hunger for the transcendental and the ineffable, yet his verse is remarkably limpid. It is distinguished by a fine economy and by a masterful use of metaphor and allusion. He can evoke a mood of serene contemplation, notably in confronting the natural scene, but his most characteristic lyrics are the product of a mind bent over itself "on the threshold of double being." The ordered world upon which falls the light of common day is for him but appearance. True reality is "the hundred-eyed beast" that night is, "ancient chaos," which is ready to engulf man, his petty works and pitiful longings. Tyutchev does not turn away from the black abyss. Rather he lives in constant awareness of it, vainly seeking the resolution of the tragic duality either in passionate love or in Christian faith, two leading themes in his poetry.

Pushkin's mantle fell not upon Tyutchev, who wrote for posterity (recognition came long after his death), but upon Mikhail Lermontov. This brilliant, egotistical youth was a lyricist of rare gifts. His verse follows patterns different from Pushkin's, but the effect of music and magic is as strong. His poetry is of an essentially romantic cast, expressive of a longing for the unattainable and inexpressible. The growing civic bias of the mid-century made it possible to put a social interpretation on the disquietude that pervades his work and that sometimes breaks out in vitriolic satire, although he revolted less against the Czar of all the Russias than against the God of heaven and earth. His imagination was haunted by the somber figure of a rebel angel vainly seeking regeneration through the love of a maiden. He had, however, moods of serenity and piety, and his verse, as indeed that of other Russian romantics, could be sober and earthy. A realistic strain runs deep in the grain of the Russian temperament.

As he was approaching maturity, Lermontov, like Pushkin, tried his hand at prose, producing a remarkable novel, *The Hero of Our Time*, which was published in 1840. On a May morning two years later Gogol's *Dead Souls* appeared in the bookshops. The day of prose had dawned. The period, one of the most fruitful in literary history, lasted about half a century, coinciding with the better part of the Victorian age. In the course of it fiction held the center of the stage, the taste for poetry undergoing progressive deterioration. There was one poet, however, who rivaled in popularity, if not in importance, the contemporary novelists: Turgenev, Dostoevsky, Tolstoy. This was Nikolay Nekrasov. He made articulate the conscious-ness—and the conscience—of the period of reform and inchoate revolt which had set in with the death, in 1855, of Nicholas I. His was, he said truly, "the Muse of grief and vengeance." His troubled, uneven verse dwells upon the miseries of the op-pressed and plundered masses, particularly the peasants. It voiced the aspirations of the democratic intelligentsia, as well as the *peccavi* of the gentry, painfully sensible of their debt to the people. At its best, his verse powerfully conveys profound self-scorn and bitter compassion for the victims of injustice. In denouncing social evils, he threw untransmuted into his poems —occasionally satirical, some of them parodies—the raw stuff of *feuilleton* and pamphlet. With great skill he reproduced the diction and swing of the folksong by using trisyllabic feet and dactylic rhymes.

Nekrasov set the fashion for the middle decades of the cen-tury. A socially indifferent poetry became anathema. In radical circles the utilitarian view of literature as a vehicle of enlighten-ment prevailed, and verse-making was rather looked down upon.

In the serious sixties an iconoclastic "Nihilist" critic advocated the abolition of all art and laid impious hands on the laurels of Pushkin himself.

In this unfriendly atmosphere several authors continued to carry on the tradition of pure poetry. Maikov achieved a small excellence in his genre pictures of the native scene and in his imitations of the ancients. Alexey Tolstoy had among his various gifts a talent for neat and graceful lyrics. Fet's work was furthest removed from the concept of utilitarian art. His poems have the insubstantial quality of reverie. It has been said of this etherealist that he could have paraphrased the familiar dictum thus: I dream, therefore I am. So absorbed is he in the mood of the moment, that time abdicates for him. Indeed, some of his most successful pieces are verbless. He does not state but adumbrates, suggests. He employs a delicate imagery in an effort to reach out toward the supersensuous and to present nature as the cosmic context of human life.

These poets professed allegiance to the principle of art for art's sake. Nevertheless, with the exception of Fet, they all wrote some political verse, as did also Tyutchev, preaching a pietistic and reactionary variety of nationalism. The perform- ance of both the civic-minded realists and the aloof esthetes reached its nadir during the eighties and the better part of the nineties, and so did the taste of the public. Those were years of bloodless, pretty, slovenly verse of plaints and platitudes, twitterings and stammerings.

As the century moved to its close a change made itself felt in the cultural atmosphere. When the Yellow Book was brighten- ing London bookstalls, a new literary trend began to develop in Petersburg (Leningrad) and Moscow. It went by the name of Modernism. The term was soon supplanted by Symbolism, while those who disliked the movement were apt to refer to it as Decadence, thus singling out its strain of mingled estheti- cism, eroticism, and morbidity. Although clearly the response to a stimulus from abroad—its detractors branded it a warmed- over French dish—it was also a reaction against native provin- cialism, lack of craftsmanship, and devotion to the Social Muse. Modernism was both a fresh beginning and a revival, at first not without puerile affectations intended to confound the Philistine.

Its advent was preceded by a flourish of hortatory writing: articles inveighing against the subservience of literature to the cause of social betterment, advocating individualism in Nietzschean accents, and exalting art over life. An early apostle of Modernism was Dmitry Merezhkovsky. In a muddle-headed essay published in 1893 the young author called for a poetry marked by heightened sensory perceptiveness but also by idealism and mysticism, an art engaged with absolutes and ultimates. Further, he urged using the language of symbols, without clearly defining the term. Indeed, he gave the title *Symbols* to a sheaf of poems issued at about the same time and echoing Poe and Baudelaire. But verse was not to be his vehicle.

Others dominated the movement for which Merezhkovsky had spoken. The oldest of them was Fyodor Sologub. He came closest to being a Decadent of Baudelaire's stripe. There is something eerily obsessive, if not perverse, about his poems. They are weighted down with *tædium vitae* and with the sense that life, when it is not a dismal menagerie, is what Dostoevsky called "the Devil's vaudeville." From his "tormenting fatherland" Sologub escapes into "a valley of dreams," an enchanted world of his own imagining. Thence the sick and humorless phantast emerges only to utter threats to the sun, prayers to Satan, hymns to Death the Deliverer. True, he knows moods when earthly existence presents itself as a rung of "an endless ladder of perfection." But his hosannas are far less compelling than his curses.

If there is a strong strain of morbidity in the small body of verse left by Innokenty Annensky, it is qualified by grim humor, by courageous confrontation of invalidism and the thought of death waiting on the doorstep. Evening and autumn are his favored death symbols, but winter and even spring serve the same purpose, the poet hearing "the call of death in the Easter hymn." Though free of self-pity, his lyrics dwell on waning, ailing, dying: his habitual cast of mind is one of anguish and hopelessness. Sometimes he is drawn to what he fears. He plays variations on such themes as loneliness, insomnia, dreams (chiefly nightmares). As might be expected of a Modernist who translated some of the French Symbolists, Annensky readily turns to music and moonlight and flowers (withering ones). Beauty redeems existence for him but, alas, life holds little of it, and that little is fragile. Poetry, like music, can adumbrate it faintly. Yet words are so inadequate that the making of verse is a torment, mitigated by the exhilaration of attempting a well-nigh impossible task. Although he occasionally touches upon the ideal world and his poems sometimes have an esoteric quality, there is nothing mystical about them. He wanted poetry to be concrete, dealing with three-dimensional objects and avoiding riddles, but he did not always practice what he preached.

A leading poet of the new school was Konstantin Balmont. His claim to being a Symbolist is founded largely on those lyrics in which he seeks to capture elusive moods. Furthermore, he grandiloquently celebrates the individual exulting in his own freedom. "My only fatherland," he declares, "is my desert soul." One of his early collections bears the title *Let Us Be Like the Sun*. A spontaneous, exuberant, all too facile, all too prolific poet, he composed hymns to the elements, a series of poems about colors, verses for children, retold exotic myths, and adapted spells and folksongs in many tongues. Not for nothing did he develop, in a turgid essay published in 1915, the thesis that poetry is in essence magic. He also turned out a vast body of translations, chiefly verse. Unfortunately, his skill with rhyme, rhythm, and tone color saves little of his work from vacuity.

Shortly after the publication of Merezhkovsky's *Symbols*, three fascicules of a miscellany entitled *Russian Symbolists* appeared under a Moscow imprint. It was virtually an anthology of French verse. The translations and imitations were for the most part from the pen of a university student named Valery Bryusov. At twenty-two he bestowed upon eternity, to use his own words, the first collection of his poems, modestly entitled *Chefs d'Oeuvre*. Like Balmont, the young man was "a Narcissus of the ink bottle." In an early lyric he advised the poet to sympathize with no one, to love himself "boundlessly," and to worship art alone. For him life was but material for the fashioning of verbal patterns that would endure by virtue of their formal excellence. He continued to protest his allegiance to "Beauty," but with time his verse took on a degree of concreteness. Further, he became aware of contending social forces, and he responded to such public crises as the abortive revolution of 1905–06 and the World War. Like Emile Verhaeren, a friend and master, whom he translated—Bryusov was a prolific translator—but with far less success he sought to bring the modern city into his verse. He had early scandalized and amused the critics and the public, not only by his self-vaunting but also by parading an unprecedented eroticism. But by 1905 he was a prominent literary figure, the acknowledged *maître* of the Moscow Symbolists. In an essay entitled "The Keys to Mysteries" he restated the thesis of the French Symbolists that poetry should use language to suggest the transcendent meaning of what the senses apprehend, should seek to glimpse eternity behind the fleeting moment and to penetrate to the secret heart of things. Yet he rarely adopted the vatic pose. He was not a visionary but a conscientious if uninspired craftsman, deeply concerned with verse technique. He likened his labors as a poet to the toil of an ox urged on by the plowman's heavy whip. The range of his subject matter is enormous. Russia is, of course, an inevitable theme. And having no allegiance to any one faith, he was able to declare: "Pantheon, the temple dedicated to all gods, has always been my dream." In accordance with the Symbolist canon, his style is metaphorical and allusive. Yet the language of some of his poems about the World War is so archaic that they struck a contemporary as the product of a gray-haired witness of the Crusades. Too much of his work is flawed by rhetoric and a weakness for such abstractions as Man, Time, Pride, Madness. Nevertheless, during the first decade of the century Bryusov's verse had a considerable vogue.

From the first, as has been noted, the advocates of the new poetry were drawn toward a religiosity tinged with mysticism. This was evident in the work of Merezhkovsky, but he was a devotee of a factitious faith that he called "the religion of the Third Testament," a synthesis of Christianity and paganism. Bryusov, too, employed religious imagery—as did Balmont—

but for him Symbolism was distinct alike from science and from religion. As for Sologub, he was inclined toward the inverted religiosity that takes the form of satanism. It is the work of Vyacheslav Ivanov that has the private and ecstatic character associated with genuine mysticism. The word, he wrote, is "the cryptogram of the ineffable." If the other Modernists were influenced by French poetry, he was indebted to German romanticism, the Christian stance of Dostoevsky and the thinking of Vladimir Solovyov. The latter was a visionary of an apocalyptic temper who made a major contribution to theology and also wrote a number of rather tenuous lyrics of soaring spirituality. Their main theme is the worship of the Feminine Principle, which he called Sophia—Divine Wisdom—and which, he taught, generates and governs all life. He devoutly looked forward to its incarnation at the imminent Second Coming, when the body politic would become a theocracy. In sum, this theologian held that his role as a poet was both priestly and prophetic, and so, too, did his disciple, Ivanov. Unlike his fellow Symbolists, Ivanov called in question the adoration of beauty and rejected the other cult that had inspired the Modernist revolt—that of the ego. Indeed, he regarded his verse as the crystal chalice of collective consciousness.

The pontiff of Russian Symbolism, Ivanov was the master of a monumental, quasi-ecclesiastical style. Some of his poems are marked by Byzantine pomp and ornateness. Others are cast in the Grecian and Latin mold (he was an accomplished classical scholar, at home in the antique world). They are apt to suffer from abstruse erudition. Yet there is a clear loveliness about certain of his lyrics, and a few, vibrant with his faith, burn with a pure flame.

Vyacheslav the Magnificent, as he was nicknamed, was the most notable figure in the Symbolist circles of the capital. Every Wednesday, from 1907 to 1912, he presided over night-long gatherings in his sixth-floor flat, known as the Tower (one thinks of Yeats and Mallarmé). The air at these assemblies must have been charged with portents, and words like "mystery," "eternity," "abyss," were as cheap as turnips. Among those who frequented these symposia on religion and poetry was Maximilian Voloshin. Since his middle twenties he had been contributing verse to Modernist periodicals. Like his host, he was drawn toward the sacred and the mystical, and shared the former's affection for, if not his knowledge of, classical antiquity, calling the Mediterranean "the fatherland of my spirit." As a poet he owed much to the French, but to the Parnassians rather than the Symbolists. His lines have something of the intense color and plasticity of Hérédia, from whom he claimed to have learned the art of verse. Like Hérédia, he was an expert sonneteer. It is noteworthy that he was a painter in a small way, limiting himself to watercolors. His most evocative poems bear witness to the vigor of his visual imagination. His Crimean landscapes have a rare splendor. He also made verbal engravings, as it were, of figures from the past, and transposed into verse such works of art as the stained-glass windows of the Rouen cathedral. Neither the events of 1905–06 nor the World War dislodged him from his ivory tower.

Holding that symbols reveal the parallelism of the phenomenal and the noumenal worlds, Ivanov accorded reality to both. For Andrey Belyi, on the other hand, the physical world was a realm of shadows and echoes of the supersensual, which alone was real and which the poet could glimpse at the moment of inspiration. He regarded Symbolism as "a system of mystical experiences," and he was an ardent disciple of Vladimir Solovyov. Small wonder, then, that his first book of verse, like the prose poems that preceded it, celebrates Sophia, envisioning the glory of her imminent advent. *Gold in Azure*, the title of the book, describes his palette. Within a few years he was to lose his faith, and harsh realism was to invade his anguished verse. Cries of adoration gave way to laments and to curses upon Russia's material and moral wretchedness. A man of unstable temperament, he swung between euphoric anticipations and presentiments of doom. His style is frenetic, abounding in synesthetic, explosive imagery and enlivened by neologisms. His poems show sharp attention to tone color, and indeed his imagination seems to have been largely auditory. None of the other members of the group took so much to heart the conviction that poetry is allied to music, since that art comes closest to voicing the inexpressible. Belyi began by writing "symphonies": sequences of pieces in cadenced prose, elaborated in the manner of musical compositions. At the same time he was writing conventional verse. In his late twenties he bade farewell to youth, and gave up his former medium for prose, of which he made remarkable uses, returning to verse briefly after the Revolution. All he had ever written, he declared in a foreword to one of his late books—he was an incorrigible preface writer—formed a whole, the tenor of which was "a quest for truth." It was a quest that he conducted in terms too abstract and cryptic to promote the enterprise.

Linked to Andrey Belyi by a stormy friendship was a major poet who was prominent in the Symbolist movement, Alexander Blok. In his youth he, too, had belonged to Solovyov's following. The lyrics collected in *Poems About the Lady Beautiful*, Blok's first book (1904), have a singular unity of mood and tone. The prevailing attitude is one of worship, the atmosphere that of a vigil, a tense waiting upon mystic illumination, the miracle of contact with the ideal world. The Lady Beautiful, the object of the young poet's passion, is, of course, an alias for "Sophia" and is almost pure spirit, not visualized but wistfully foreknown. The sensuality that colors Blok's adoration is highly rarefied. At the time, like several mystically oriented friends, he actually believed in the imminent dawn of a new era under the aegis of Divine Wisdom: "Sophia." Before long, however, this belief was shattered, presumably under the impact of a crisis in his marriage and the failure of the quasi-revolution of 1905, when he had been sufficiently committed to head a demonstration, carrying a red flag. A poem of that year announced the Lady's departure "forever." As a matter of fact, some of the earlier lyrics he had addressed to his discarnate mistress suggest doubt and distrust, forebodings of fatal estrangement.

The poet now descends from the empyrean and finds himself in the physical world inhabited by creatures of flesh and blood. He takes increasing cognizance of his surroundings, his times, his civic responsibilities. The city with its fogs and fevers looms up in his pages. The object of his youthful adoration has undergone a degrading metamorphosis. Without ceasing to be beautiful, she has become a creature of evil, a deceiver, a prostitute, seen through the haze of intoxication. Again, she appears in the guise of a plain-featured girl, a snow woman, a cardboard doll. Is she consubstantial with Russia? His country inspires the poet with a profound emotion, of mixed love and loathing. And is not Russia's martyrdom strangely identified with his own, indeed with Christ's? Blok sees himself actually crucified, or else as a fallen angel scorched by hell fire. (This does not prevent him from describing himself in a later poem as "the child of kindness and light.") Prayer is supplanted by irony, ecstasy by despondency, even despair. The reader often finds himself in a confessional, overhearing an anguished sinner's avowals. Blok can write a lyric breathing a childlike faith or he can turn out a piece of light verse, but for the most part his poems record disillusionment, self-pity, self-disgust, horror. He gave a sequence of lyrics the title "The Terrible World."

Blok's verse is not centered solely on his private distresses. Now and then, as noted above, the note of social concern is sounded. Furthermore, like Belyi and to a lesser extent Bryusov, he was troubled by forebodings of public disaster, of a catastrophe that would lay waste civilization. As mankind moved closer to the World War, his sense of doom grew keener. Perhaps this was an echo of Solovyov's eschatological ideas, or the sentiment may have been fed by his half-conscious sense that the generation to which he belonged was under sentence. Faith in the Russian people alone sustained the poet. With this went a strong anti-bourgeois animus. Nevertheless, with characteristic inconsistency, he hopefully anticipated the industrialization of Russia, its transformation into "a new America."

As Blok approached maturity he conceived a distaste for whatever smacked of mysticism. "We need reality," he jotted in his notebook, and he did not mean the reality *behind* appearance, but that of the actual world. He gave up making poems out of the "astral dreams" of his youth and found more substantial material in the raw stuff of ordinary experience. Yet there is something spectral about many of his realistic poems— they form the bulk of his *oeuvre*—and they gain depth from undertones of the mysterious and enigmatic. This is enhanced by the rich texture of his verse. He hoped against hope for a miracle that would make the poet a whole man. But to the end of his life he remained a divided soul, a late devotee of realism who seems to have longed for the realm from which he had exiled himself, and who believed his finest poems to be transcripts of silent music coming from "other worlds."

The Symbolists' claims for their art were extravagant, and their performance, though ample and varied, leaves something to be desired. Yet they did quicken poetry and enrich it. An enhanced sense of the mystery and ambiguity of life deepened their work. Allusion and implication supplanted flat statement, sentimental or sententious. They made more effective use than had been made hitherto of the resources of the language. Subject matter expanded in scope and complexity. By translation, too, they widened poetic horizons. Imagery was relieved of outworn tropes and similes and enlivened by color. Preoccupation with structure and style made for a higher standard of craftsmanship. The Symbolists experimented with a stanza composed in varying metres, employed triple rhythm and stress prosody, which had seldom been used by their predecessors, and wrote free verse as well. The practice of Bryusov and Blok legitimized the off-rhyme, previously tolerated as a poetic license. Indeed, varieties of off-rhyme have become an established feature of Russian versification. The monotony and rigidity of much nineteenth-century verse was happily reduced by these innovations.

The best talents gravitated toward Symbolism. Ivan Bunin was one of those who definitely did not. When as a young man he first came upon the Modernists, he described them as "sick boys with complete chaos in their heads." He was himself a traditionalist in an age of innovation, a realist in a neoromantic generation, a sober man among the God-intoxicated. Religious feeling may enter into his poems without blurring their firm outlines. His lyrics offer landscapes and neat genre pictures that evoke the melancholy charm of vanished things and are touched with a longing for the distant. A strong exotic strain fills some of his work with Oriental color, fragrance, heat. Yet his poems can be examples of economy and precision.

Shortly before the World War a reaction against Symbolism began to declare itself. Early in 1913 two essays appeared which amounted to the manifesto of a new literary trend, Adamism, better known as Acmeism. Its adherents had for some time been banded together in a short-lived association that they called The Guild of Poets, to underscore their workmanlike concern with their craft. Though they emphasized their antipathy to Symbolism, they inherited some of its strategies. Yet they preferred a visible, tangible, solid world to the insubstantial shadow of a higher reality. Furthermore, while not lacking in piety toward the ineffable and the unknowable, they wanted to keep poetry separate from the mysteries of faith. Confrontation of the external world, not the exploration of arcane regions; detachment, not ecstasy; the precise word, the graphic image, not the hazy allusion; a balance of the elements of poetry, rather than the primacy of music; not Germanic obfuscation, but Mediterranean light that separates objects, bringing them into focus. Such were the main precepts of Acmeism; they were not always followed. All this indicated a penchant for the classical, akin to that of the French Parnassians, as against the neoromanticism of the Symbolists.

The new trend was represented by several gifted poets. The *maître* was Nikolay Gumilyov, the Russian Chénier. A loyal subject of the Czar and a faithful son of the Church, he was an imperialist with a Nietzschean streak who was drawn to the exotic, for all his classicism. His poems exalt the explorer and the conquistador—the dedicated and the daring. He set himself the task of rescuing Russian poetry from the effete state to which, he believed, Symbolism had reduced it.

Another prominent member of the group was his wife, known as Anna Akhmatova, who wrote intimately personal, chamber poetry. She endeared herself to the public by her finely wrought, limpid, fastidious lyrics which combine indirection with an admirable economy. They center on what Henry James called "the great constringent relation between man and woman." When the World War broke out, she voiced an intense patriotism colored, like Gumilyov's, by religious faith.

Mikhail Kuzmin, though usually grouped with Symbolists of the Decadent stripe, was close to the Acmeists in that he preached "beautiful clarity" and practiced poetry not as a sacred ritual but as a "gay métier." An esthete and a hedonist, to whom nightmares and beatific visions were alien, his elegant lyrics have a piquant charm, some of them discreetly celebrating love, both hetero- and homosexual. One of the few Russian poets to write free verse, he delighted in assuming the masks of varied stylization.

A professed Acmeist was that greatly gifted poet, Osip Mandelshtam. His first book, made up of verse that dates from the years 1908 to 1915, bears the title *Stone*, which suggests a Parnassian predilection for working with hard, heavy, durable materials. Curiously enough, the volume opens with poems that, far from exhibiting this preference, are notable for a gossamer, weightless quality. They move on a timeless level and have the veiled, nebulous character associated with Symbolism. The abundance of negatives is striking. The themes are loneliness, sadness, silence, emptiness. "Can it be that I am real?" the poet asks. In "Silentium" he urges Aphrodite to remain foam and the word to return to music. His tendency is to attain what Gumilyov called "the periphery of consciousness."

On the other hand, some of the later poems in *Stone* have substantiality, density, gravity, an almost lapidarian stamp. The poet's eye is focused on works of architecture: the Petersburg Admiralty, "this chastely builded ark," Russian cathedrals, Hagia Sophia, Notre Dame. The lines on the last-named conclude with the presage that some day he, too, will create beauty out of "hostile ponderousness." In keeping with the Acmeist canon is devotion to classical antiquity. This is amply evidenced in *Stone*. Several poems have to do with the city of the Caesars and the Popes, a symbol of the perdurable might of State and Church. It is an imagined Rome (Mandelshtam, it appears, was never in Italy), conjured up by means of expressive, parsimoniously chosen, concrete details. Russia's northern capital, which had been Mandelshtam's home for years and which had a powerful hold on him, is evoked with equal economy and an unparalleled freshness of vision. There are also chiseled stanzas on such diverse themes as an ice-cream vendor, a Lutheran funeral, an American female tourist, the organ music of Bach, "the irate interlocutor," and a reflection on the change of Europe's "mysterious map," dated 1914.

Almost simultaneously with Acmeism, another post-Symbolist, distinctly *avant-garde* development arose. This was Futurism. Both the Symbolists and the Acmeists spurned certain of their predecessors, but they appreciated the masters of many ages and countries. The Futurists, on the contrary, repudiated the cultural heritage lock, stock, and barrel, though their animus was directed chiefly against the nineteenth century. They had nothing but abuse for their contemporaries, and when in 1914 Marinetti visited Russia, at least some of them denounced the master of the school to which they owed their name (if little else). It was formally adopted in 1913, though occasionally it had been used earlier. The first manifesto of these frantic iconoclasts, entitled A *Slap in the Face of Public Taste*, appeared in a pamphlet issued under a Moscow imprint in 1912. "We are the face of our time," it announced, going on to say that "Academia and Pushkin are less intelligible than hieroglyphs" and that Pushkin, together with "Dostoevsky, Tolstoy, etc.," must be thrown overboard from "the steamship of modernity," an image that dates. The Futurists were "new people of the new life." Their hatred of the "stifling" past extended to the language itself. They declared war on Russian spelling, punctuation, syntax.

The opuscule that opened with the manifesto was the second collection of Futurist verse. Others followed. They were brought out by feuding splinter groups, into which the movement had promptly broken up and which made doctrinal confusion worse confounded. The eccentric titles, the weird metaphors, the grotesque juxtaposition of words—all were meant to bewilder and shock the Philistines. Neologisms were an outstanding feature of the verse written by this harum-scarum *avant garde*. The Symbolists and Acmeists occasionally produced coinages; the Futurists "ordered" the public "to respect the poet's right to expand the vocabulary with arbitrary and newly coined words."

Indefatigable in minting them was Velimir Khlebnikov, a signatory of A *Slap in the Face of Public Taste*, and one of the most improbable figures in literary annals. He made up thousands of words, derived from Slavic roots—when it came to vocables of foreign stock he behaved like a fanatical xenophobe. Alas, not one of his inventions has passed into the language. Since a newly coined word is imprecise, its semantic mold not having hardened, so to speak, its use is in keeping with his doctrine of *samovitoe slovo* (word as thing in itself), which subordinates meaning to the purely physical features of the vocable. This principle is, indeed, the heart of Futurist poetics. Khlebnikov also originated the idea of what he called the "metalogical, alias transmental, tongue" (*zaum*), a potentially universal language composed of separate phonemes, each denoting a cluster of related variants of a concept, expressed in geometric terms. Some of his fellow poets not surprisingly misinterpreted this delightful invention, and produced "metalogical" verse by stringing together "freely made" words, mostly monosyllabic, devoid of meaning, in short, a kind of jabberwocky.

For a man who died young (at the same age as Pushkin), and who devoted a large part of his energy to chimerical pursuits other than literary, Khlebnikov left behind a substantial body of writing. Some of his work is lost (during one of his stays in the country, peasant boys stole a sackful of his manuscripts "for cigarettes"); much consists of fragments, rough drafts, unfinished pieces. Coinages, sometimes incomprehensible, are numerous in his early efforts and are never absent from his pages. A relatively simple example of an almost wholly neologistic text is "Incantation By Laughter." For the most part he uses ordinary vocables, of the kind he called "day, or sun words," conventional names of objects, in contradistinction to "night, or star words," which denote what he felt to be the essences of things and which would seem to be somehow related to the "metalogical tongue." Now and then elements of it, in the form of enigmatic single capital letters, figure in his texts, as do numbers that had a private significance for him. He is quite ready to treat words in the dictatorial fashion of Humpty Dumpty. The surrealistic incongruities and idiosyncrasies of his style are prominent alike in his shorter poems and in the dozen lengthy verse narratives that he wrote before the Revolution. These are marked by helpless formlessness and sometimes have the absurd illogic of dreams. His innovations include what he called "supertales," each a kind of collage made up of pieces on diverse themes, written in verse or prose, at diverse times. His last work was such a supertale, entitled *Zangezi*, the name of the hero, who is the author's double.

Insofar as he avidly experimented with language in an attempt to shape a new vehicle for poetry, he belonged in the camp of the Futurists. In certain basic ways, however, his attitude was at variance with theirs. One finds in his work a strong note of nostalgia for the primitive world, and he was hostile to industrialism and all it entails. Besides, being something of a recluse, he was inclined to stay away from the gatherings of the coterie and shun the discussions. Nevertheless, he was looked up to even by the most outstanding member of the group, another signatory of A *Slap in the Face of Public Taste*, Vladimir Mayakovsky. The Futurists gave frequent public readings (at which Khlebnikov rarely appeared). To scandalize their audiences more thoroughly, they affected such eccentricities as boutonnières of wooden spoons, while Mayakovsky is said to have painted roses on his cheeks.

This young man's poems—five collections of them, with such titles as A *Cloud in Pants*, appeared between 1913 and 1917—were beginning to attract attention. There was a vitality in his riotous, cacophonous lines, with their bold imagery, broken rhythms, clever off-rhymes, their mixture of the colloquial and the neologistic. For all the persiflage and saucy exhibitionism in his work, it carries overtones of sharp social satire and asserts humane values with Bohemian exuberance and far from Bohemian earnestness.

On the fringe of the Futurist group moved an author named Boris Pasternak, then in his twenties. He was repelled by the brashness and self-vaunting of these iconoclasts, yet he found congenial their free way with language. His first two books of verse, which appeared during the World War, revealed an authentic and original talent. He was to develop into one of the major poets of our time.

With the outbreak of the war Futurism went into a decline. It would probably have shared the fate of an ephemeral fashion, had it not been for the Revolution.

.   .   .

The establishment of the Soviet regime in October* 1917 forms the great divide in the history of Russian poetry, as in that of every phase of Russian art and life. Verse did manage to reach the public either in printed form or through recitals at literary gatherings, but the publication of fiction practically ceased in the general disruption. As a matter of fact, the misery and bloodshed that marked the stormy dawn of the new era, the breakdown of the routine of living, the giant hopes and fears, the apocalyptic visions—all this created an atmosphere rather favorable to poetry. True, there were those among the older poets who, seeing their world crumble about them, were paralyzed by despair, or who, abhorring the objectives and methods of Bolshevism, felt called upon to oppose it. Shortly after the outbreak of the Revolution some escaped abroad, there to eat the bitter bread of exile. Such was the case of Merezhkovsky, Balmont, Bunin. As the work of the expatriates was proscribed, it was effectually excluded from their country's literature. Others became exiles at home and continued to write without making any concessions to the radically changed intellectual climate. Kuzmin, after issuing a book of poems in his usual vein in 1923, published nothing more. A year earlier Sologub had brought out a little collection of frivolous *bergerettes*, a gesture of such complete disdain for the *Zeitgeist* as to be audacious. This was his last appearance in print.

The Revolution put an end to Voloshin's aloofness from public issues. In 1919 he published a sequence of poems which was a survey of Russia's past from the vantage point of a retrograde and mystical nationalism. As for the Revolution, he envisaged it as a "fiery furnace" in which the country was being tempered to "a diamond hardness." He also contributed to the émigré press some pieces depicting the horrors of the upheaval. A Soviet critic described these as "counterrevolutionary," but instead of siding with the Whites, Voloshin called for reconciliation of the two camps. He continued to live in the Crimea, where he was practically unmolested by officialdom. But he was not heard from for years before he withdrew into the final silence.

---

* November, according to the Gregorian calendar, which the Soviet Government adopted in 1918.

Believing that the Revolution had religious roots, Vyacheslav Ivanov welcomed it. For some time, in fact, he occupied the post of Vice-Commissar of Education in the Azerbaijan Soviet Republic. His cycle of "Winter Sonnets," which appeared in 1920, belongs to his finest work. These poems realize the physical privations that made living so hard at this period. Yet they are buoyant with faith in the integrity of the poet's "true self," while their patent genuineness, their simplicity and directness help to make them the moving lyrics that they are. As time went by, Ivanov found existence under communism increasingly distressing, and in 1924 he expatriated himself, settling in Italy.

Bryusov, on the other hand, resolutely threw in his lot with the Bolsheviks. Back in the troubled year 1905, when reproached for writing poems without social significance, he had stammered an absurdly helpless reply in verse. The same year he composed a piece in which he told the revolutionaries: "Destroy with you I will, build—no!" Now he underwent a complete change of heart. He made a pathetic effort to pour the new wine into old bottles. In his critical essays he took to using Marxist terminology; he versified on scientific themes in the vein of dialectical materialism, hymned Lenin in an erudite hyperbolic style, and apostrophized Soviet Russia and its emblem in manic metaphors.

Not unnaturally, Andrey Belyi's political stance was an equivocal one. He hailed the new era with his customary exultation and in the field of culture collaborated with the Bolsheviks. Although in 1909 he had concluded a lyric thus: "Go, vanish, Russia, my Russia, / Vanish away into space!," in 1917 he ended another lyric: "Oh, Russia, my Russia, Messiah of the days to come!" The next year he published a lyrical sequence, "Christ Is Risen," which the public took to be a stuttering hallelujah to the Revolution. In later years he was to insist that it dealt with "very intimate personal experiences, independent of country, party and astronomical time." This work was followed in 1921 by a remarkable semi-autobiographical verse narrative, having to do with his early life. Thereupon he expatriated himself, but after two years in exile he returned to Russia. In the decade left him he made a further effort to move toward acceptance of Bolshevism, but without success. He had by then abandoned verse for prose.

Alexander Blok greeted the Revolution with enthusiastic acclaim. He had long since come to loathe official Russia, both Church and State, and the middle-class civilization of the West repelled him equally. It has been noted that he was haunted by forebodings of impending catastrophe. The prospect of the collapse of the world in which his own being was rooted did not appall him. He accepted the violence and destruction of revolution in the belief that it had the power to replenish the deepest sources of the people's vitality. For him, as apparently for Andrey Belyi, too, here was something other than a change of government or the adoption of a new system of economy. Rather was it the prelude to the creation of a new heaven and a new earth, where life would be "just, clean, gay, beautiful."

It was in this mood that early in 1918, hot upon the heels of the epochal events, Blok wrote a long poem, "The Twelve." Its full meaning was not clear to the poet himself, but it was not, he was certain, a political piece—he had a profound contempt for politics. It held, he wrote, no more than "a drop of politics." We have his word for it that while he was composing "The Twelve," and for some days afterward, he perceived with his "physical ear a great, composite noise, probably the noise of the old world crashing." The poem reverberates with that harsh music. Among the writings spawned by the Revolution, "The Twelve" stands out, a monument to the days that shook the world. Couched partly in a coarse ballad style, new to the delicate and sophisticated lyricist, it harmonizes its heterogeneous elements and maintains a mood of revolutionary fervor, closing with a religious apotheosis, which, recognizing its mawkishness, he came to dislike, but never changed.

"The Twelve" was promptly followed by "The Scythians," a rhetorical, confused piece, in which the poet assumes the unaccustomed role of one who speaks in the name of his people, and which was a response to the threat of foreign intervention. In his last three years he said nothing further in verse. His mentality was wholly at variance with that which was beginning to assert itself in Soviet Russia. A few months before his death he made this entry in his diary: "The louse has conquered the whole world, that's already an accomplished fact." He foresaw changes, but all in the wrong direction, and he was well aware of the dangers to literature that lurked in the new regime. In his last public address, delivered in February 1921, on the anniversary of Pushkin's death, he sounded a prophetic warning against the bureaucrats who were "preparing to direct poetry into channels of their own, attempting upon its secret freedom and preventing it from accomplishing its mysterious purpose." Nevertheless, Blok's works are reprinted and accorded praise as one of the glories of Soviet letters.

Two weeks after Blok's death Gumilyov was executed for alleged participation in a conspiracy against the Government. The verse of his last years, which belongs to his best work, was, as before, remote from the life of the day. Anna Akhmatova, her powers heightened, clung to her sensitive, intimate, backward-looking art. After 1924 her name vanished from the public prints, reappearing in 1940, when the verse she had written during the previous sixteen years came out between covers. Mikhail Zenkevich, a member of the quondam Guild of Poets, accepted the Revolution as an elemental force and continued to compose tight, colorful lyrics on subjects of no topical interest. The poems of Nikolay Tikhonov were marked by exaltation of virile action and a predilection for the exotic, which allied them to Gumilyov's verse. But the young Red Army volunteer, who was to become a pillar of the Establishment, had had no personal contact with the Acmeists.

The last representative of the trend that a Soviet critic dismissed as "a Petersburg disease" was Mandelshtam. Few writers were by temperament so sharply antagonistic to Bolshevik totalitarianism. He remained in Russia, however, and continued to write. If he hailed Kerensky in a poem, at first he was inclined to accept the Soviet order. Yet as his "Twilight of Liberty" suggests, he recognized that he was paying a high price for acquiescence: "ten heavens for the earth." Concern with what he called "my age, my beast" was now not totally excluded from his work. As time passed, the beastly nature of the age became increasingly present to him. His defiance of the official ideology took the form of withdrawal. By and large his verse was apolitical. Classical antiquity continued to exert a spell over him. His second book of poems (1923) is entitled *Tristia,* with a bow to Ovid. A wag nicknamed him "Gaius Julius Osip Mandelshtam." Furthermore, his style was completely at variance with that to which a proper Soviet writer was expected to adhere. The idiosyncrasy from which his early work was not free had grown with the years. Imagery, syntax, sequential development—all are affected. The language is often extremely private. One peculiarity of the diction adds to the difficulty of deciphering some pieces which are, after all, communications: on the fascinating theory that in the union between the word and what it signifies, the former is the master and that it is free to choose its denotation, the poet ascribes an arbitrary and arcane meaning to ordinary vocables, like "swallow," "salt." In reading the later Mandelshtam, the utmost acumen is on occasion futile. He wrote jokingly in a late letter that he was "becoming intelligible to positively everyone," adding: "This is horrible." As a measure of defense against the ubiquitous censor, the poet may have half consciously intensified the obscurity of an elliptical style natural to an exceedingly eccentric mind. This applies particularly to the verse that he wrote in his last years, when he lived as a deportee under police surveillance in a provincial city lost in the steppes. One hears in these remarkable pieces, published posthumously abroad, a strangled outcry, a farewell to the culture of the West, in which he was at home, the moan of one longing to flee a place intolerable to him, as when he asks for "an inch of blue sea, just enough to fill a needle's eye."

There are those of Mandelshtam's poems that are models of cryptic utterance, outdoing the surrealism of Khlebnikov, to whom he was, in fact, indebted. They have, however, what Khlebnikov lacks: emotional impact, and the verbal magic, the enchantment that the *avant-garde* poet today is content to miss. For Mandelshtam is an esoteric poet possessed of an extraordinary mastery of language. A friend of his recalled that, hearing him recite his verse, he felt "a kind of chill, fear, shudder, as if in the presence of the supernatural. Never in my life," he wrote, "have I witnessed such a manifestation of the unalloyed essence of poetry as in this reading and in this man." Even in cold prose some of his lines can make the skin prickle.

Of late he has become the subject and to a degree the victim of a cult, both at home, where his unpublished verse is circulated clandestinely in manuscript, and in the Russian diaspora.

As a group the Acmeists appear not to have survived Gumilyov. By the time he died other trends were developing. The early years of the Soviet era witnessed a proliferation of coteries—Russian writers had long been a gregarious lot—which kept forming and reforming their ranks and fighting among themselves. Some of them were offshoots of Futurism. Before 1924 there existed, among others, expressionists, luminists, fuists, forme-librists, biocosmists (they issued their program from a *creatorium*), nothingists (*nichevoki*), even rubbishists (*yerundisty*). Each splinter group claimed to speak for the poetry of the age. Most of them had a shadowy existence on the lunatic fringe of literature and produced little beyond their pretentious and often unintelligible manifestoes.

There were also Constructivists and Imagists. The latter—they were unrelated to the Anglo-American group of that name—tried to outdo the Futurists in the choice of striking metaphors, but they preached the poet's duty to romanticize and idealize life. In fact, between 1922 and 1924, when the confraternity dissolved, their rallying point was a meager review that flaunted the title *A Hostelry for Travelers in the Beautiful*. The group included several minor verse-makers, notably Marienhof, and one poet of consequence, Sergey Yesenin. This half-educated village lad had a fresh and authentic if frail talent, but he did not quite fulfill the rich promise of his youth. His work is rooted in his rural background, and so, in a class-conscious society, he and several other writers were lumped together as peasant poets. They were by no means simple-minded rustics who composed their songs as they followed the plow, but they did operate with the details of the peasant's life and faith, drawing upon immemorial folklore and on the imagery of the Church books that had long been the sole reading matter of the masses.

Yesenin greeted the coming of the new order ecstatically. To him, as to Kluyev, the other noted peasant poet, the Revolution was a mammoth *jacquerie*, an elemental conflagration.

They hoped that out of the ashes a *muzhik* Utopia would arise. They courted disillusionment. Anticipating the urbanization and industrialization of the country, and welcoming it in spite of the fact that this doomed his world, Yesenin decided that he was "the last poet of the village." This does not account for his suicide but seems in key with it. Posthumous selections from his works have been repeatedly issued under Soviet imprints, but some critics have not hesitated to brand him and Kluyev as *kulak* poets.

The Constructivists began by repudiating all art as passive and consequently unsuitable to a society in process of drastic transformation. Eventually they reconciled themselves to the idea of producing literature—that is, chiefly verse. They sought to ground it on science and technology, to saturate it with the here and now, to make it a genuine factor in the building of a socialist culture. They have to their credit the introduction of so-called Time Prosody. In this system the lines are of approximately equal duration, the number of syllables varying and having no set pattern of stresses. It was meant not to replace but to supplement the traditional modes of versification, thus making for greater rhythmic freedom and flexibility. A number of Soviet poets have used this prosody. The moving spirit of the Constructivist group was a poet of considerable inventiveness, Ilya Selvinsky. His talent, which was not without a vein of humor, thrived in the atmosphere of experimentation and of seemingly unlimited possibilities that prevailed when the Revolution was young.

By 1930 the Constructivist group was no more. At one time it had included Eduard Bagritzky, a conscientious if uneven poet of unusual originality and power. His intimate lyrics gave place to verse inspired by fervor for the Communist cause. When the civil war reached his native southwest, he turned from pieces influenced by Futurist works and Gumilyov's exotic lyrics to Soviet propaganda. Though matters of public interest were not his sole themes, to the end of his short life he remained a poet of the Revolution. Nevertheless, he clung to his private vision of the world, and his tense, full-blooded poetry is not seldom obscure.

.   .   .

In addition to the groups enumerated above, the Futurists were still on the scene, and prominently so. They had embraced the revolutionary cause from the first. While others were hostile or hung back, these young bohemians leaped to the support of the new regime. They, too, were for a complete break with the past, were they not? Obviously they could provide an appropriate literature for the victorious proletariat. Not without some misgivings, the Bolsheviks welcomed this ally. Because the term Futurism trailed unsavory associations, it was rejected in 1923 in favor of LEF (Left Front of the Arts). Marxist critics had much to object to in LEF's theory and practice, but they gave their unqualified approval to the work of its leader, Vladimir Mayakovsky.

He was becoming a towering figure. Under the new dispensation he stopped clowning, curbed his weakness for the bizarre and the extravagant, without, however, giving up all his odd ways with words, and stepped, as he put it, on the throat of his song. He made himself the megaphone of Bolshevism, the loudspeaker, in more senses than one, of the Revolution. He hymned it, he composed marching songs for it, he eulogized Lenin and the Party: "the million-fingered hand clenched in a crushing fist"; he vociferated against the enemies of the Soviets. In numerous pieces, some written to order, he exhorted, explained, jeered, boasted, threatened—all on behalf of Soviet policy. There was no task too mean for him. He wrote poems urging his fellow citizens to brush their teeth and, also for the sake of hygiene, to avoid handshaking; to visit the new Moscow planetarium, patronize communal restaurants, observe fire regulations, refrain from celebrating Easter. He wrote advertisements for the department stores and denounced the mills for the poor quality of the socks they turned out. By his own account he produced six thousand rhymed slogans, which appeared on posters, three thousand of them painted by himself, or which were used in other ways—on candy wrappers, for example. "I am not a poet," he wrote in 1927, "but first of all a man who has put his pen at the service—mind you—the service of the present hour, the immediate actuality and its builders: the Soviet Government and the Party." Yet if he subordinated to the political requirements of the hour the poet's concern for craftsmanship, he still retained it. His skill with off-rhymes was extraordinary. He paid attention to typographical effects. He spurned traditional metres, branding iambics and trochaics as White Guardist, himself using stress prosody. Some of his poems combine what is virtually prose with lines in that prosody and in disguised conventional metres. He wielded his powerful pen now as a weapon, now as a tool, always in fulfillment of what LEF theoreticians called "a social assignment." His verse, with its posteresque crudities, its oratorical exuberance, its raucousness and didacticism, was a complete denial of the lyrical graces, the subtleties, the intimacies belonging to the poetry of the age that lay behind him.

Khlebnikov, too, ranged himself on the side of the Soviet regime. The Revolution and the civil war figure in the verse narratives that he wrote in his last four years and that were, for the most part, published posthumously. In one of them Lenin, not named, is described as "your new image, Time," and the White soldiers as "sons of deceit." In another long piece, capitalism is destroyed by "divine explosions." He projected a socialist utopia of his own, in which songs and smiles are used instead of money; nutriment is introduced into lakes so that the water, on boiling, becomes *shchee**; whales are employed as draught animals. These and other such innovations are retailed in iambic pentameter without any suggestion that the poet is out to emulate Baron Münchhausen. His new order is ruled by Futurists. On the other hand, in one of his last short poems this self-appointed President of the Globe† announces that he will "never, no, never, become a ruler." Attitudes at variance with Bolshevism are discernible in his writings. He did try his hand at propaganda but partisanship was alien to him. "Night Search" (1921), a dramatic sketch which deals with a brutal episode of the Red Terror, involving a crew of "holy murderers," is a politically ambiguous piece, faintly echoing Blok's "The Twelve." It stands out among Khlebnikov's writings as a psychologically sophisticated, nearly finished product. The other compositions are in his usual outlandish vein. One of them

* Cabbage soup.
† See bio-bibliographical note on Khlebnikov.

is a narrative poem subtitled "An Incantation by the Double Flow of Speech, Double Convex Speech." Each of its 408 lines is a palindrome.

It could not have been such a tedious *tour de force* as this that led Mayakovsky to declare Khlebnikov "the Columbus of new poetic continents." The lands he discovered in his fantastic voyagings have not remained wholly unexplored or uncultivated. His wild vagaries and idiosyncrasies notwithstanding, his work, together with that of other Futurists, has been influential in encouraging the use of synesthetic, eccentric imagery and in enhancing concern for verbal texture and word play. As for the recent upsurge of regard for Khlebnikov (his body was lately transferred to Moscow), it may be a manifestation of the violent reaction against the blinkers and shackles of "socialist realism."

It has been stressed that Mayakovsky became "the big-mouthed agitator" that he called himself. He was also a vitriolic satirist. His thrusts at bureaucrats, pedants, parasites—not only in his poems but especially in his two plays, *The Bedbug* and *The Bathhouse*—earned him powerful enemies. It is not impossible that he would have become another victim of the bloody purges of the thirties, had he not killed himself. Exactly what drove him to take his own life when he was at the height of his powers is a matter for conjecture. Five years earlier he had publicly condemned Yesenin for committing suicide. Posthumously he was enshrined as the poet laureate of the regime. A Moscow square in which his statue stands was named for him. Most of the comment on his writing was in the nature of homilies on a text supplied, in 1935, by Stalin himself: "Mayakovsky was and remains the most talented poet of the Soviet epoch, and an indifferent attitude toward his memory and his works is a crime." Many years later Boris Pasternak was to write that Mayakovsky was being forced on the public. He added: "That was his second death."

The work of the two poets offers striking contrasts. Pasternak, too, accepted the Revolution. The poems that he wrote in 1917—they belong to his best—give expression, he declared, to "everything unprecedented and elusive that can be learned about revolution." In fact, he even attempted to deal with themes having obvious political implications, as in the long poem about Lieutenant Schmidt, who headed a naval mutiny in 1905. Yet he did not feel it incumbent upon himself to celebrate the new faith or to persuade anyone of its worth. His concern was the contemplation of life, not the will to alter it. Endowed with an extremely alert sensibility, on one occasion he defined poetry as a sponge, yet he conferred on the fleeting impressions that it absorbed the quality of essences under the aspect of eternity. In a day and a generation demanding from poetry, as from the other arts, participation and even partisanship, he managed to remain virtually above the battle. He clung to an idealistic estheticism in a society which has conferred official status on the materialistic outlook. He went further: he hinted that poetry, with its concern for what is unique in the individual, is incompatible with collectivism.

His verse deals with a narrow range of ordinary events and not unusual situations: a summer rain, a sunrise, a mountain landscape, a thaw, an incident in an intimate personal relationship. Yet it is poles removed from conventional discourse. It is a kind of shorthand, which not infrequently defies transcription. Pasternak made no attempts to coin words, and his rhythmic patterns are by no means new, nor is his virtuosity with tone color or his ingenious elaboration of off-rhyme unique. What gives his verse individuality is the juxtaposition of words establishing connections and, often, paradoxical similarities between the most heterogeneous objects and concepts. His work thus illustrates Wallace Stevens' definition of poetry as "a satisfying of the desire for resemblance." Here is a highly studied, personal style, dense and opaque, the vehicle of saltatory, idiosyncratic thinking. Following it entails strain but is also exhilarating. To find analogous work in English one must turn to the performance of such poets as Gerard Manley Hopkins or Dylan Thomas. Pasternak's metaphors and metonymies are as fresh and as bold. Sometimes delightfully homely, more often they tax the imagination, demanding a difficult traffic in abstractions and violently dislocating habitual associations. His style is marked by an uninhibited and most effective indulgence in what Ruskin denounced as the pathetic fallacy, which Pasternak sometimes reverses, translating the behavior of sentient

beings into terms taken from the nonhuman sphere. This practice is founded on the tacit but firm assumption that the world
of man and the world of nature are at one. The total effect of
exposure to his work is at once to remove us from the daily
commonplace and to intensify our sense of reality.

In the spring of 1922 Pasternak came upon a little book of
verse from the pen of Marina Tsvetayeva and was struck by
what he felt to be the close affinity between this young woman's
work and his own. She had just accepted the bitter lot of the
dépaysé writer by expatriating herself, and she was to die a
tragic death some two decades later. Speaking of her poems
shortly before his own end, Pasternak ranked them with the
purest and most vigorous achievements of the Russian Symbolists. According to him, much of her work had remained unknown and, if ever published, would be "a great triumph and
a great discovery." A fairly generous selection from her poems
appeared in 1961 under a Moscow imprint. Unless it is wholly
unrepresentative, one must conclude that Pasternak had been
overly enthusiastic. Tsvetayeva was intensely emotional and
intransigent, a born extremist, "a rebel in head and guts," as
she phrased it. Her published writings include several plays
and a number of perceptive essays. Hers is the work of an
obfuscating poet, a virtuoso of compactness, using a breathless,
hysterical idiom, exclamatory, incantatory, and stubbornly re-
sisting translation. She saw the Revolution as an eruption of
the forces of evil. A sequence of her lyrics laments the defeated
White troops, but in one poem she writes of the fallen soldiers
of both camps lying indistinguishable one from another: the
Whites reddened by blood, the Reds whitened by death. The
bulk of her verse has to do with her private drama.

There was yet another school that enlivened the literary scene
and for years dominated it: the proletarian writers. Poems and
stories on working-class themes written by working-class people
from a working-class viewpoint had found their way into print
before the Revolution. Fifty volumes of "proletarian" verse
were published between 1908 and 1915. Under the new regime
this sort of writing blossomed out fully in the sun of public
encouragement. From the first, proletarian writers, the majority
of them versifiers, were nursed along by "Proletarian Cultural-

Educational Organizations" (Proletcults), which had originated shortly before the October Revolution. They issued books and magazines, and set up classes, seminars, and studios where poetry and the other arts were taught and practiced and which attracted not only beginners but people whose work had already seen publication.

The number of Proletcults kept growing and their prospects seemed bright, but their heyday was brief. Their leaders argued that since there was an unbreakable nexus between art and the class struggle, the literature of the new age could be created only by writers who were flesh of the flesh and bone of the bone of the revolutionary vanguard, the industrial workers. Here was a thesis in line with Marxism. But these ideologists had the temerity to claim for the organizations immunity from Party control. The Party rejected this claim, at Lenin's instigation. He, for one, preferred the development along socialist lines of the best elements in bourgeois culture. Other influential Communists, notably Trotsky, denied on theoretical grounds the very possibility of a proletarian culture. In December 1920 the Proletcults were placed under the Commissariat of Education and made subject to the directives of the Central Committee of the Party. This was the start of their decline, and by 1922 they were definitely on the way out.

Long before their activities ceased, associations of proletarian writers had sprung up outside those organizations. The Smithy was formed in 1920 in Moscow, where another group, called October—the month sacred to the Revolution—which included secessionists from The Smithy, came into being two years later. Similar associations arose in Petrograd and in the provinces. They warred with each other and issued rival manifestoes, much like their despised nonproletarian *confrères*. Nevertheless, in 1925 these bodies managed to set up an All-Russian Association of Proletarian Writers. By that time they had given up any claim to immunity from Party control.

Early proletarian verse exultantly celebrated the might and glory of the working class, the joy of collective labor freed from exploitation, Russia as "the mother of Soviets" rocking "the cradle of beautiful centuries." Steel, concrete, electricity were glorified in hyperbolic rhetoric, and so was the machine, "the iron Messiah." With the millennium seemingly at the door and man about to move mountains and command the stars, why should not a poet urge revolution on a global, indeed on a cosmic scale? Several Leningrad proletarian versifiers banded together as Cosmists. One poem urged the erection of a "Palace of World Freedom" beside the canals of Mars.

The retreat from socialism signalized by the New Economic Policy, inaugurated at the end of the civil war, had a sobering effect. At least one versifier suggested that NEP was a betrayal of the Revolution. But such kill-joys were few and far between. As reconstruction got under way, the scene was increasingly dominated by poets, many of them proletarian in name only, who did not question the wisdom of the Party and took every occasion to proclaim their devotion to communism. Mostly sanguine young people who had become articulate since the Revolution, they employed a realistic style and were engrossed in such matters as production costs and the state of the currency. Distrustful of lyricism, they were developing a penchant for rhymed narratives. While recently Balmont and Bryusov, as well as Verhaeren and Walt Whitman, had been the poets' models, now it was Mayakovsky, though some preferred more conventional metres than his. Straightforward propaganda, like that turned out for the dailies by the indefatigable Demyan Bednyi, gains in comparison with the more ambitious, if uninspired, performance of most of his fellows.

When the first Five-Year Plan was launched in 1928, the poets, like other soldiers of the pen, applied themselves dutifully to the task of promoting industrialization and rural collectivization. Alexander Tvardovsky, a gifted newcomer, glorified collective farming in long narrative poems written in a style echoing Nekrasov's and that of the native folk tales. Verse, however, was by this time quite overshadowed by fiction and semi-fictional reportage. Most of the literary schools that had added to the stir and excitement of the early twenties now folded up and the factional fury abated. The distinction between proletarian and nonproletarian (fellow traveler) writing lost its meaning, and in 1932 the Party abolished the Association of Proletarian Writers on the ground that all the authors had achieved an ideological homogeneity which made that organization unnecessary. It was replaced by a single all-embracing Union of Soviet Writers, which is still functioning. According to its statutes, its basic aim is "the creation of works of high artistic significance, permeated by the heroic struggle of the international proletariat and by exultation over the victory of socialism, and reflecting the great wisdom and heroism of the Communist Party." The statutes also impose upon writers a uniform way of treating their material, declaring that "the cardinal method" of Soviet literature is "socialist realism." This nebulous formula, attributed to Stalin, bolsters the doctrine that the proper task of the literary art as a handmaiden of the Party-State is to assist in the building of "socialism."

The trend now was toward simple, accessible, obvious verse, innocent of irony and paradox, eschewing eccentricities of style and all experimentation. In addition to conventional lyrics and variations on the inexhaustible theme of the civil war, many poems were written in connection with and furtherance of specific Soviet policies. There were pieces that carried a patriotic message and extolled stubborn strength and readiness to bear the brunt of battle; that paid homage to the heroism of the pilot Chkalov, and the labors of Michurin, the Russian Burbank; there were encomiums of Lenin and more particularly of Stalin. Writing assumed a made-to-order look. Few of the poets who had lent luster to the first dozen years of the Soviet period had survived. The newcomers were of lesser stature.

The thin sheaf of poems, under the promising title *Second Birth,* brought out by Pasternak in 1932, failed to justify the hope in authoritative quarters that he would fall into line with his colleagues. His work continued to defy the Party directives on literature. For the next ten years he published practically no original verse. A man of independent spirit in an atmosphere of abject conformism, he maintained his integrity as a writer by withdrawing into silence. Now and then critics held him up to scorn, and on one occasion he had to make a public apology for some of his lines. Yet, oddly enough, he was unscathed by the witch-hunt and terror of the thirties. He occupied himself chiefly with turning English, French, and German poetry, and—at second hand—Georgian verse, into Russian. His fellow writers, notably Tikhonov, translated verse from the many languages spoken in the Union. As in the past, translation was an important function of the poet, but now its purpose was less to make world masterpieces accessible to Russian readers than to strengthen the bond holding together the various Soviet nationalities.

"The arming of the souls of our fellow citizens with flaming love of our country and searing hatred of the enemy," the Union of Soviet Writers, anticipating victory, declared in a message to Stalin in February 1944, "has become the content of all our work in the days of the Great Fatherland War."* The verse-makers' contribution to this effort bulked large. Intended to stiffen the morale of both soldiers and civilians, the war poetry addressed itself to the more elementary emotions in simple, direct language. Much of it was what Louis MacNeice called "slogan poetry." A novel note was the acknowledgment of man's spiritual resources and even an appeal to religious feeling. Practically every established poet was moved to utterance by the conflict, and a number of novices—the versatile Konstantin Simonov, for one—found their subject matter there. Tvardovsky, who virtually chronicled the war in prose and verse, achieved immense popularity with a poem on an epic scale, the hero of which, affectionately delineated in his usual style, is the Russian equivalent of G.I. Joe. Vasily Tyorkin is the typical *muzhik* in uniform, a descendant of Tolstoy's Platon Karatayev. A companion piece to this is a verse narrative exalting the indomitable courage and endurance of a peasant woman, a soldier's wife. Even Pasternak composed a number of war poems, quite different from his previous work in their simplicity and directness. Selvinsky took the same road. Anna Akhmatova's name reappeared under a few lyrics, one of them a noble call for valor in the national emergency. Some of the finest and most sustained war poems, too long to be represented here, were written by women.

Control of literature was somewhat relaxed during the war, but when hostilities ended the reins were tightened again. The old injunctions were reiterated with a new urgency and intransi-

---

* It is thus that the share of the Soviet Union in the Second World War is officially styled.

gence: the writer's duty is to serve the people and the Party; he must produce ideologically impeccable works that meet the specifications of "socialist realism" and whose intention is to inspire action in furtherance of official policy; he must extol the heroism of the citizenry in battle and in peaceful labor exploits. Whatever was susceptible of being interpreted as showing the influence of—let alone sympathy with—the West was excoriated by umbrageous critics as a sure sign of bourgeois corruption, and so was any trace of "formalist," that is, apolitical and stylistically sophisticated writing. And adverse criticism implied a threat to more than prestige. Where imaginative writing is held to be a political instrument, an author's alleged fault verges on a political offense.

By way of intimidating the profession, an example was made of Mikhail Zoschenko, a popular writer of humorous short stories, and of Anna Akhmatova. In August 1946 the Central Committee of the Party discontinued the publication of a Leningrad monthly because, in addition to other "faulty works," it had printed her verse. This, permeated as it was with "the spirit of pessimism and decadence," was pronounced harmful to the young and so "not to be tolerated in Soviet literature." Forthwith, in a speech that was given the widest publicity, a high Party official vilified her as a despicable purveyor of mysticism and eroticism, whereupon she was expelled from the Writer's Union. Pasternak, though not proscribed, was denounced as out of tune with Soviet literature, and laxity in combating the popularity of his work was deplored in a resolution of the Presidium of the Union.

The verse produced in the stifling atmosphere of the first half dozen postwar years affects a facile, commonplace style and moves in traditional prosodic patterns. Nevertheless, the inexact rhyme is widely used, and one finds, if less frequently, the steplike arrangement of lines that Mayakovsky often employed. There is an abundance of occasional pieces called forth by an anniversary, an "election," an event such as the revaluation of the ruble, a speech of Stalin's. The late Generalissimo had been adulated so long, so persistently, so variously, that each new paean is a real tribute—to the versifier's inventiveness. The Party gets a generous measure of fulsome praise. There are variations on such themes as "Our flag is the world's noblest," "There are no people on the planet stronger and happier than we." War reminiscences, particularly deeds of Soviet heroism and experiences of Red Army men abroad, are a favorite subject. Nor does the Soviet Muse fail to do her bit in the cold war: verse-makers swell the chorus of anti-British and especially anti-American propaganda. They also celebrate the labor of the farmer, the miner, the steelworker, the road builder, driving home the moral that the construction front, though bloodless, is still a battlefront, demanding the utmost straining of every nerve and muscle. Promotion of the Government's forestation program is the sole purpose of a verse narrative printed in 1952. Another such work details the fortunes of a collective farm, concluding with a procession of trucks carrying a rich harvest. The last lines read: "The people are intoxicated with happiness and drink a toast to Stalin."

There are, however, during this period a number of non-political poems. These lyrics deal, some of them felicitously, with such stock themes as love and nature. But irony, skepticism, bitterness are, of course, generally absent, and the verse is expressive of the high spirits and noble sentiments believed to produce the bracing and uplifting effect mandatory for all literature.

The death of Stalin (in March 1953), while leaving the foundations of the system intact, brought about a significant shift in policies and in the methods of carrying them out. The new regime clings to the prerogative of directing all cultural activities, but it has been less coercive. To use a metaphor popularized by the title of a novel published in 1954 under a Moscow imprint, a "thaw" has been under way, intermittently and precariously, ever since the beginning of the post-Stalinist era.

The first signs of the new times were of a hortatory character. Pleas were heard for personal emotion in poetry, for sincerity and unvarnished truth in all literature, for replacing stereotypes with human beings. Protests against the regimentation of artists and the crudely mechanistic conception of the creative process were allowed to reach the public. Fiction and drama frankly suggesting that something was rotten in the state of the Soviets were not slow to appear. The unorthodox authors were sharply reproved by the watchdogs of the Party line, but no such punitive measures as imprisonment or deportation were taken against the culprits. Furthermore, the posthumous rehabilitation of victims of the purges went on, and proscribed writers continued to emerge from oblivion. In the months that followed the Twentieth Congress of the Party (February 1956), at which Khrushchev dealt a crushing blow to the cult of the dead demigod, the feeling spread that the time had arrived for a critical revaluation of received ideas, and that a long dark night was coming to an end.

The mood of the moment had its poets, among them Leonid Martynov, who envisaged the carting away of the "garbage" of "mistaken notions and false axioms" and, looking forward, exclaimed: "What bonds will be broken, / What knots cut!" The October issue of a Moscow monthly carried a candid verse narrative, "Zima Junction," by a member of the Communist League of Youth, Yevgeny Yevtushenko, of whom more later. It offers revealing glimpses of life in a Siberian town—among them alcoholism, intellectual stagnation, official corruption. Furthermore, there are thinly veiled allusions to the shattering effect of the denunciation of Stalin. The young author is deeply troubled. He has a visting Moscow journalist admit that "there have been changes" and that people talk about matters not mentioned yesterday, but add that "behind the speeches / some dark game is being played." The poet invites his readers to "think about things great and little"; he reflects on the genesis of lies, and ends by declaring that "without truth there is no happiness."

The turbulence that Khrushchev's anti-Stalin speech caused far and wide, the unrest in Poland, and the Hungarian insurrection late in the year, checked the concessive mood that had prevailed in high places. The authorities proceeded to suppress the stirrings of discontent and encouraged virulent attacks in the press on writers who went too far in stressing the seamy side of Soviet life. In an address to Moscow literati in the spring of 1957 Khrushchev referred to the role played by writers in the Hungarian uprising and is said to have added that he would not hesitate to use bullets to silence the more recalcitrant members of the writing profession at home. Two months later he delivered himself of another "tough" speech in defense of the political control of literature and the dogma of "socialist realism." There was some beating of breasts and there were protestations of devotion to the Party line.

It looked as though the frosts had returned, but they had not. True, "socialist realism" remains a cardinal communist dogma. An article by the editor of *Pravda* in the issue for February 21, 1965, allows that "genuine creativity . . . is possible only in the setting of inquiry, experimentation, free expression and clashes of opinion." In the next breath he declares that all the competing schools and trends have in common conformity to "socialist realism." Yet the bark is worse than the bite. The Soviet writer may not overtly question the basic purposes and policies of the existing order, including its tutelage over the arts, but the obligatory formula has not seldom been liberally interpreted. Furthermore, Soviet culture is to some degree losing its parochial character. There is more travel *in partibus infidelium*, greater access to foreign writings in the original as well as in translation, an organized attempt to promote personal contacts between Soviet intellectuals and their opposite numbers abroad.

In this less oppressive air, literature has begun to recover from the debilitating, corrupting effect of the political pressure to which it had been exposed since the Party-State laid rough hands on it. Within the last dozen years plays and works of fiction have appeared in which the characters behave like plausible, complex human beings, and Soviet life is presented more or less candidly. In 1962 the taboo was removed from revealing the nightmarish conditions in the Soviet concentration camps—until then the very existence of that institution could only be hinted at. As might be expected, poetry has been showing new vitality. To be sure, much verse is of the tiresome, unregenerate variety. The message, to use the words of a Soviet critic, "sticks out like a spring in an old sofa." Encomiums to the Party, "lighthouse of the planet," are numerous. One rhymester avers that there is no happier man on earth than a delegate to the Twenty-second Party Congress. Avowals of undying devotion to the Fatherland, "the world's conscience," abound. A female versifier declares that one heart is not enough to hold her love for her native land. Hosannas to Stalin have been replaced by panegyrics to Lenin. "Ilyich" is like the sun: "his warmth is felt by all." His mausoleum "is flying into eternity." There is no lack of self-congratulation even on occasions other than the Soviet penetration of outer space. If less prominently than before, the lyre is part of the cold war arsenal.

Even during the Draconian years, however, poems that failed to meet the quasi-official specifications of partisanship, social charge, wholesomeness, cheer, sometimes managed to get into print. The body of post-Stalinist verse—its bulk is staggering—includes a larger proportion of such work. It is contributed by the younger lyricists who speak for a generation in revolt, but also by a few older poets who have managed to preserve their artistic integrity. An eminent figure in this group is Anna Akhmatova. Signal distinction attaches to those of her poems that have appeared since Stalin's death. She has returned to the theme of her early lyrics: love as a woman knows it. In dealing with it, the septuagenarian shows the familiar intensity of feeling, touched sometimes by acrimony, but now the crystal clarity of her verse can be clouded by a breath from arcane regions. Some of her poems, such as those from the cycle "Secrets of the Trade," are esoteric pieces in the manner of poetry as practiced in the West. In 1963 her compatriots were first allowed to read her "Epic Without a Hero," a phantasmal "triptych" enveloped in an impenetrably misty, Hoffmannesque atmosphere. The poem, composed during the Second World War, is a farewell to the friends and lovers of her youth. Still inaccessible to the Soviet public is "Requiem," a sequence of lyrics written during the terror of the thirties and commemorating its victims, among them her husband and her son.

No less nonconformist is the poetry of the late Nikolay Zabolotzky, a stammerer among the glib. Although on occasion he protested against the poet who, "playing charades, puts on a sorcerer's cap," he was incapable of writing for the mass mind. Zabolotzky's work is the product of a pantheistic imagination that transfigures the lower forms of life—birds, insects, plants. His lyrics vibrate with feeling, keen awareness of evil, pain, and death. His bold, sometimes grotesque, imagery and elliptical style suggest the influence of the Futurists and of Pasternak. Since, as every newspaper reader knows, the author of *Doctor Zhivago* suffered proscription, not all the poems that he composed in his last years have been published at home, but they have appeared in the original abroad. They revolve chiefly about the natural scene, and they are written in the less abstruse style that he had been using since the outbreak of the Second World War.

Unlike these poets, Alexander Tvardovsky is a master of the homely, limpid style. A staunch member of the Party, he seems to hold that basic freedoms, including freedom of the press, are compatible with communism. In fact, he is the leader of an informal group of liberal writers who are at war with the neo-Stalinist die-hards. His position is manifested in two remarkable verse narratives recently published. The first, completed in 1960, is a personal, semi-autobiographical work, of the sort frowned upon in the black years, when the poet's duty was to be "the speaking trumpet of the times." In one passage Tvardovsky suggests that the fraudulence of Soviet fiction is due to the timidity of writers still living in the fearful past. In another, the author encounters a childhood friend on his way from a concentration camp, where he had spent seventeen years as an innocent victim of a purge. The second verse narrative relates the further adventures, this time "in the other world," of Vasily Tyorkin, the hero of Tvardovsky's wartime epic. A delightful blend of fantasy and humor, couched in time-honored trochaics managed with great skill, it is also a satire on the Soviet regime so biting that for two years "Tyorkin in the Other World" circulated secretly in manuscript. It was published in 1963 in the Moscow monthly edited by its author, only after it had been printed abroad earlier that year.

Other poets of the older generation, though none of them is of the first rank, are publishing work that is respectable or better. The fantastic and the whimsical have their part in it. The subject matter is apt to be private, and even when public themes are touched upon, the approach is indirect, while the tone is not aggressive and may even be quietly ironical. The poetry produced is definitely not of the kind that, in Keats's phrase, has "a palpable design upon the reader." One finds an attractive obliquity here. There is also a stronger feeling for economy, as in the work of Stepan Shchipachev, a maker of miniatures that give off fragrance and freshness. Further, some of these writers have a technical competence as well as a gift for unhackneyed imagery that can extend to inventiveness. Though sophistication is rare, their simplicity has its engaging aspect.

A poet who is on the sunny side of middle age and who stands out from his contemporaries is Yevgeny Vinokurov. Like so many of them, he was schooled by the war. If his wartime experiences made him respect blunt, forceful ingenuousness that will not be deflected from its goal, he was to repudiate this lesson. "There is nothing in this world / More terrible than simplicity," he was to write. His is a skeptical, questing intelligence, feuding with the obvious. The war, he says, robbed him of his youth, and perhaps for this reason he prizes that period of life above maturity. In any event, he has written lyrics instinct with the dynamism, the animal faith that belong to youth. But he is aware of the ubiquitousness of pain, "the tragic basis of the world," and with sobriety and wit he keeps returning to the mysteries of infinity and eternity. His reflective verse is suffused with human warmth. He longs to speak out about the horrors that he had lived through, the abysses that he had plumbed. The word has supreme potency for him. He is impatient with vacuous words ("barren bean pods") and he recognizes that "suffering is mute. Music is mute."

The range of his subject matter is wide. He vividly recalls adolescence, evokes the effect of music ("It removes the hard crust of rationality from people, the way a knife barks a birch"); he muses on the enigma of woman's beauty, on "the great and complex art of wonderment," the unpredictability of the ways of the mind as against the regularity of Nature's; he sets down an episode of the war; he speaks of his craving for truth, "as a patient craves something sour." Regardless of theme, the stance is candid, the language plain, the tone conversational, intimate. By his own account, technical matters do not interest him much. The genesis of a poem, he ventures, is like the birth of a child, adding: "The organic is dear to me."

He generally uses conventional metres and regular rhyme. Expressiveness is achieved by piling up separate, concrete, humdrum, evocative details—leaving something unsaid. Here is poetry distilled from life's prose.

Vinokurov's work is clearly in line with the verse produced by the more gifted members of the post-Stalinist generation. The performance of these young poets is most adequately represented by the writing of two friends, both born in 1933: Yevgeny Yevtushenko and Andrey Voznesensky. For all their difference, they share certain characteristics which appeal to their contemporaries: nonconformism, active self-definition, an inquiring mind, a passion for freedom of expression. Yevtushenko has already been mentioned as the author of "Zima Junction," one of the landmarks of the "thaw." This verse narrative was followed by numerous lyrics. They have brashness and verve, are alive with a lust for action, for experience. Yevtushenko is "greedy for people." His pages are dominated by the "I," so long in hiding, and are not free from posturing. Now he dwells on his failings, now speaks with unabashed pride of his endurance, gift of his Siberian origin and upbringing. He will have nothing by halves. Declaring that mediocrity is unnatural, he demands that everyone be "great." He writes, too, about grief, tenderness, and, of course, love. In one poem he has it that when love entered his life, "everything vanished, and it alone was in the world"—a sentiment scarcely befitting a Communist. And he commits a breach of Soviet proprieties, as does Vinokurov, by admitting sex into his lyrics.

For all his self-assertion, Yevtushenko is a poet much of whose work is in the nature of civic verse. He believes that he must proclaim the truth to the people. In pieces that combine the topical with the personal, he denounces Soviet society's failings, seen as Stalin's bequest: mendacity, toadying, widespread official corruption, bureaucratic abuse of power, the arrogance of the new upper class. He pleads for change, warns against a return of Stalinism, the dead hand of the past, urges freedom of expression. It is largely this verse that has won Yevtushenko an immense and ardent following and has spread his renown far beyond the confines of the Soviet Union. What may be effective as platform poetry in cold print sometimes gives the impression of rhymed journalism. Such is the case of "Babiy Yar," commemorating the massacre of thirty-four thousand Jews by the Germans in a ravine near Kiev, "unmarked by any memorial." As an impassioned outcry against Soviet anti-Semitism, it was a courageous act which has justly had ample resonance; as a poem, it is wanting. Yevtushenko can be heavy-handed in driving home his message, and occasionally spontaneity and improvisation result in slovenliness.

There is nothing in his writing that implies disloyalty to the regime or deviation from the fundamentals of ideological orthodoxy. What he inveighs against is not communism but the betrayal of that ideal in all its pristine purity. His versified account of a journey, composed in 1958, is the work of a patriot deeply attached to his native region and enraptured by the might of his country, for which he envisages a revolutionary mission in the world. He and his contemporaries, he declares, will match the exploits of their fathers without jeering at their (unspecified) errors, but without committing them, either. He adds: "We enter life angrily and bravely / As befits the young. / We want not half-truths, or untruths, / But the whole truth." In another poem, however, he is at pains to dissociate his generation from the angry young men of the West. They have no faith in anything, he argues, and despise even themselves, but he, for one, believes in "Lenin's truth." More recently he has explicitly affirmed his devotion to communism and was one of the writers who signed a statement to the effect that all Soviet poets, regardless of age, are fighting for Lenin's cause. In the spring of 1965 he published a poem running to thousands of lines, entitled "The Bratsk Hydroelectric Station." He opens it by prayerfully calling upon the help of the "immortal" poets, from Pushkin to Pasternak. The foreword states the theme: the clash between pessimism and faith in mankind's future, symbolized respectively by the Pyramid and the mammoth Siberian plant. His declared purpose is to urge his contemporaries to carry on the tradition of insurgency. To that end he evokes the native revolutionaries, concluding with Lenin, "the man dearest to all of us."

There is no doubt that some poets, apparently a small minority of more clear-sighted and critically-minded youths, sharply disagree with Yevtushenko's stand. They hold that the more odious features of Soviet life, not least the debasement of arts and letters, stem directly from the regime hammered out by the Revolution. This view finds expression in the clandestine writings, mostly, it seems, the work of students, which, at serious risk to the authors and readers, have been circulating in manuscript or mimeographed and hectographed copies since the turbulent year 1956, if not earlier. To judge by the samples that have reached the West, much of this literature is verse. The uncensored thoughts voiced in these poems are tinged with horror of life in "a prison built on bones," with forebodings of disaster, hunger for a new faith, despair, hope. There are love lyrics, but the prevailing note is rebellion. One writer predicts that when the decisive hour strikes, the poet will find his place in the ranks of the rebels; another has it that a crisis brings forth poets, and they mold fighters. The style of these pieces is obviously a reaction against the official canon. It faintly echoes Pasternak, Tsvetayeva, the early Mayakovsky, Khlebnikov. Here is a rare instance of political and stylistic extremism coexisting. It is not surprising to find in a 1961 issue of the underground journal bearing the sanguine title *Phoenix* an open letter to Yevtushenko, dismissing him as "a new type of chameleon," a man "lacking firm convictions" and "too ready to forgive the errors of the fathers."

One can conceive the contempt with which the disaffected young regard Voznesensky. A group of poems that he published in 1963 outdoes in uninhibited extravagance the adulation lavished through the years upon Lenin—no small feat of inventiveness. It is hard to credit this young sophisticate with believing that "Lenin answers all questions" or that in the mausoleum the mummy's "transparent brow shines sunnily and passionately." Be that as it may, Voznesensky's work is in sum a denial of the totalitarian temper generally, and of the Leninist policy in the area of culture particularly. Unmistakably original, emphatically subjective, his is not poetry for the millions. He writes as if he had never heard of "socialist realism." The poet, he intimates, is given to smashing codes and dogmas. Authority does not awe Voznesensky. His full-blooded, highly charged poetry, compounded of feeling, fantasy, and wit, is the product of an ebullient, independent nature and a subtle intelligence. A verbal virtuoso, he puns richly, juggles with words, plays with the aural elements of language: alliteration, and diverse forms of assonance, consonance, and dissonance. He is one of those poets whom Francis Thompson described as "drunkards in words," and not unnaturally his excitement is sometimes in excess of its occasion. Like other incantatory poets, melody is of first importance to him. "Music in verse is indispensable," he wrote to a friend; "it is like a signal, a siren, directing the reader's attention to the highest meaning of the poem." His verse does not readily yield meaning, of whatever order. Sometimes he gives the impression of deliberately avoiding clarity. His cloudy sequences move elliptically, veiled in ambiguity. The imagery is eccentric, not without anachronisms and bold incongruities; the juxtaposition of words is startling, the allusions and implications are sometimes impenetrable. All this links him to Western writers now in vogue. He is obviously a modern, not only by reason of his peculiarly private style, but also because he is at home in the atomic age and exults in the speed and the technological marvels that are its notable features (this is at variance with the note of nostalgia for the old rural simplicities and of aversion to the mechanical that is heard in recent Soviet poetry). In fine, Voznesensky is the leader of the incipient poetic vanguard in the Soviet Union.

Specimens of Voznesensky's work at its most extreme and a poem in a similar style by Vladimir Tsybin have appeared in the columns of the Moscow monthly that addresses itself to youth. That such verse has managed to clear the barrier of censorship is proof enough that in Russia poetry has been allowed to arrive at a *modus vivendi*, tolerable if precarious. Further, there are now not a few writers who are certain to make the most of whatever freedoms are being granted or such as may be granted in the future. This group, which finds a huge and enthusiastic if not yet very discriminating public, is composed of several older poets of stature and a number of younger practitioners of verse, men and women who have either made a distinctive contribution to their art or who give promise of doing so. They are seeking to assert themselves but are innocent of the sense of alienation that haunts the Western artist. And none of these writers starts from scratch: there is behind them a humane tradition—marked by an inveterate concern for the collective as well as for the individual, increasingly devoted to the word, and not without that historical sense which, in Eliot's phrase, "makes a writer most acutely conscious . . . of his own contemporaneity." This tradition, having survived the rigors of the Stalinist era, is apparently being recovered.

A . Y .
May, 1965

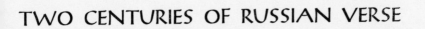

TWO CENTURIES OF RUSSIAN VERSE

MIKHAIL LOMONOSOV

Inscription for a Statue of Peter the Great

Behold the sculpture here of him, who, most audacious,
Most wise, forewent his ease to serve, supremely gracious
Toward his people: chose the rank of lowliest knave,
And reigned—exemplar, he upheld the laws he gave;
He put his scepter by, reached, rather, for the spanner;
His power he hid, unfurling science's bright banner.
He built a city; none bore battle's brunt as he;
He visited far lands, and journeyed oversea;
To gather artists, to train soldiers was his doing,
The enemies at home, as those abroad, subduing:
There's Peter, father of the fatherland, in brief;
An earthly deity our Russia is adoring;
Many the altar fires before this figure soaring,
The hearts beholden to him, many beyond belief.

Not later than 1747

Verses Composed on the Way to Peterhof

*Whereto the Author was Riding in 1761 to Solicit a Signature
to a Franchise for the Academy, He having Traveled Thither
Many Times Previously upon the Same Errand**

Dear grasshopper, how truly fortunate thy lot,
How happier far art thou than humans are, I wot!
Amidst the softest grass thy easy life thou spendest,
And honey dew's the fare upon which thou dependest.

* All lines save the final one are in imitation of "The Grasshopper," an
Anacreontic piece well known to readers of English poetry in Cowley's
version.

Though many view thee as a despicable thing,
Compared to us thou art, yea, verily, a king.
Incarnate angel, thou, nay—incorporeal being!
Thy leap is free, thy song with Nature's voice agreeing;
Whate'er thou seest is thine, at home wherever met,
Thou dost solicit naught, thou art to none in debt.

1761

GAVRIIL DERZHAVIN

On the Emperor's Departure, December 7, 1812*

Lo, my prophetic dreams are very truth at last:
France bows to Russia's might and Europe is laid low.
The glory we may claim no nation has surpassed!
The gift of peace 'tis in our power to bestow.
Be the Greek Alexander renowned as great in war,
But who brings peace on earth, his soul is greater far!

[1812]

"Time's River" †

Time's river carries on its current
All the affairs of men; it flings
To the abysm of oblivion
Drowned nations, kingdoms even as kings.

* On that day Alexander I, receiving word that the Russian army had
entered Vilna, left the capital for Kutuzov's headquarters to hearten the
troops by his presence.
† Derzhavin's last lines, penned three days before his death.

And if the voice of lyre and trumpet
Awhile holds aught above the spate,
That, too, eternity will swallow,
That, too, await the common fate.

[1816]

VASILY ZHUKOVSKY

Remembrance

How many dear companions who enlivened for us
The world's rough road are gone, each fellow traveler
   Much missed; yet say not sadly: they have left us!
   But rather say, with gratitude: they were.

[1821]

DMITRY VENEVITINOV

Fatherland*

How ugly nature is here, truly:
Fields whose meek flatness gives offense
(It seems the very land in Russia
Takes height as an impertinence);
Mean huts and taverns; bare legs taking
Big-bellied wenches on their way;
Poor peasants shod with bast that's rotting;
Roads that facilitate delay;
And steeples, oh, what endless steeples—
Enema tubes in effigy;
And wretched views from manor houses
Of landscaping bizarrerie;
Filth, vileness, stench, cockroaches swarming,
The knout supreme on every hand—
And that is what our countless boobies
Keep calling, "sacred fatherland."

[1826]   1924

* There is some doubt as to the attribution of this poem, discovered
nearly a century after it was written.

KONDRATY RYLEYEV

Citizen

Am I the one who in these fateful days
Will tarnish the proud name of citizen,
And follow in your ways, degenerate Slavs,
Who are no longer of the race of men?
No, I cannot deliver up my youth
To idleness, lust shall not capture me,
My fiery spirit was not born to bear
The heavy irons of autocracy.
Let careless youths who have misread their fate,
Blind to the struggle we dare not deny,
Be found unready at the heroic hour
When freedom sternly bids us act, or die.
Let such as those look with indifference
Upon their country's anguish, nor foresee
Their shameful portion in the time to come,
The just reproaches of posterity.
They will repent when, rising in revolt,
The people strain to break the inveterate chain
And seek among those slothful libertines
A Brutus, a Riego—but in vain.

[1825] 1861

ALEXANDER PUSHKIN

To Chaadayev

Not long we basked in the illusions
Of love, of hope, of tranquil fame;
Like morning mist, like dreams' delusions,
Youth's pastimes vanished as they came.
But still, with strong desires burning,
Beneath oppression's fearful hand,
The bidding of the fatherland
We are impatiently discerning;
In hope, in torment, we are turning
Toward freedom, wishing she were near,
As a young lover waits his dear
And looks and longs, consumed with yearning.
While freedom fires the blood, and now
While honor summons us—O hear it!
Friend, to our country let us vow
The noble strivings of the spirit.
Comrade, believe: joy's star will leap
Upon our sight, a radiant token;
Russia will rouse from her long sleep;
And where autocracy lies, broken,
Our names shall yet be graven deep.

[1818]

To N. N.

From Aesculapius escaping,
I'm lean and shaven, but alive;
His cruel paw no more torments me,
And there is hope that I may thrive.

Now health, the light friend of Priapus,
And sleep, are entering my door,
And in my plain and crowded corner
Repose becomes my guest once more.
Then humor this poor convalescent,
You, too—he longs to see again
Your face, you lawless carefree creature,
Parnassus' lazy citizen,
The son of Freedom and of Bacchus,
Who worships Venus piously,
A master hand at every pleasure.
From Petersburg society,
Its chilly charms, its idle bustle,
Its clacking tongues that nothing stills,
Its various and endless boredom,
I'm summoned by the fields and hills,
The shady maples in the garden,
The bank of the deserted burn,
The liberties the country offers.
Give me your hand. I shall return
At the beginning of October:
We'll drink together once again,
And o'er our cups with friendly candor
Discuss a dozen gentlemen—
We'll talk of fools and wicked gentry,
And those with flunkeys' souls from birth,
And sometimes of the King of Heaven,
And sometimes of the czar on earth.

[1819]

Gay Feast

I love the festive board
Where joy's the one presiding,
And freedom, my adored,
The banquet's course is guiding;

Where "Drink!" half drowns the song
That only morning throttles;
Where wide-flung is the throng,
And close the jostling bottles.

[1819]

Grapes

I shall not miss the roses, fading
When springtime's hurrying days are done;
I love the grapes whose clusters ripen
Upon the hillsides in the sun—
The glory of my fertile valley,
They hang, each lustrous as a pearl,
Gold autumn's joy, oblong, transparent,
Like the slim fingers of a girl.

[1820]

A Nereid

Below the dawn-flushed sky, where the green billow lies
Caressing Tauris' flank, I saw a Nereid rise.
Breathless for joy I lay, hid in the olive trees,
And watched the demigoddess ride the rosy seas.
The waters lapped about her swan-white breast and young,
As from her long soft hair the wreaths of foam she wrung.

[1820]

The Coach of Life

Though often somewhat heavy-freighted,
The coach rolls at an easy pace;
And Time, the coachman, grizzly-pated,
But smart, alert, is in his place.

We board it lightly in the morning
And on our way at once proceed;
Repose and slothful comfort scorning,
We shout: "Hey, there! Get on! Full speed!"

Noon finds us done with reckless daring,
And shaken up. Now care's the rule.
Down hills, through gullies roughly faring,
We sulk, and cry: "Hey, easy, fool!"

The coach rolls on, no pitfalls dodging.
At dusk, to jolts more wonted grown,
We drowse, while to the night's dark lodging
Old coachman Time drives on, drives on.

[1823]

"A Sower"*

"Behold, a sower went forth to sow."

A sower—in the waste—of freedom,
Before the star of morning showed
I cast into the slavish furrow,
With clean and blameless hand, the load
Of seeds that quicken where they're sowed;
My loss was only time and labor
And thoughts by noble hopes bestowed.

Graze as you must, you peaceful peoples!
You will not rouse at honor's horn.
Can flocks enjoy the gifts of freedom?
Their lot is to be killed or shorn,
Wear the belled yoke tame sires had worn,
The legacy of generations,
And bear the whip that they had borne.

[1823]

---

* In a letter dated December 1 (Old Style), 1823, Pushkin described
this poem as "an imitation of a parable by that moderate democrat,
Jesus Christ."

The Demon

In days when each of life's impressions
For its sheer freshness gave delight—
When a girl's eyes, a grove's susurrus,
The nightingale's pure voice at night;
When every noble impulse, freedom,
And glory, and inspired art
Were powerful as love to waken
A quicker motion of the heart—
With sudden anguish having shadowed
The hours of hope, of ecstasy,
Forthwith a certain evil genius
Would visit me in secrecy.
Those meetings made for desolation:
His gaze, bizarre, his very smile,
His caustic words would pour cold venom
Into my soul, till all was vile.
With what exhaustless denigration
He tempted Heaven, naught was exempt:
The beautiful he called a figment,
Held inspiration in contempt,
Believed in neither love nor freedom,
Mocked life in all its variousness,
And there was nothing in all nature
That he could bring himself to bless.

[1823]

On Count M. S. Vorontzov*

Half hero and half ignoramus,
What's more, half scoundrel, don't forget.
But on this score the man gives promise:
He's apt to make a whole one yet.

[1824]

* Pushkin's superior in Odessa.

"Though Soporific Not a Little"

Though soporific not a little,
He's so pugnacious, you would think
That with a mad dog's foaming spittle
This critic thins his opiate ink.

[1824]

"Beneath the Azure"

Beneath the azure of her native skies she drooped,
  To fade, to vanish past returning;
It may be the young ghost above me briefly stooped
  And swept me with a shadowy yearning.

But now between us lies a line I may not cross.
  I cannot rouse the old devotion:
Indifferent lips were those that told me of my loss,
  I learned of it without emotion.

So that is she who set my spirit all afire
  With love that mingled tender sadness
And grievous straining, weary ache of sharp desire,
  That was heart's torment and mind's madness!

Where is the torment now, the love? Alas, the host
  Of memories that thus outlive you
Can stir no tears, you credulous, poor ghost,
  In one with no regrets to give you.

[1825]

Winter Evening

Storm clouds dim the sky; the tempest
Weaves the snow in patterns wild;
Like a beast the gale is howling
And now wailing like a child;
On the worn old roof it rustles
The piled thatch, and then again
Like a traveler belated
Knocks upon the windowpane.

Sad and dark our shabby cottage,
Indoors not a sound is heard.
Nanny, sitting at the window,
Can't you give me just a word?
What is wrong, dear? Are you wearied
By the wind, so loud and rough?
Or the buzzing of your distaff—
Has that set you dozing off?

Let us drink, dear old companion,
You who shared my sorry start;
Get the mug and drown our troubles:
That's the way to cheer the heart.
Sing the ballad of the titmouse
That beyond the seas had gone,
Or the song about the maiden
Fetching water just at dawn.

Storm clouds dim the sky; the tempest
Weaves the snow in patterns wild;
Like a beast the gale is howling
And now wailing like a child.
Let us drink, dear old companion,
You who shared my sorry start;
Get the mug and drown our troubles:
That's the way to cheer the heart.

[1825]

The Prophet*

Athirst in spirit, through the gloom
Of an unpeopled waste I blundered,
And saw a six-winged Seraph loom
Where the two pathways met and sundered.
He set his fingers on my eyes:
His touch lay soft as slumber lies—
And like an eagle's, scared and shaken,
Did my prophetic eyes awaken.
He touched my ears, and lo! they rang
With a reverberating clang:
I heard the spheres revolving, chiming,
The angels in their soaring sweep,
The monsters moving in the deep,
The vines low in the valley climbing.
And from my mouth the Seraph wrung
Forth by its roots my sinful tongue,
The idle tongue that slyly babbled,
The vain, malicious, the unchaste,
And the wise serpent's sting he placed
In my numb mouth with hand blood-dabbled;
And with a sword he clove my breast,
Drew forth the heart that shook with dread
And in my gaping bosom pressed
A glowing coal of fire instead.

Upon the wastes, a lifeless clod,
I lay, and heard the voice of God:
"Arise, O prophet, look and ponder:
Arise, charged with my will, and spurred!
As over roads and seas you wander,
Kindle men's hearts with this, my Word."

[1826]

* See Isaiah 6:1–10.

Message to Siberia*

Deep in the Siberian mine,
Keep your patience proud;
The bitter toil shall not be lost,
The rebel thought unbowed.

The sister of misfortune, Hope,
In the under-darkness dumb
Speaks joyful courage to your heart:
The day desired will come,

And love and friendship pour to you
Across the darkened doors,
Even as round your galley beds
My free music pours.

The heavy-hanging chains will fall,
The walls will crumble at a word;
And Freedom greet you in the light,
And brothers give you back the sword.

[1827] 1874

Arion

We numbered many in the ship;
Some trimmed the sails, while some, together,
Pulled on the oars; we had fair weather.
The rudder in his steady grip,

* This poem is addressed to the participants in the abortive armed uprising
against the autocracy, which occurred in December 1825. Pushkin handed
it to the wife of one of the Decembrists who was leaving to join her
husband in Siberia. In reply to this message one of the exiles, Prince
Alexander Odoyevsky (1802–1839), wrote a poem which at one time was
very popular in revolutionary circles. In it he assured "the bard" that the
Decembrists were proud of their chains and that their faith in the cause
of freedom was unshaken:

> Our grievous labors were not all in vain:
> A flame will yet be kindled from the spark.

The last line is printed at the masthead of *The Spark,* the central organ
of the Russian Social Democratic Workers' Party, which in 1900–1903
was edited by Lenin abroad and smuggled into Russia.

Our helmsman silently was steering
The heavy galley through the sea,
While I, in blithe serenity,
Sang to the crew . . . when savagely
A gust swooped, sudden waves were rearing. . . .
The helmsman and the crew were lost!
No sailor by the storm was tossed
Ashore—but I who had been singing.
Lifting my voice in song once more,
I shed my garments, wetly clinging,
To sun them on the rocky shore.

[*1827*]

Three Springs

Three springs in life's immense and joyless desert
Leap into light from a mysterious source;
The spring of youth, boiling in bright rebellion,
Bubbles and sparkles ere it runs its course;
Life's exiles at the clear Castalian fountain
Drink draughts more pure, more heady than the first;
But 'tis the deep, cold wellspring of oblivion
That slakes most sweetly ecstasy and thirst.

[*1827*]

Remembrance

When noisy day at last is quieted
   And on the hushed streets of the town,
Half diaphane, night's shadow lies, and sleep,
   The wage of toil, is handed down,
Then in the silence how the hours drag out
   My weary vigil; then up start
Snakes of remorse nocturnal torpor wakes
   To livelier flame that stings the heart.

Dreams eddying, surge; anguish crowds the mind
   With wounding thoughts that press too close;
In silence memory unrolls for me
   A scroll as long as it is gross;
I read and loathe the record of the years,
   Shake, curse the grim display;
My groans are bitter, bitter are the tears
   That wash no sorry line away.

[1828]

Poltava

From Canto III

The east is bright with dawn. Already
On field and hill the cannon roars.
The purple smoke in swirl and eddy
Toward a cloudless heaven soars
To meet the beams that morning pours.
The ranks are closed. The marksmen scatter—
They lie in ambush even yet.
The balls go rolling, bullets spatter,
And coldly slants the bayonet.
The Swede, long crowned with victory's favors,
Tearing through trench fire, never wavers.
The frantic cavalry in force
Rides forth—the infantry, impassive,
With solid tread and firm front massive,
Moves forward to support the horse.
And here the battlefield is burning,
And there the fatal thunder lours;
But now the tide of war is turning,
And fortune, it is plain, is ours.
The fire beats off the troops, defeating
The broken ranks that strew the field.
Rosen slips through the gorge, retreating,
Impassioned Schlippenbach must yield.

Our hosts press on till we have crowded
The Swedes, who, panicked, perish thus,
The glory of their banners clouded:
The God of Battles sides with us.

Then, like the voice of Heaven, urging
The victors, Peter's voice sounds clear:
"Now, with God's help, to work!" And here,
His favorites about him surging,
Comes Peter from the tent. His eyes
Ablaze, his face commands surrender.
His step is swift. A tempest's splendor
Alone with Peter's splendor vies.
He goes. They bring his charger, panting;
High-strung, yet ready to obey,
He scents the fire of the fray
And quivers. Now, his eyeballs slanting,
Into the battle's dust he fares,
Proud of the rider that he bears.

Noon nears. The blazing heat bores deeper.
The battle rests—a tired reaper.
Some Cossacks prance, and by design.
The regiments fall into line.
No more is martial music sounding,
And on the hills the hungry roar
Of the calmed cannon breaks no more.
And lo! across the plain resounding,
A deep "Hurrah!" rolls from afar:
The regiments have seen the Czar.

[*1828*]

"The Man I Was of Old"

*Tel j'étais autrefois et tel je suis encore.**

The man I was of old, that man I still remain:
Lighthearted, quick to fall in love. My friends, 'tis vain

* The epigraph is from André Chénier.

To think I can behold the fair without elation
And timid tenderness and secret agitation.
Has love not played with me and teased me quite enough?
The Cyprian's nets deceive, so soft and yet so tough,
Have I not struggled there like a young hawk who's cheated?
Forgetting injuries a hundred times repeated,
Unto new shrines I bring my old idolatries. . . .

[1828]

Portrait

When she, that soul of fire, appears,
O women of the North, among you,
It is a radiant challenge flung you,
Your dull conventions, worldly fears.
She spends herself as, brightly daring,
She flies, disdainful of those bars—
How like a lawless comet flaring
Among the calculable stars!

[1828]

"Night Lays Its Pall"

Night lays its pall upon the hills of Georgia;
I watch Aragva's waters rushing past.
Sad but serene, I feel my sadness lightened:
A sadness filled with you, holding you fast.

You, only you. . . . And pain has lost its power;
Burdened my spirit, yet exalted, too:
My heart is quick once more with love's sweet fever,
Because not love is what I cannot do.

[1829]

"Lovely Youth"

(Camp on the Euphrates)

Lovely youth, when war drums rattle
Be not ravished: seal your ears;
Do not leap into the battle
With the crowd of mountaineers.
Well I know that death will shun you,
And that where the sabers fly
Azrael will look upon you,
Note your beauty, and pass by.
But the war will be unsparing:
Surely you will come to harm—
Lose your timid grace of bearing,
Lose your shy and languid charm.

[*1829*]

"I Loved You Once"

I loved you once, nor can this heart be quiet,
For it would seem that love still lingers here;
But do not you be further troubled by it:
I would in no wise sadden you, my dear.
I loved you without hope, a mute offender;
What jealous pangs, what shy despairs I knew!
A love as deep as this, as true, as tender,
God grant another may yet offer you.

[*1829*]

"Here's Winter"

Here's winter. Far from town, what shall we do? I question
The servant bringing in my morning cup of tea:
"How is the weather—warm? Not storming? The ground's
        covered
With freshly fallen snow?" Come, is it best to be

Astride a horse at once, or shall we, until dinner,
See what the neighbor's old reviews may have to say?
The snow is fresh and fine. We rise, and mount our horses,
And trot through fields agleam with the first light of day.
We carry whips; the dogs run close behind our stirrups;
With careful eyes we search the snow, we scour the plain
For tracks, ride round and round, and tardily at twilight,
After we've missed two hares, at last turn home again.
How jolly! Evening comes: without, the storm is howling;
The candlelight is dim. The heart is wrenched with pain.
Slow drop by drop I drink my boredom's bitter poison.
I try a book. The eyes glide down the page—in vain:
My thoughts are far away . . . and so I close the volume,
Sit down, take up my pen, force my dull Muse to say
Some incoherent words, but harmony is wanting,
The sounds won't chime. . . . The devil! Where now is the way
I had with rhyme? I can't control this curious handmaid:
The verse is shapeless, cold, so lame it cannot walk.
So I dismiss the Muse: I am too tired to quarrel.
I step into the parlor where I hear them talk
About the sugar works, about the next election;
The hostess, like the weather, frowns, her only arts
Are plying rapidly her long steel knitting needles,
Or telling people's fortunes by the king of hearts.
How dismal! Thus the days go by, alike and lonely.
But if, while I play draughts at twilight in my nook,
Into our dreary village a closed sleigh or carriage
Should just by chance bring guests for whom I did not look:
Say, an old woman and two girls, her two young daughters
(Tall, fair-haired creatures, both), the place that was so dull,
So Godforsaken, all at once is bright and lively,
And suddenly, good heavens, life grows rich and full!
Attentive sidelong looks, and then a few words follow,
There's talk, then friendly laughter, and songs when lamps
        are lit,
And after giddy waltzes there are languid glances,
There's whispering at table, gay and ready wit;
Upon the narrow stairs a lingering encounter;
When darkness falls, a girl steals from her wonted place

And out onto the porch, bare-throated, chest uncovered—
The wind is up, the snow blows straight into her face!
Unhurt in northern blasts the Russian rose will blow.
How hotly burns a kiss in keen and frosty weather!
How fresh a Russian girl abloom in gusts of snow!

[1829]

"Along the Noisy Streets"

Along the noisy streets I wander,
Enter a crowded church, maybe,
What hours with witless lads I squander—
Still the same thoughts are haunting me.

This year will fly, the next will follow,
And all who press around you here
Be sure eternity will swallow—
For some the moment now draws near.

I need but see a lone oak thriving
To be reminded of decay:
Mine, while that patriarch will survive me
As it survived my fathers' day.

"I yield my place to you," I'm thinking,
When I caress a tiny tot;
The years march on, there is no blinking,
Your time to bloom is mine to rot.

Each year I question: Is this fated
To be the last that I shall see?
Which day will be commemorated
As my death's anniversary?

And when death comes, where will it find me?
Fighting, at sea, upon the road?
That valley, has it been assigned me
For my clay's final chill abode?

The body has no inkling of it,
But rots among its fellow dead,
Yet secretly, in truth, I covet
Some loved place for my final bed.

Then in the grave I'll not be friendless,
If young life is its careless guest,
And neutral Nature spreads her endless
Beauty about my place of rest.

[1829]

To the Poet

Be deaf, Poet, to popular acclaim;
The tumult of applause and praise will die;
The laughter of the crowd, the dullard's blame,
In your serene austerity, put by.

With kingship a brave loneliness accords.
Move freely where your spirit bids you tread.
Let the fruit ripen that long thoughts have fed,
And, having labored nobly, scorn rewards.

They are yours to give, you are the highest court,
Sternest of judges, if your work falls short.
Are you content? It is for you to say.

Are you content? Then let the mob that spurns
Spit on the altar where your fire burns,
And shake your tripod in its childish play.

[1830]

Evil Spirits

The clouds are scurrying and spinning;
The moon, though hidden, throws her light
Upon the flying snow; the heavens
Are troubled, troubled like the night.

I drive across the naked country,
The bell rings ting-a-ling; in vain
I try to check my terror, viewing
The enormous, unfamiliar plain.

"Drive faster, fellow!" "There's no help, sir,
The horses find the going rough;
The blizzard pastes my eyes together.
The roads are buried, sure enough.
There is no track for me to follow;
We've lost our way. What can we do?
A devil's leading us in circles
Across the plain—one of a crew.

"Look, there he is! He's playing with us;
He spat at me, you might have seen;
And now he's here, maddening the horses,
He'll push them into the ravine.
That milepost sprang up out of nothing—
He took that shape: and now a spark
Flashed horridly—'twas he—and vanished,
And left us in the empty dark."

The clouds are scurrying and spinning;
The moon, though hidden, throws her light
Upon the flying snow; the heavens
Are troubled, troubled like the night.
We have no strength to go on circling;
The bell falls silent suddenly;
The horses halt. . . . "What's that out yonder?"
"Who knows? A stump? A wolf, maybe?"

The blizzard wails, the blizzard rages;
Nervous, the horses snort, oh, hark!
He's there—he's dancing in the distance,
Alone his eyes burn in the dark.
The horses, wild, are dashing onward,
The bell rings ting-a-ling again.
Those throngs I see are evil spirits
Assembled on the whitening plain.

Variform, innumerable,
Hideous spirits fill the night,
Whirled round like leaves in deep November
Beneath a faint moon's pallid light.
Countless! But whither are they driven?
Their chant has such a plaintive pitch.
Is it a house-sprite they are burying,
Or do they marry off a witch?

The clouds are scurrying and spinning;
The moon, though hidden, throws her light
Upon the flying snow; the heavens
Are troubled, troubled like the night.
The evil spirits, swarming, swirling,
Rush, frantic, through the topless sky.
It tears the heart of me to hear them,
Their desolate, long, lamenting cry.

[1830]

On the Translation of the *Iliad*

Sacred, sonorous, is heard the long-muted speech of the
    Hellenes;
Shaken, my soul knows thee near, shade of the mighty old
    man.

[1830]

Work

Here is the long-looked-for hour: the labor of years is accom-
    plished.
Why does unsearchable sadness secretly weigh on my heart?
Is it that, idle at last, I must stand like a workman unwanted,
One who has taken his pay, stranger to tasks that are new?
Is it the work I regret, the silent companion of midnight,
Friend of the aureate Dawn, friend of the gods of the hearth?

[1830]

Elegy

Though quenched, the mirth that once was madly bubbling,
Like fumes of last night's cups, is vaguely troubling;
Not so the griefs that choked my throat with tears—
Like wine, they grow more potent with the years.
Before me lie only my barren morrows:
A tossing sea, portending cares and sorrows.
And yet I do not wish to die, be sure;
I want to live—to suffer, think, endure;
And I shall know some savor of elation
Amidst the woes, the burdens, the vexation:
Sometimes I shall grow drunk on music, thrill
To a sad tale at which my eyes will fill,
And, even as dusk folds down about my story,
Love's farewell smile may shed a parting glory.

[1830]

To My Critic

"You rosy-gilled good fellow, as quick as thought to offer
Our wistful Muse affront, you plump, pot-bellied scoffer,
Come here, I beg, sit down, and have a little nip;
Together we may get the better of the hyp.
Look at those wretched huts: a view to feast your eyes on,
Beyond, black earth—the plain that slopes to the horizon;
Above the hovels hang low clouds, thick-massed and gray.
But the bright meadows, friend, the dark woods—where are
    they?
Where the blithe brook? Beside the low fence in the court
Two trees rejoice the eye; they're of a meager sort,
Such pitiable things, the two of them together,
And one has been stripped bare by autumn's rainy weather,
The other's yellow leaves wait, sopping, to be strewn
On puddles by the wind that will be raging soon.
There's not a living cur. True, here a peasant trudges
Across the empty court, tagged by two kerchiefed drudges.

The coffin of a child beneath his arm, no hat
On that rough head—he calls to the priest's lazy brat
To bid his dad unlock the church—'You've legs to run with!
Be quick! We're late—high time the funeral was done with!'
Why do you frown, my friend?" "You've kept this up too long;
Can't you amuse us with a jolly sort of song?"
"Where are you off to now?" "To Moscow, best be setting
Out for the birthday ball!" "But are you quite forgetting
That we are quarantined? There's cholera about.
Come, cool your heels, as in the mountainous redoubt
Your humble servant did—there's nothing else to do now.
Well, brother, you don't scoff: so you've got the hyp too now!"

[1830]

Parting

For one last time my thought embraces
Your image, all but lost to me;
The heart with wistful longing traces
A dream that hour on hour effaces,
And dwells upon love's memory.

Our years roll onward, swiftly changing;
All changes; we change in the end—
Far from your poet you are ranging,
And darkness like the tomb's, estranging,
Has drawn you from that passionate friend.

This heart its leave of you has taken;
Accept, my distant dear, love's close,
As does the wife death leaves forsaken,
As does the exile's comrade, shaken
And mute, who clasps him once, and goes.

[1830]

"Abandoning an Alien Country"

Abandoning an alien country,
You sought your distant native land;
How could I stop the tears at parting
When sorrow was beyond command?
With hands that momently grew colder
I tried to hold you, wordlessly
I begged that our farewells, our anguish,
Might be prolonged eternally.

But from the bitter kiss and clinging
You tore away your lips; and from
The gloomy land of lonely exile
To a new country bade me come.
You said: "When we are reunited,
Beneath a sky of endless blue,
In the soft shadow of the olives,
Then, lip to lip, I'll solace you."

But yonder, where the blue is radiant,
And where the olives from the shore
Cast tender shadows on the waters,
You fell asleep, to wake no more.
Within the funeral urn your beauty
Lies hidden with your suffering now—
But the sweet kiss of our reunion
I wait . . . I hold you to your vow.

[1830]

Verses Written During a Sleepless Night

Sleepless in the dark I lie
While the earth is wrapped in slumber;
Only weary tickings number
Hours that emptily drag by.

Fate, with your glib female mutter,
Night, in sleep atwitch, aflutter,
Life, that rustles mousily,
Why will you not let me be?
What, dull whisper, are you saying—
Protest or reproach conveying
Of a day that's lost to me?
Your demands I cannot reckon;
Do you prophesy or beckon?
If your meaning I but knew!
Would that I could fathom you. . . .

[1830]

"No, Never Think"

No, never think, my dear, that in my heart I treasure
The tumult of the blood, the frenzied gusts of pleasure,
Those groans of hers, those shrieks: a young Bacchante's cries,
When writhing like a snake in my embrace she lies,
And wounding kiss and touch, urgent and hot, engender
The final shudderings that consummate surrender!

How sweeter far are you, my meek, my quiet one,
What a tormenting bliss when, the long contest done,
And you, in answer to my endless pleading,
You give yourself to me, to my deep need conceding
With bashful tenderness, so shy you turn away,
Seemingly cold, and barely hearing what I say,
Responding, growing warm, oh, in how slow a fashion,
To share, unwilling, yet at last to share my passion!

[1830]

"When I Have Locked Your Slender Body"

When I have locked your slender body
Close in my arms, and tenderly
Pour out to you the words of love that
Well up from my ecstasy,

You free your supple form in silence
From the tightening grip I take,
And a distrustful smile, my darling,
Is all the answer that you make.

Your memory diligently hoarding
The sad lore of unfaithfulness,
Betrayals, oaths forsworn, you listen
With inattentive, cold distress.

I curse youth's criminal maneuvers,
The dogged chase after delight,
The trysts impatiently awaited
In the hushed fragrance of the night.

I curse love's softly whispered discourse,
The enchantment of melodious verse,
The gullible young girls' caresses,
Their tears, their late laments, I curse.

[1830] 1857

Autumn

(*A Fragment*)

"What does not then pass through my drowsy mind?"
—DERZHAVIN

I

October has arrived. The grove is shaking
The last reluctant leaves from naked boughs.
A breath of autumn cold—the road is freezing;
The millpond, glazed with ice, is in a drowse,
Though the brook babbles; with his pack my neighbor
Makes for the distant field—his hounds will rouse
The woods with barking, and his horse's feet
Will trample cruelly the winter wheat.

2

This is my time! What is the spring to me?
Thaw is a bore: mud running thick and stinking;
Spring makes me ill: my mind is never free
From dizzy dreams, my blood's in constant ferment.
Give me instead winter's austerity,
The snows under the moon—and what is gayer
Than to glide lightly in a sleigh with her
Whose fingers are like fire beneath the fur?

3

And oh, how jolly, on the placid river
To glide steel-shod, swiftly, with easy grace!
The shining stir of festivals in winter!
But there's a limit—nobody could face
Six months of snow—even that cave dweller,
The bear, would growl "enough" in such a case.
Sleigh rides with young Armidas pall, by Jove,
And you turn sour with loafing by the stove.

4

Oh, darling summer, I could cherish you,
If heat and dust and gnats and flies were banished.
You dull the mind, the heart grows weary, too.
We, like the meadows, suffer drought and wither.
Drink is our only thought, and how we rue
Old woman Winter, at whose funeral banquet
Pancakes and wine were served, but now we hold
Memorial feasts of ices, sweet and cold.

5

They say ill things of the last days of autumn:
But I, friend reader, not a one will hear;
Her quiet beauty touches me as surely
As does a wistful child, to no one dear.
She can rejoice me more, I tell you frankly,
Than all the other seasons of the year.
I am a humble lover, so I should
Find singularly much in her that's good.

6

How shall I make it clear? I find her pleasing
As you, perhaps, may like a sickly girl,
Condemned to die, poor creature, who is drooping
And without one word of reproach to hurl
At life, forsaking her. Upon her pallid
Young lips a little smile is seen to curl.
She does not hear the grave's abysmal yawn.
Today she lives—tomorrow she is gone.

7

Oh, mournful season that delights the eyes,
Your farewell beauty captivates my spirit.
I love the pomp of Nature's fading dyes,
The forests, garmented in gold and purple,
The rush of noisy wind, and the pale skies
Half-hidden by the clouds in darkling billows,
The early frost, the sun's infrequent ray,
And threats of grizzled Winter far away.

8

Each time that autumn comes I bloom afresh;
For me, I find, the Russian cold is good;
Again I go through life's routine with relish;
Sleep comes in season, and the need for food;
Desire seethes—and I am young and merry,
My heart beats fast with lightly leaping blood.
I'm full of life—such is my organism
(If you will please excuse the prosaism).

9

My horse is brought; far out onto the plain
He carries me; the frozen valley echoes
To his bright hooves with resonant refrain;
The ice creaks under him and as he gallops
In the keen wind he waves his streaming mane.
But day soon flickers out. At the forgotten
Hearth, where the fire purrs low or leaps like wind,
I read, or nourish long thoughts in my mind.

10

And I forget the world in the sweet silence,
Imagination lulls me, and once more
The soul oppressed by the old lyric fever
Trembles, reverberates, and seeks to pour
Its burden freely forth, and as though dreaming
I watch the children that my fancy bore,
And I am host to the invisible throngs
Who fill my reveries and build my songs.

11

And thoughts stir bravely in my head, and rhymes
Run forth to meet them on light feet, and fingers
Reach for the pen, and the good quill betimes
Asks for the foolscap. Wait: the verses follow.
Thus a still ship sleeps on still seas. Hark: Chimes!
And swiftly all hands leap to man the rigging,
The sails are filled, they belly in the wind—
The monster moves—a foaming track behind.

12

It sails. But whither shall we sail? . . .

[1833]

From Eugene Onegin

Tatyana's Letter

I write you; is my act not serving
As an avowal? Well I know
The punishment I am deserving:
That you despise me. Even so,
Perhaps for my sad fate preserving
A drop of pity, you'll forbear
To leave me here to my despair.
I first resolved upon refraining
From speech: you never would have learned
The secret shame with which I burned,
If there had been a hope remaining

That I should see you once a week
Or less, that I should hear you speak,
And answer with the barest greeting,
But have one thing when you were gone,
One thing alone to think upon
For days, until another meeting.
But you're unsociable, they say,
The country, and its dullness, bore you;
We . . . we don't shine in any way,
But have a hearty welcome for you.

Why did you come to visit us?
Here in this village unfrequented,
Not knowing you, I would not thus
Have learned how hearts can be tormented.
I might (who knows?) have grown contented,
My girlish dreams forever stilled,
And found a partner in another,
And been a faithful wife and mother,
And loved the duties well fulfilled.

Another! . . . No, my heart is given
To one forever, one alone!
It was decreed . . . the will of Heaven
Ordained it so: I am your own.
All my past life has had one meaning—
That I should meet you. God on High
Has sent you, and I shall be leaning
On your protection till I die. . . .
I saw you in my dreams; I'd waken
To know I loved you; long ago
I languished in your glance, and oh!
My soul, hearing your voice, was shaken.
Only a dream? It could not be!
The moment that I saw you coming,
I thrilled, my pulses started drumming,
And my heart whispered: it is he!

Yes, deep within I had the feeling,
When at my tasks of charity,
Or when, the world about me reeling,
I looked for peace in prayer, kneeling,
That silently you spoke to me.
Just now, did I not see you flitting
Through the dim room where I am sitting,
To stand, dear vision, by my bed?
Was it not you who gently gave me
A word to solace and to save me:
The hope on which my heart is fed?
Are you a guardian angel to me
Or but a tempter to undo me?
Dispel my doubts! My mind's awhirl;
Perhaps mere folly has created
These fancies of a simple girl
And quite another end is fated. . . .
So be it! Now my destiny
Lies in your hands, for you to fashion;
Forgive the tears you wring from me,
I throw myself on your compassion. . . .
Imagine: here I am alone,
With none to understand or cherish
My restless thoughts, and I must perish,
Stifled, in solitude, unknown.
I wait: when once your look has spoken,
My heart once more with hope will glow,
Or a deserved reproach will show
The painful dream forever broken!

Reread I cannot. . . . I must end. . . .
The fear, the shame, are past endurance. . . .
Upon your honor I depend,
And lean upon it with assurance. . . .

[1833]

The Bronze Horseman

Proem

Upon the shore he watched the swell
Of barren waves that rose and fell,
And gazing, grandly meditated.
Where the broad river rushed pell-mell
A poor lone skiff sped by, belated.
On mossy, marshy banks showed black,
Set here and there, the sorry shack
Sheltering the wretched Finn; protected
From the sun's beams by mist and wrack,
The forest hummed.

                Thus he reflected:
"From here we shall outdare the Swede;
And here a city shall be founded
To spite our haughty neighbor's greed;
Here Fate with Nature has compounded
To have us cut a window through
To Europe, command ocean, too.
Ships of all flags audaciously
Shall cross strange seas to reach this port;
Here we shall give these guests good sport,
Rejoice, and revel spaciously."

A century passed—there the sublime
Young city stood, graceful and stately,
The marvel of the northern clime,
Where swamp and somber woods reigned lately.
Where once from the low-lying bank
The Finnish fisherman, ill-fated
Stepson of Nature, glumly sank
His ragged net, and, lonesome, waited,
Now on the lively shore there crowd
The soaring grace and bulk of proud
Towers and palaces that span it;
From the earth's ends across the seas
Throng hurrying ships to these rich quays;

Neva has clothed herself in granite;
Her waters mirror bridges, all
Her islands now are greenly dusky
With pleasances, abloom and bosky.
Old Moscow has grown sadly faded,
A dowager, whose purple here
Is somewhat shadowily paraded,
With the fresh young czarina near.

I love you, sprung of Peter's orders,
Your look of trim severity,
Neva's grand stream and granite borders,
Your railings' iron tracery,
Your limpid twilight, and the shimmer
Of your hushed, brooding, moonless night,
When, with no lamp nor taper's glimmer,
I keep my room, and read, and write;
And in the empty streets each building,
Asleep, bulks large and clear, and gilding
The Admiralty needle, one
Dawn hurries to replace a dawn,
Not letting darkness touch the golden
Fair heavens, so that for a bare
Half hour night may be beholden.
I love the frost and the still air
Your winter, harsh but grand, imposes;
By broad Neva the racing sleighs,
Girls' faces, rosier than roses,
And balls, their sparkle, hum, and haze;
And, when a stag party is thriving,
The foaming goblets' hiss, the blue
Flame with the bowl of punch arriving;
Mars' playing fields—I love them, too:
The warlike vigor, the brisk manners,
The sounds as foot and horse parade,
The ranks in ordered rhythm swayed,
The rags of those victorious banners,

The glitter of the brazen helms
All pocked with shot; I love the snorting
And smoke of fortresses reporting,
O martial capital, the realm's
Northern czarina has presented
To the czar's house a son, or when—
The enemy once more prevented,
Having surrendered arms and men—
Our Russia celebrates again;
Or when, at last, her blue ice broken,
Neva is bearing out to sea
The splintered chunks, exultantly
To the first scents of spring awoken.

Bedazzle, Peter's city—stand,
As Russia stands, unshakable!
That conquered element command,
And know a peace unbreakable;
May waves that washed the Finnish strand
No more remembrance coldly keep
Of ancient thralldom, angry riot,
Nor with vain rancor vex the quiet
Of Peter's everlasting sleep!

[1833]

The Tale of the Golden Cockerel*

In a realm that shall be nameless,
In a country bright and blameless,
Lived the mighty Czar Dadon,
Second in renown to none.
In his youth he would belabor
Without scruple every neighbor.
But he fancied, as he aged,
That enough wars had been waged—
Having earned a rest, he took it.

* The libretto of Rimsky-Korsakov's opera Le Coq d'Or is based on this
tale.

But his neighbors would not brook it,
And they harassed the old czar,
And they ruthlessly attacked him,
And they harried and they hacked him.
Therefore, lest his realm be lost,
He maintained a mighty host.
Though his captains were not napping,
They not seldom took a rapping:
In the south they're fortified—
From the east their foemen ride;
Mend the breach, as is commanded—
On the shore an army's landed
That has come from oversea.
Czar Dadon, so vexed was he,
Was upon the point of weeping,
Didn't find it easy sleeping.
Never was life bitterer!
So to the astrologer,
To the wise old eunuch, pleading
For his help, an envoy's speeding.
To the eunuch he bows low,
And the mage consents to go
At Dadon's behest, appearing
At the court: a sign most cheering.
In his bag, as it befell,
He'd a golden cockerel.
"Set this bird," the mage directed,
"On a pole that's soon erected;
And my golden cockerel
Will protect thee very well.
When there is no sign of riot,
He will sit serene and quiet,
But if ever there should be
Threat of a calamity,
Should there come from any quarter
Raiders out for loot and slaughter,
Then my golden cockerel
Will arouse: his comb will swell,

He will crow, and up and doing,
Turn to where the danger's brewing."
In return the mage is told
He shall have a heap of gold,
And good Czar Dadon instanter
Promises the kind enchanter:
"Once thy wish to me is known,
'Twill be granted as my own."

On his perch, by the czar's orders,
Sits the cock and guards the borders—
And whenever danger's near
As from sleep our chanticleer
Rises, crows and fluffs his feathers,
Turns to where the trouble gathers,
Sounds his warning clear and true,
Crying: "Cock-a-doodle-doo!
Slug-a-bed, lie still and slumber,
Reign with never care or cumber!"
And the neighbors dared not seek
Any quarrel, but grew meek:
Czar Dadon there was no trapping,
For they could not catch him napping.

Peacefully two years go by,
And the cock sits quietly.
But one day, by noises shaken,
Czar Dadon is forced to waken.
Cries a captain: "Czar and Sire,
Rise, thy children's need is dire!
Trouble comes, thy realm to shatter."
"Gentlemen, what is the matter?"
Yawns Dadon. "What do you say?
Who is there? What trouble, pray?"
Says the captain: "Fear is growing,
For the cockerel is crowing:
The whole city's terrified."
Then the czar looked out and spied
The gold cockerel a-working—
Toward the east he kept on jerking.

"Quickly now! Make no delay!
Take to horse, men, and away!"
Toward the east the army's speeding
That the czar's first-born is leading.
Now the cockerel is still,
And the czar may sleep his fill.

Eight full days go by like magic,
But no news comes, glad or tragic:
Did they fight or not? Dadon
Has no message from his son.
Hark! Again the cock is crowing—
A new army must be going
Forth to battle; Czar Dadon
This time sends his younger son
To the rescue of his brother.
And this time, as at the other,
The brave cockerel grows still.
Now no news comes, good or ill.
And again eight days go flying,
And in fear the folk are sighing;
And once more the cockerel crows,
And a third host eastward goes.
Czar Dadon himself is leading,
Not quite certain of succeeding.

They march on, by day, by night,
And they soon are weary, quite.
Czar Dadon, in some vexation,
Vainly seeks an indication
Of a fight: a battleground,
Or a camp, or funeral mound.
Strange! But as the eighth day's ending,
We find Czar Dadon ascending
Hilly pathways, with his men—
What does his gaze light on then?
'Twixt two mountain peaks commanding,
Lo! a silken tent is standing.
Wondrous silence rules the scene,
And behold, in a ravine

Lies the slaughtered army! Chastened
By the sight, the old czar hastened
To the tent. . . . Alas, Dadon!
Younger son and elder son
Lie unhelmed, and either brother
Has his sword stuck in the other.
In the field, alackaday,
Masterless, their coursers stray
On the trampled grass and muddy,
On the silken grass now bloody. . . .
Czar Dadon howled fearfully:
"Children, children! Woe is me!
Both our falcons have been taken
In the nets! I am forsaken!"
All his army howled and moaned
Till the very valleys groaned—
From the shaken mountains darted
Echoes. Then the tent flaps parted. . . .
Suddenly upon the scene
Stood the young Shamakhan queen!
Bright as dawn, with gentle greeting
She acknowledged this first meeting
With the czar, and old Dadon,
Like a night bird in the sun,
Stood stock still and kept on blinking
At the maid, no longer thinking
Of his sons, the dead and gone.
And she smiled at Czar Dadon—
Bowing, took his hand and led him
Straight into her tent, and fed him
Royally, and then her guest
Tenderly she laid to rest
On a downy couch, brocaded,
And by silken curtains shaded.
Seven days and seven nights
Czar Dadon knew these delights,
And, of every scruple ridden,
Did, bewitched, what he was bidden.

Long enough he had delayed—
To his army, to the maid,
Czar Dadon was now declaring
That they must be homeward faring.
Faster than Dadon there flies
Rumor, spreading truth and lies.
And the populace have straightway
Come to meet them at the gateway.
Now behind the coach they run,
Hail the queen and hail Dadon,
And most affable they find him. . . .
Lo! there in the crowd behind him
Who should follow Czar Dadon,
Hair and beard white as a swan,
And a Moorish hat to top him,
But the mage? There's none to stop him;
Up he comes: "My greeting, Sire."
Says the czar: "What's thy desire?
Pray, come closer. What's thy mission?"
"Czar," responded the magician,
"We have our accounts to square;
Thou hast sworn, thou art aware,
For the help that I accorded,
Anything thy realm afforded
Thou wouldst grant me—my desire,
As thy own, fulfilling, Sire.
'Tis this maiden I am craving:
The Shamakhan queen." "Thou'rt raving!"
Shrieked Dadon forthwith, amazed,
While his eyes with anger blazed.
"Gracious! Hast thou lost thy senses?
Who'd have dreamed such consequences
From the words that once I said!"
Cried the czar. "What's in thy head?
Yes, I promised, but what of it?
There are limits, and I'll prove it.
What is any maid to thee?
How dare thou thus speak to me?

Other favors I am able
To bestow: take from my stable
My best horse, or, better far,
Henceforth rank as a boyar;
Gold I'll give thee willingly—
Half my czardom is for thee."
"Naught is offered worth desiring,"
Said the mage. "I am requiring
But one gift of thee. I mean,
Namely, the Shamakhan queen."
Then the czar, with anger spitting,
Cried: "The devil! 'Tis not fitting
That I listen to such stuff.
Thou'lt have nothing. That's enough!
To thy cost thou hast been sinning—
Reckoned wrong from the beginning.
Now be off while thou'rt yet whole!
Take him out, God bless my soul!"
The enchanter, ere they caught him,
Would have argued, but bethought him
That with certain mighty folk
Quarreling is not a joke,
And there was no word in answer
From the white-haired necromancer.
With his scepter the czar straight
Rapped the eunuch on his pate;
He fell forward: life departed.
Forthwith the whole city started
Quaking—but the maiden, ah!
Hee-hee-hee! and Ha-ha-ha!
Feared no sin and was not queasy.
Czar Dadon, though quite uneasy,
Gave the queen a tender smile
And rode forward in fine style.
Suddenly there was a tinkling
Little noise, and in a twinkling,
While all stood and stared anew,
From his perch the cockerel flew

To the royal coach, and lighted
On the pate of the affrighted
Czar Dadon, and there, elate,
Flapped his wings, and pecked the pate,
And soared off . . . and as he flitted,
Czar Dadon his carriage quitted:
Down he fell, and groaned at most
Once, and then gave up the ghost.
And the queen no more was seen there:
'Twas as though she'd never been there—
Fairy tales, though far from true,
Teach good lads a thing or two.

[1834]

"I Visited Again"

               . . . I visited again
That corner of the earth where once I spent,
In placid exile, two unheeded years.
A decade's gone since then—and in my life
There have been many changes—in myself,
Who from the general law am not exempt,
There have been changes, too—but here once more
The past envelops me, and suddenly
It seems that only yesterday I roamed
These groves.

          Here stands the exile's cottage, where
I lived with my poor nurse. The good old woman
Has passed away—no longer do I hear
Through the thin wall her heavy tread as she
Goes on her busy rounds.

                  Here is the hill
Upon whose wooded crest I often sat
Motionless, staring down upon the lake—
Recalling, as I looked, with melancholy,
Another shore, and other waves I knew. . . .
Among the golden meadows, the green fields,
It lies as then, that blue and spacious lake—

A fisherman across its lonely waters
Is rowing now, and dragging after him
A wretched net. Upon the sloping shores
Are scattered hamlets—and beyond them there
A mill squats crookedly—it scarcely stirs
Its wings in this soft wind....

                              Upon the edge
Of the ancestral acres, on the spot
Where the rough road, trenched by the heavy rains,
Begins its upward climb, three pine trees rise—
One stands apart, and two are close together,
And I remember how, of moonlit nights,
When I rode past, their rustling greeted me
Like a familiar voice. I took that road,
I saw the pines before me once again.
They are the same, and on the ear the same
Familiar whisper breaks from shaken boughs,
But at the base, beside their aged roots
(Where everything had once been bare and bald),
A glorious young grove had risen up,
A verdant family; the bushes crowd
Like children in their shadow. And apart,
Alone as ever, their glum comrade stands,
Like an old bachelor, about whose feet
There stretches only bareness as before.
I hail you, race of youthful newcomers!
I shall not witness your maturity,
When you shall have outgrown my ancient friends,
And with your shoulders hide their very heads
From passers-by. But let my grandson hear
Your wordless greeting when, as he returns,
Content, lighthearted, from a talk with friends,
He too rides past you in the dark of night,
And thinks, perhaps, of me.

                              [1835]

"The Eremites of Old"

The eremites of old, all of the world unspotted,
That they might reach the heights to holy saints allotted,
That they might fortify the heart against life's stress,
Composed such prayers as still comfort us and bless.
But none has ever stirred in me such deep emotion
As that the priest recites at Lententide devotions;
The words which mark for us that saddest season rise
Most often to my lips, and in this prayer lies
Inscrutable support when I, a sinner, hear it:
"Oh, Lord of all my days, avert Thou from my spirit
Both melancholy sloth and poisonous love of power,
That secret snake, and joy in gossip of an hour.
But let me see my sins, O God, and not another's,
Nor sit in judgment on the lapse that is my brother's,
And quicken Thou in me the breath and being of
Forbearance and of meekness, chastity and love."

[1836]

"In Vain I Seek To Climb"

In vain I seek to climb to Zion's beckoning height:
Rapacious sin pursues, hard on my panting flight;
Thus, dusty nostrils thrust in yielding sand, with sure
Intent the lion tracks the musk deer's pungent spoor.

[1836] 1857

"When, Lost in Thought"

When, lost in thought, I roam beyond the city's bounds
And find myself within the public burial grounds,
The fashionable tombs behind the railing squatting,
Where the great capital's uncounted dead are rotting,
All huddled in a swamp, a crowding, teeming horde,
Like greedy guests that swarm about a beggar's board;

Officials' sepulchers, and merchants', too, all fizzles:
The clumsy products of inexpert, vulgar chisels,
Inscribed in prose and verse with virtues, service, rank,
Outlandish ornaments displayed on either flank;
A widow's fond lament for an old cuckold coffined;
The posts, their urns unscrewed by thieves, the earth that's
        softened
And slippery, where graves are gaping dark and wide
To welcome tenants who next day will move inside—
All this brings troubled thoughts; I feel my spirits fail me
As I survey the scene, and evil blues assail me.
One wants to spit and run!
                            But how it pleases me—
When the autumnal sky sheds pure serenity—
To find a churchyard where, in dignity reposing
Among their simple forebears, the country dead seem dozing!
There, unadorned, the graves have ample elbow room;
At midnight no pale thief creeps forth to rob the tomb;
The peasant sighs and says a prayer as he passes
The timeworn stones o'ergrown with yellowed moss and grasses;
No noseless angels soar, no blowsy Graces here,
No petty pyramids or idle urns appear;
But a broad oak above these dignified graves brooding
Bestirs its boughs in music. . . .

                                        [*1836*]

"Unto Myself I Reared a Monument"

Exegi monumentum

Unto myself I reared a monument not builded
With hands; a track thereto the people's feet will tread;
It raises higher than the Alexandrian pillar
        Its noble and unbending head.

I shall not wholly die—but in my songs my spirit
Will, incorruptible and bodiless, survive—
And I shall be renowned as long as under heaven
        One poet yet remains alive.

The rumor of my fame will sweep through vasty Russia,
And all its peoples speak this name that yet shall gain
Regard from Slav unborn, the Finn, the savage Tungus,
    The Kalmuck horseman of the plain.

For years to come the people will lovingly remember
What kindly thoughts my lyre awoke in every breast,
How in this cruel age I celebrated freedom,
    And pled for ruth toward those distressed.

O Muse, obey the Lord's commandments, never fearing
An insult, both to praise and blame indifferent,
Demanding no reward, sing on, and meeting folly,
    Do not descend to argument.

[1836]

Secular Power*

When the supreme event had come to pass, and He,
Our God, upon the cross had died in agony,
On either side the tree two gazed at one another:
One, Mary Magdalene, and one, the Virgin Mother—
        In grief two women stood.
But now whom do we see beneath the holy rood,
As though it were the porch of him who rules the city?
Not here the holy twain, borne down by pain and pity,
But, shakos on their heads and bayonet in hand,
Beside the crucifix two bristling sentries stand.
Are they set here to guard the cross as 'twere State cargo?
Do you fear mice or thieves? Wherefore this strict embargo?
Would you add dignity unto the King of kings?
What honor do you think your patronage thus brings,
You mighty of the earth, what help by you is rendered
To Him who's crowned with thorns, to Him who freely
        tendered

* This poem seems to have been occasioned by the fact that when a
painting by K. P. Bryullov depicting the Crucifixion was placed on view,
sentries guarded the canvas from the press of spectators.

His body to the scourge, without complaint or fear,
The Christ who had to bear the cross, the nails, the spear?
You dread the mob's affront to Him who won remission
Of sins, and saved the race of Adam from perdition?
Is it to keep the way for strolling gentry clear
That thus the common folk are not admitted here?

[*1836*] *1870*

" 'Tis Time, My Friend"

'Tis time, my friend, 'tis time! For rest the heart is crying.
The days go swiftly by, hour after hour flying
Bears off some shred of life—yet still we wish to live,
Though death must come, how soon? And joy is fugitive.
Not happiness, but peace and freedom may be granted
On earth; this is my hope, who by one dream am haunted—
A weary slave, I plan escape before the night
To the remote retreat of toil and pure delight.

[*1836*]

YEVGENY BARATYNSKY

The Road of Life

When Fate equips her sons, us fools, to take
The road of life, she would be kind, it seems,
For to each one she gives what is his due
In golden dreams.

The years post swiftly by and as they go
New stations beckon, greet us and are lost;
And with those golden dreams we duly pay
The journey's cost.

[1826]

"My Gift Is Small"

My gift is small, my voice makes no large sound,
But I am a living man, and here on earth
Is one to whom my being does have worth;
It may be that my selfhood will be found
By some remote descendant: he will see
His own soul, hear his heart beat in my rhyme,
And I who knew a friend in my own time,
May win a reader in posterity.

[1828]

The Muse

Truly, I am not dazzled by my Muse.
They will not call her beautiful; the young,
Regarding her, will not crowd after her,
Rushing to be the blest she moves among.
She has no guile, no gift for the allure
That sparkles in the fine folds of a dress,
In witty words, in play of glances. Yet
The world, at whiles, feels its complacency
Troubled by the uncommon look she wears,
Her mild simplicity of speech, and pays
Not the expected tribute of barbed scorn
But rather honors her with casual praise.

[1830]

"Phyllis"

Phyllis, as the nights grow colder,
With every winter that she sees,
Bares further her appalling shoulder,
A skeleton that strives to please;

And, a sepulchral Venus, brightly
Approaches the last couch of all,
As though before she slept she lightly
Let, one by one, her garments fall.

1838?

"Of What Use Are You, Days?"

Of what use are you, days? There can be nothing
  New for the mind to greet;
The world is full of things and all familiar,
  And time can but repeat.

Not vainly did you strive in your impatience,
  O frantic soul, to gain
Your full development before the body,
  Which cannot slip its chain.

Since you have long since locked the sorry circle
  Of sights beneath the moon,
You drowse, fanned by recurrent dreams; the body,
  Accorded no such boon,

Must stupidly watch dawn arrive, relieving
  The night for naught, and mark
A barren dusk, crown of a day that's empty,
  Drop down into the dark.

1840

Prayer

King of Heaven, make me whole:
Grant Thy peace to my sick soul!
Banish from my memory
This poor world's perversity,
And give my heart the strength to rise
To Thy austere Paradise!

1844

FYODOR TYUTCHEV

Autumn Evening

In autumn, evening's clarity, serene
And touching, charms beyond all saying. . . .
The trees in motley with their eerie sheen,
The languid airs through crimson leafage playing;
The tranquil azure that hangs dim and far
Above the earth wan with an orphan's sorrow,
And sometimes chilly gusts of wind that are
The harsh forerunners of a stormy morrow;
A withering, a waning, over all
A wistful smile that yields while it beseeches:
The look that in a rational soul we call
The sublime shyness only suffering teaches.

[1830]

"As Ocean Holds the Globe"

As ocean holds the globe in its embrace,
Round earthly life a sea of dreams is sweeping;
Night comes, and the sonorous billows chase
Each other, on the coast of darkness leaping.

That voice of dream, how urgently it sounds!
Alert, the magic skiff prepares to wander;
The tide swells swiftly, now the white sail rounds,
And we are borne to shoreless waters yonder.

Lo, the high heavens, starred and luminous,
Mysteriously from the deeps are gazing,
And we sail onward, while surrounding us
On every side the strange abyss is blazing.

                                        1830

"We Drive Knee-Deep"

We drive knee-deep in sand that sifts and scatters. . . .
The hour is late—rapidly daylight dims;
The shadows of the pine trees by the roadside
Flow into one shadow that overbrims.

The deep woods have become darker and denser—
How heavy on this landscape sadness lies!
From every bush now sullen night is peering
Like a beast that has a hundred eyes.

                                        1830

Reconcilement

The storm was over—the tall oak, still smoking,
Lay where the bolt had struck; its gray as warm
As breasts of doves, smoke drifted from the branches,
Their foliage sparkling, freshened by the storm.

But the grove has already long been thrilling
With birdsong, resonant in birch and larch,
And overhead a rainbow has been resting
Upon green crests the foot of its brave arch.

1831

Silentium

Be silent, private, and conceal
What you may fancy or may feel.
Within your soul your dreams should rise
And set as the stars in the skies
How soundlessly follow their route.
Behold, admire them, and be mute.

How can a heart at will unfold
Its secret? Who will grasp, if told,
Whatever you are living by?
Spoken, a thought becomes a lie.
The springs men force they but pollute.
Drink of those waters, and be mute.

Within yourself learn how to live;
A world of thoughts not fugitive
Is there: mysterious, spellbound,
That worldly clamor will have drowned,
Dispersed by the day they dispute;
Heed that hushed music, and be mute.

[1833]

"The Service of the Lutherans"

The service of the Lutherans is pleasing,
The rites they use are simple and austere;
These naked walls, this empty tabernacle
I like; I find their lofty lesson clear.

But look you: Faith has made her preparations
To leave; not long will she be lingering there;
She has not yet put foot across the threshold,
Already, though, her house stands stripped and bare.

She has not yet put foot across the threshold,
Nor shut the door as one who goes away.
Ah, but the hour has sounded. . . . Say your prayer:
For this is the last time that you will pray.

[1834] 1879

Twilight

Dove-colored, the shadows melt and mingle,
Color fades and sound has gone to sleep;
Motion is dissolved in distant rumors,
Undulant the dark, with life at neap. . . .
Beating the nocturnal air, a night moth
Is in flight, softly, invisibly. . . .
Hour of unutterable longing!
I am in the all, the all in me.

Gentle twilight, slumber-lidded twilight,
Brim my being with your quietness,
Let your silent, tender, fragrant langor
Rise in flood to tranquilize and bless.
Give my senses over to the darkness
Of pure self-forgetfulness to keep.
Let me taste annihilation, mix me
With the universe that lies asleep.

[1831-36] 1879

"What Do You Howl Of, Night Wind?"

What do you howl of, night wind, endlessly?
What do you mourn with such a wild lament?
Your voice is strange, what does it mean, as now
Plaintive and low, again a roar unpent?

You harp on unintelligible woe
In language that the heart has known, how long!
Over and over you complain, and then
You touch off in the heart a savage song.

Oh, hush the terror of these strains that tell
Of ancient Chaos, our familiar!
The world of the nocturnal soul is keyed
To the beloved tale, and leans to hear.
That soul would issue from the mortal breast,
So longing for the infinite. . . . Ah, no!
Do not arouse the storms that lie asleep.
Old Chaos stirs below.

[1836]

"Tears"

Tears, human tears, that pour forth beyond telling,
Early and late, in the dark, out of sight,
While the world goes on its way all unwittingly;
Numberless, stintless, you fall unremittingly,
Pouring like rain, the long rain that is welling
Endlessly, late in the autumn at night.

1850

July 14, at Night

Still the heat of mid-July
Lay upon night's glimmering air,
And above dim earth the sky
Shivered, as the storm drew nigh,
With heat lightnings' fitful flare.

Heavy lashes, so it seemed,
Parted, and the eyes they fringed,
When the swift heat lightnings gleamed,
On the earth abruptly beamed
With a look so fierce it singed.

1852

Last Love

How tenderly, how superstitiously
We love when time has told its story. . . .
Shine, shine, departing light, and be
Crowned, late last love, with sunset's glory!

Long shadows cover half the sky,
Alone the west warm splendor casting;
Delay, delay, dusk, our good-by,
Enchantment, oh, be everlasting!

Let blood run thinner in the vein,
Heart's tenderness is not abated. . . .
Last love, you are the pitch of pain,
Of rapture and despair created.

                    1854

"I Love Spring Thunderstorms"

I love spring thunderstorms, my heart leaps up
Hearing the heavens rumble in early May,
When, while the sky's still blue, the thunder peals,
Noisily tumbling about as though in play.

Young thunders crash, dust's flying in the wind,
And now a shower patters, the sky sheds
Liquid luster: each raindrop is a pearl,
And sun comes suddenly to gild the threads.

A stream is rushing nimbly down the slope,
And in the grove the birds will not be still,
The thunders have gay echoes in the woods'
Bird-throated noise and on the clamorous hill.

You'd say that giddy Hebe, shaken by
Laughter, when the eagle of Zeus must sup,
Involuntarily spilled on earth
Heaven's thunder-seething cup.

                    1854

"Oh, Vatic Soul"

Oh, vatic soul, oh, heart astir
And aching with your heavy trouble,
Upon the threshold of this double
Being, you waver, as it were.

And so two alien worlds you plumb:
Your day of morbid, passionate living,
Your sleep, vague revelations giving
Of heavenly visions yet to come.

Then let the tortured bosom beat
With fatal passion, mad vagary;
The soul is ready, even as Mary,
To cling forever to Christ's feet.

[1855]

"Sorry Hamlets"

Sorry hamlets, niggard Nature,
Land that, patient, bears its yoke—
These are mine, this is my country,
Land of my own Russian folk!

Haughty foreign eyes can never
See your glory, never guess
The pure light that glimmers shyly
Through your humble nakedness.

Like a slave the King of Heaven
Tramped your roads on every hand;
Burdened with His cross He blessed you
Everywhere, my native land.

[1855]

"When Autumn Pauses"

When autumn pauses upon entering,
A glorious season, soon to pass, sets in;
The whole long day the air is crystalline,
And softly lucent every evening.

Now all is vacancy—the scene is bare
Where sickles swung and where the corn was piled;
Upon the furrow, idle as the wild,
Glitters alone the cobwebs' finespun hair.

No bird is heard—air's fallow as the weald,
But winter storms are far, hidden from view,
And the immaculate, warm, liquid blue
Pours its pure grace upon the resting field.

[*1857*]

"I Knew Her"

I knew her in those fabled years
When, so it seems, the morning nears
And, as the hint of its first rays
Upon the azuring sky appears,
There sinks the star of primal days.

And in those sparkling early hours
The freshness wherewith Nature dowers
The dark in which the morning stirs
And dew falls softly on the flowers,
Unheard, unseen—that charm was hers.

Her life was then a perfect thing,
A whole that asked no ripening,
From all our earthly fret so far,
I see it as not perishing
But only setting—like a star.

[*1861*]

"Ocean Has Music"

Est in arundineis modulatio musica ripis.
—AUSONIUS

Ocean has music that his combers make,
The elements, though storming, harmonize,
And in the swaying bulrushes arise
Sweet sibilances that now hush, now wake.

Full consonance inheres in nature: there
Is imperturbable serenity;
In our illusory freedom, only we
Dissent, of difference bitterly aware.

Whence did this discord come, how did it grow?
Why does the song of ocean leave the soul
Like some deaf-mute, with no part in the whole?
The thinking reed protests it does not know.

A voice is crying in the wilderness,
The desperate soul, intransigent, asks, why?
And from earth to the farthest stars the cry
Reëchoes: why? Reëchoes, answerless.

1865

"Tonight the Sky Is Sullen"

Tonight the sky is sullen, everywhere
It glowers, yet it does not threaten hurt,
Nor is it meditative: this is sleep,
But dreamless, joyless as it is inert.
Only at measured intervals the dark
Is seared with fire where heat lightnings flare,
As if some deaf-mute demons, who were else
Invisible, were holding converse there.

Abruptly then a strip of sky's alight,
As at a signal, and there is a gash
In the heavens: fields and forests far away
Break from the darkness in a livid flash.
Then all grows black once more, and all is hushed
In the attentive dark; as though, without speech,
Some matter of mysterious import were
Being decided—high beyond man's reach.

1865

"Not with the Mind"

Not with the mind is Russia comprehended,
The common yardstick will deceive
In gauging her: so singular her nature—
In Russia you must just believe.

[*1866*]

ALEXEY KOLTZOV

An Old Man's Song

I shall saddle a horse,
A swift courser, he,
I shall fly, I shall race,
Lighter than a hawk,
Over fields, over seas,
To a distant land.
I shall overtake there
My first youth again.

I shall spruce myself up,
Be a blade again,
I shall make a fine show
For the girls again.
But alas! no road leads
To the bygone years,
And the sun will not rise
Ever in the west.

[1835]

MIKHAIL LERMONTOV

The Angel

An angel was winging his way through the night,
    And softly he sang on his flight.
The moon and the stars and the clouds crowded near,
    That marvelous music to hear.

He sang of the bliss that is known by the blest
    Where the shadows of Paradise rest;
He sang of the greatness of God as he flew,
    His praise ringing holy and true.

He bore a young soul in his arms that must know
    The tears of the world and its woe.
Yet deep in that soul there lived, wordless and strong,
    The heavenly sound of his song.

Long years in the world were to sadden and tire
    One haunted by wondrous desire,
And dull earthly songs could not ever supplant
    For her that celestial chant.

[1831]

A Sail

A far sail shimmers, white and lonely,
Through the blue haze above the foam.
What does it seek in foreign harbors?
What has it left behind at home?

The billows romp, and the wind whistles.
The rigging swings, the tall mast creaks.
It is not happiness he flees from,
Alas, it is not joy he seeks!

Below, the sea, like blue light flowing,
Above, the sun shines without cease,
But it is storm the rebel asks for,
As though in storm were peace.

                                        [1832]

"See How He Gallops"*

See how he gallops, with what dash and daring:
White hair is sometimes a delusive sign;
Thus an old, cobwebbed, mold-encrusted bottle
May hold a ready stream of sparkling wine.

                                        [1836]

"When the Yellow Rye Field"

When the yellow rye field billows in the breezes
And the fresh woods answer to the wind's low thrum,
And deep in the orchard, hiding in the shadow
Of a cool green leaf, hangs the purpling plum;

---

* These lines were written under the portrait of an elderly officer of the
Hussars, a colleague of the poet.

When, at rosy dusk or in the first gilt hours,
Sprinkled with fresh-fallen, sweetly smelling dew,
From beneath the bushes, with a silver nodding
Lily-of-the-valley welcomes me anew;

When a cold brook ripples romping through the valley
And my thoughts are plunged, as its saga flows,
Into dim imaginings of the peaceful country
Whereof it is singing, land where it arose—

Then repose is granted to my troubled spirit,
Then no more with wrinkled brow I mope and plod,
And I can conceive of happiness on earth here,
And I can believe that in Heaven I see God.

[1837]

Gratitude

My thanks for all Thou gavest through the years:
For passion's secret torments without end,
The poisoned kiss, the bitterness of tears,
The vengeful enemy, the slanderous friend,
The spirit's ardor in the desert spent,
Every deception, every wounding wrong;
My thanks for each dark gift that Thou hast sent;
But heed Thou that I need not thank Thee long.

[1840]

"Land of Masters"*

Land of masters, land of slaves, farewell,
Unwashed Russia, it's good-by I say:
You in your blue uniforms, and you
Who were fashioned only to obey.

* Probably written when the poet was for the second time transferred to the Caucasus. Some MS copies have "czars" instead of "pashas" in line 5.

From your pashas I may hide at last
Once the Caucasus between us rears,
And be safe from those all-seeing eyes
And unheard by those all-hearing ears.

[1840] 1887

Testament

I'd like to be alone with you,
Brother, of course you won't say no:
The hours left me now are few;
I know it, they have told me so.

You'll soon be going home again,
So listen to me. . . . Oh, but then,
There's no one, to speak honestly,
Who cares much what becomes of me.

If someone asks . . . no matter who,
Just how it was that I went west,
Say I was wounded in the chest,
A bullet got me: I was through.

And tell them that I served the czar,
And honorably, understand;
Say, too, how poor our doctors are,
And that I greet my native land.

Father and mother won't be found,
I fear, by this time above ground,
And it is sorry I would be
Were grief to come to them through me.

So if you see one of them, say
That I am lazy with the pen,
And that we're in the field, and they
Should not expect me soon again.

They have a neighbor . . . time does fly,
It's long ago we said good-by,
And ask for me she never will,
I'm very sure of that. . . . But still,

Tell her the truth and no white lie,
That empty heart you will not wring;
Just spill it, man, and let her cry—
Sure, tears to her don't mean a thing.

[1840]

My Country

I love my country, but that love is odd:
My reason has no part in it at all!
Neither her glory, bought with blood,
Nor her proud strength hold me in thrall;
No venerable customs stir in me
The pleasant play of reverie.
Ask me not why I love, but love I must
Her fields' cold silences,
Her somber forests swaying in a gust,
Her rivers at the flood like seas.
I love to rattle on rough roads at night,
My lodging still to find, while half awake
I peer through shadows left and right
And watch the lights of mournful hamlets quake.
I love the smoke above singed stubble rising;
I love a caravan that winds forlorn
Across the steppe; I love surprising
Two birches white above the yellow corn.
A well-stocked barn, a hut with a thatched roof,
Carved shutters on a village window: these
Are simple things in truth,
But few can see them as my fond eye sees.
And on a holiday, from dewy dusk until
Midnight, it is a boon for me
To watch the dancers stomping to the shrill
Loud babble of the drunken peasantry.

[1841]

From The Demon: *An Eastern Tale*

On the vast aerial ocean,
Through the mist how calmly steers
Star on star, to fill the heavens
With the music of the spheres.

Through the infinite blue meadows,
Through the boundless fields of space,
Clouds in shaggy flocks are straying,
Fugitives that leave no trace.

Hour of meeting, hour of parting,
Neither gladden them nor fret;
Theirs no yearning toward the future,
Theirs no haunting of regret.

On the dark day of misfortune
These remember, far away;
Be beyond earth's reach as they are,
And indifferent as they.

                    [1841] 1860

A Dream

The heat of noon, a gorge in Daghestan—
I lay there with a bullet in my chest.
My deep wound was still steaming, and my blood
Oozed, drop by drop by drop, over my breast.

I lay alone within the sandy gorge,
The terraces of rock above my head;
Sun scorched their sulphurous summits, and scorched me;
But I slept on, as men sleep who are dead.

And I dreamed of a feast, alive with lights,
A night of pleasure, in my own country,
And girls were there, all garlanded with flowers,
Smiling and talking merrily of me.

But one of them sat sunk in thought, apart,
Letting the merry conversation stream
Beyond her, and her tender soul was plunged,
'Tis God knows why, in a most mournful dream.

She dreamed she saw a gorge in Daghestan. . . .
There one she knew lay dead, and there, behold,
A black wound in his breast was steaming still,
And the blood flowed that now was growing cold.

1841

NIKOLAY NEKRASOV

"On Passing Through the Haymarket"

On passing through the Haymarket last night
Somewhere near six o'clock, I chanced to see
A woman being whipped: a peasant girl
She was, who bore the lashes quietly.

No cry was forced from her, the only sound
Came from the whip that whistled through the air.
I called my Muse to me and bade her look:
"There is your sister—there!"

[1848]

"The Capitals Are Rocked"

The capitals are rocked with thunder
Of orators in wordy feuds.
But in the depths of Russia, yonder,
An age-old awful silence broods.

Alone the wind in wayside willows
Stirs with unceasing restlessness,
And in the endless fields the billows
Of arching stalks stoop to caress
The earth that cherishes and pillows.

[1857]

"My Verses!"

My verses! Living witnesses of tears
    For this forlorn earth shed!
Born in those moments when the stormwind rears
    That fills the soul with dread,
Against the hearts of men you beat—who hears?—
    Like waves on cliffs as dead.

[1858]

Freedom*

Ah, Mother Russia, never yet have I
Traveled across your plains with heart so high!

I see a baby at its mother's breast
And by this stirring thought I am possessed:

Child, you were blest in these times to be born;
Please God, it will not be your lot to mourn.

Free, and in dread of no man from the start,
You will yet choose the work after your heart;

You may remain a peasant all your years,
Or soar, with only eagles for your peers.

Perhaps my dream will cause a doubtful smile:
Man's mind is subtle and is full of guile;

* The emancipation of the serfs, which took place on February 19, 1861
(Old Style).

Though serfdom's nets are broken, well I know
New snares have been contrived, as time will show;

But these the people will more readily
Break loose from: Muse, great freedom hopefully.

[*1861*]

Newlyweds

So after the wedding, the husband
Must show off his goods to the bride:
"Look, woman, we've got a good cowshed,
But the cow—God would have it so—died!

"We've no featherbed and no bedstead,
But the bench here is warm, you can feel;
And though we've no calves, we've two kittens:
Just hark at them now, how they squeal!

"There are vegetables out in the garden:
Horseradish and onions I grew.
And if it is brassware you're wanting,
Here's a cross and a brass button, too."

[*1866*]

From Who Lives Happily in Russia?

The Salt Song

There's nobody left but God. . . .
Maybe He knows the cure:
Not a mouthful my little one takes.
Ah, he will die for sure.

I gave him a bit of bread,
I gave him another bit.
He does not eat, he cries:
"Salt! Put salt on it!"

There is no salt in the house,
Never a pinch of it here.
"Try some flour," said God.
God whispered it in my ear.

The little one took a bite,
He made a face as he bit.
He cried, the tiny boy:
"Put more salt on it!"

I floured the crust again,
My tears rained on the bread.
The little one ate it up,
The little son was fed.

She boasted of her ruse:
She had saved him, it appears.
Ah, mother, mother,
Those were salty tears!

1876

PYOTR VYAZEMSKY

Spring

"Ah, Spring, sweet Spring, chief pride of Nature!"
The air is foul, the ground is sludge;
Men curse the mud when they go walking,
And plunged in muck, a horse can't budge.

The cab breaks down, so does the carriage;
Season of colds in chest and nose,
To you, fair Spring, is reverence tendered
By cartwrights and by medicos.

1866

ALEXEY K. TOLSTOY

"Soldier of Neither Camp"

Soldier of neither camp, a casual guest in both,
I would rejoice to draw my sword in a just cause,
But secretly I chafe: both factions give me pause,
And neither can persuade these lips to take the oath.

My full allegiance, then, they cannot ever know—
My soul is still my own, though I choose either side:
The partial zeal of friends unable to abide,
I'd fight to keep unstained the banner of the foe.

[1858]

"A Well"

A well, and the cherry trees swaying
Where bare girlish feet lately trod;
Nearby a damp imprint betraying
A heavy nailed boot on the sod.

Hushed now is the place of their meeting,
But nothing the silence avails,
In my brain passion's echo repeating
Their whispers, the splash of the pails.

1858

"My Little Almond Tree"

My little almond tree
Is gay with gleaming bloom;
My heart unwillingly
Puts forth its buds of gloom.

The bloom will leave the tree,
The fruit, unbidden, grow;
And the green boughs will be
By bitter loads brought low.

1867

APOLLON MAIKOV

"Upon This Wild Headland"

Upon this wild headland, crowned meanly with indigent rushes
And covered with pitiful brush and the green of the pine trees,
The aged Meniskos, a fisherman, laid in his sorrow
His son who had perished. The sea had maternally nursed him,
That sea whose wide lap took him back, who resistlessly bore
        him
In death, and who carefully carried the young body shoreward.
Then mourning Meniskos went forth, and beneath a great
        willow
He dug him a grave, a plain stone he set for a mark on the
        cliffside,
And hung overhead a coarse net he had woven of willow—
A fisherman's wreath to be poverty's bitter memento.

[1840]

Art

Idly I cut me a reed by the shore where the sea heaves and
    thunders,
Dumb and forgotten it lay in my simple, my wind-beaten cabin.
Once an old traveler passed who remained for a night in our
    dwelling
(Foreign his dress and his tongue, an old man who was strange
    to our region).
Seeing the reed, he retrieved it, and cut the round ventages
    needful,
Lightly his lips he applied to the holes he had fashioned:
    responding
Swiftly, the reed was alive with the magical noise that would
    fill it,
When at the edge of the sea, gentle Zephyros, ruffling the
    waters,
Touched the rough rushes to music and flooded the beach with
    the sea-sound.

[1841]

Summer Rain

"Golden rain! Golden rain! Out of the sky!"
Children sing out and run after the rain.
"Quiet, my children, we'll reap it again,
Only we'll gather the gold in the grain—
In the full granaries fragrant with rye."

[1856]

The Hay Harvest

The smell of hay is on the field,
    And singing as they go
The women toss the heavy yield
    And spread it row by row.

And yonder where the hay is dry
   Each man his forkful throws,
Until the wagon loaded high
   Is like a house that grows.

The poor old horse who draws the cart
   Stands rooted in the heat,
With sagging knees and ears apart,
   Asleep upon his feet.

But little Zhuchka speeds away
   In barking brave commotion,
To dip and flounder in the hay
   As in a grassy ocean.

AFANASY FET

"A Magic Landscape"

A magic landscape,
My heart's delight:
A full moon's brightness,
A plain, sheer white,

The high sky lighted,
The snow's pure ray,
And far-off gliding,
A lonely sleigh.

      [1842]

"I Come Again"

I come again with greetings new,
   To tell you day is well begun;
To say the leaves are fresh with dew
   And dappled in the early sun;

To tell you how the forest stirs
   In every branch of every brake,
And what an April thirst is hers,
   With every whistling bird awake;

To say, as yesterday, once more,
   With love as passionate and true,
My heart is ready as before
   To serve our happiness and you;

To tell how over every thing
   Delight is blowing on the air—
I know not yet what I shall sing;
   I only know the song is there.

[1843]

"Whispers"

Whispers. Timid breathing. Trilling
Of a nightingale.
And below the runnel rocking,
Sleepy, silver-pale.

Strange nocturnal lights and shadows,
Shadows that enlace.
Row on row of magic changes
On the dearest face.

Smoky cloudlets, rose and purple,
With a tinge of fawn.
Kisses. Ah, and tears among them.
And the dawn, the dawn!

[1850]

At the Fireside

The embers sink to ashes. In the dusk
A small transparent flame is wavering;
Thus on a scarlet poppy will a moth
Flutter an azure wing.

Drawn by a train of motley images,
The tired gaze is charmed, while all unclear,
Faces that alter as they flash and fade,
From the gray ashes peer.

The joy, the grief that were, arise once more,
Caressingly commingled, nor depart.
He lies who would deny the aching need
Of all that haunts the heart.

                                    [1856]

Address to Death

I know what fainting means, the heady sweetness
When the pain stops and dark comes in its stead;
And so quite fearlessly I can await you,
You night without a dawn, eternal bed.

Your hand may touch my head, and from life's records
You may expunge me, but I testify,
Before that hour, while yet my heart is beating,
Our powers are equal, and the victor: I.

A shadow at my feet, a faceless specter,
You, while I breathe, are subject unto me,
You are merely a thought that I am thinking,
The frail toy of my anguished reverie.

                                    [1884]

Swallows

Calm Nature's idle spy, I follow
Her paths with pleasure; free and fond,
I watch the arrow-winged swift swallow
That curves above the dusking pond.

It swoops, its darting shadow smutching
The glassy surface, till one fears
Those perilous waters will be clutching
The sudden wing before it veers.

And once again the same quick daring,
And once again the same dark stream. . . .
Is not this flight our human faring?
Is not this urge our human dream?

Thus I, earth's creature, vainly chidden,
Seek out the alien way, and try
To enter the unknown, forbidden,
And scoop one drop of mystery.

[1884]

VLADIMIR SOLOVYOV

"Through Morning Mists"

Through morning mists with wavering steps I made
For a shore of marvels and mysteries. The first gleams
Of dawn contended with the last of the stars,
Dreams were still hovering. And my soul prayed
To unknown gods, my soul in the grip of dreams.

The hour is cold and candid; I tread as before
A lonely road in an unknown land. With day
The mist has lifted and the eye sees clearly
How difficult is the mountain track that rises sheerly,
And all I saw in dreams how far, how far away.

And until midnight I shall still be walking
Fearlessly toward the shore of my desire,
To where, beneath new stars, on a mountain height
My arcane temple awaits me, blazing higher
With light on triumphal light.

1884

FYODOR SOLOGUB

"Austere My Verse"

Austere my verse: therein are heard
Strange echoes, distant and despairing.
Are not my shoulders bowed in bearing
My inspiration's bitter word?

The dim day rests as shadows fall.
No road before me is unwinding:
My promised land I'll not be finding.
The world rears round me like a wall.

At times from that far land a vain
Faint voice resounds like distant thunder.
Can the long waiting on a wonder
Obliterate the long bleak pain?

"I Do Not Crave"

I do not crave for resurrection,
I have no need of Paradise.
No sadness will be mine in dying,
No wings be given on which to rise.

I shall put out the lights I lived by,
Shall shut my lips, at last shall win
To incommunicable being,
There to forget all that had been.

1900

"We Are Weary"

We are weary of steering a course,
We are spent, it is rest that we crave,
We are ripe
For the grave.

Then as meek as the babe that is laid
In its cradle, there let us descend,
To molder there soon,
To no end.

The Devil's Swing

Beneath a shaggy pine,
Where the loud waters sing,
The hairy-handed fiend
Pushes his fiendish swing.

He shoves and gives a crow:
To and fro,
To and fro.
The board creaks as it sags,
The rope is taut and drags
Against the heavy bough.

The weak, unsteady board
Creaks warningly and slides;
The devil can afford
To roar; he holds his sides.

In agony I swing:
        To and fro,
        To and fro,
I swing and cling and try
To look away, but no,
He holds me with his eye.

Above the darkening pine
The blue fiend's tauntings ring:
"The swing has trapped you—fine!
Then, devil take you, swing!"

Beneath the shaggy pine
The demon voices sing:
"The swing has trapped you—fine!
Then, devil take you, swing!"

The fiend will not let go,
The dizzy board not stay
Until that dread hand strikes
And I am swept away.

Until the hemp, rubbed thin
And frayed, breaks suddenly,
Until the broad black ground
Comes rushing up to me.

Above the pine I'll fling
And plop! into the mire.
Then swing, devil, swing—
Higher, higher, higher!

[1907]

INNOKENTY ANNENSKY

September

Gardens adorned with gold that yet are sickly,
Slow ailments wearing purple's siren suit,
And, in short arcs, the sun's delaying ardor,
Helpless to spend itself in fragrant fruit.

Rough traces left on silken, yellow carpets,
The falsehood of the final meeting bared,
And, in the parks, black ponds, unfathomable,
For perfect suffering long ago prepared.

But the heart senses loss only as beauty,
Feels only rapture in ensorcelled strength,
And those who have tasted of the lotus tremble—
Autumn's furtive aroma real at length.

1904

Black Spring

To brazen knells a funeral
Was being held, and weird
And waxen, from the coffin's head
A nose distinctly reared.

It wished, perhaps, to fill the lungs
From which all breath was gone?
The snow was soiled, the squelchy road
Was hard to walk upon.

Alone by turbid hoarfrost was
Decay obscurely glazed;
Into the jelly of the eyes
A black Spring dully gazed

From shabby roofs, from quaggy pits,
From faces like green curds. . . .
And yonder, in the lifeless fields,
From wings of sodden birds.

Oh, men! the rutted roads of life
Make going less than sweet,
But grief is heaviest to bear
When two deaths meet.

1906

Poppies

The joyful day is blazing. . . . The limp grass
Here throngs with poppies, poppies like the cries
Of avid impotence, like lips that tempt
And poison, like strange scarlet butterflies.

The joyful day is blazing. . . . But the weeds
Usurp a garden done with pleasuring.
And poppies, withered like old women's heads,
Are sheltered beneath heaven's shining wing.

1910

"I Thought that My Heart"

I thought that my heart was of stone,
A hollow, insensible heart;
Let tongues of fire lick it—
There would be no sign of smart.

And truly, I felt no pain,
Or if pain—the merest bit.
Yet—better extinguish the flame
While you still can master it.

The heart is dark as a grave.
The blaze has been quenched, as you see;
Well, now—we've put out the fire,
And the smoke is choking me.

1923

Winter Dream

The late edition has the notice, framed
In black; propriety will have its say.
There is no doubt about my having died,
Alas! in quite an ordinary way.

The family steps cautiously, as though
I were still ailing. But I'm not in bed;
And should I, then, savor the dignity
Of lying on the table here, instead?*

All day, all night, the psalms will be intoned
By priests in furs; tears will be duly shed
Amid gold braid and camlet cloaks that lend
Their luster to the office of the dead.

They have ordered candles three feet high, to weep
In soot beside my face. And there will be
A moment of tense silence, broken as
The deacon swings the censer noisily.

If anything remains of what was I,
What will you do with it? You are allowed
To touch this horror, this pity, only if
You wrap them in a shroud.

---

* It is a Russian custom to place the body on a table before laying it in
the coffin.

Go bury that white bundle before dawn
In a white field, and be concerned about
Its lot no more. . . . Meanwhile, have a heart:
Those basses in the study—get them out!

1923

KONSTANTIN BALMONT

"With My Fancy I Grasped"

With my fancy I grasped at the vague shadows straying,
At the vague shadows straying where the daylight had fled;
I ascended a tower, and the stairway was swaying,
And the stairway was swaying underneath my light tread.

Ever higher I climbed, ever clearer were rounded,
Ever clearer were rounded dreaming hilltops aglow;
And from heaven to earth twilight voices resounded,
Twilight voices resounded from above and below.

And the higher I rose, strange horizons defining,
Strange horizons defining, did the summits appear;
And my eyes as I gazed were caressed by their shining,
Were caressed by their shining, their farewell, sad and clear.

Now the night had appeared; earth in darkness lay dreaming,
Earth in darkness lay dreaming, like a slumbering star,
While the smoldering sun, his dim embers still gleaming,
His dim embers still gleaming, shone for me from afar.

I had learned to ensnare the vague shadows far straying,
The vague shadows far straying, where the daylight had fled:
Ever higher I rose, and the stairway was swaying,
And the stairway was swaying underneath my light tread.

[*1894*]

VALERY BRYUSOV

"Radiant Ranks"

Radiant ranks of seraphim
Stir the air about our bed.
With their pinions cool and dim
Our hot cheeks are comforted.

Low the circling seraphs bend,
And we tremble and rejoice
At hosannas that ascend,
Winged with their unearthly voice.

Cloudy luminous faces hover,
And the wing-swept candles wane,
And our fiery breasts they cover
With a viewless holy rain.

                              [1905]

The Coming Huns

"Trample their Eden, Attila!"
        —VYACHESLAV IVANOV

Where do you wait, coming Huns,
Who weigh on the world like a cloud?
Under the Pamirs' suns
Your cast-iron tread is loud.

Swoop down in a drunken horde
From your dark tents on the plains,
Let a wave of blood be poured
Into these empty veins.

O slaves of freedom, raise
Your tents on the palace site;
Where once the throne would blaze,
Let your grainfields glow as bright.

Heap books to build a fire!
Dance in the merry light.
The holy place bemire:
You are children in our sight.

And we, the poets, the wise,
Shall be true to the treasures we save,
Hiding the torch you despise
In catacomb, desert, and cave.

Where angry lightnings glance,
Where tempests raven and tear,
What will the play of chance
From our long labors spare?

All that we alone knew
May be blotted out by your whim.
Yet you who destroy me, you—
I salute with hosanna and hymn.

[1905]

The Last Feast

The shadows pale. Behind the shutters
Dawn shows her shameless face, in vain:
That new day is not sovereign for us,
Who live in this last moment's reign.

Over the pavement's heavy cobbles
A stray cart rumbles by, unseen.
Whiter than snow, your face's pallor,
Your look is somber, yet serene.

The guests, a herd of drunken centaurs,
All sleep a hideous sleep, pell-mell,
And wreaths of roses, wreaths of laurel,
Lie crushed and wine-drenched where they fell.

Upon the pelts of bears and ounces,
Oblivious, drowsy slaves are cast. . . .
The time has come for us to conquer
The dark genius of Fate at last.

You've lifted the Falernian phial
And let it drop. . . . The sign I mark!
My soul is faithful: you have summoned—
I go, prepared, into the dark.

Beneath our garments' folds, our heartbeats
Are regular. . . . As we refrain
From fear and hope, so we shall suffer
No panic terror and no pain.

Above the couch two blades will glitter,
A moan sound like a dreamer's sigh—
Falling, we'll not vex the dull slumber
In which the drunken centaurs lie.

[1906]

The Tryst

Where, by Nile's slow-moving waters, flaming Ra's dominion
     glitters, mirrored in Lake Moeris' sheen,
In the days of yore you loved me, loved as Isis loved Osiris, my
     companion, sister, queen!
And the pyramidal shadow o'er our twilight tryst would lean.

Oh, the mystery—remember our encounter in the temple, when
     the dances held us dazed
And, the candles quenched, we lingered in a fabulous enchant-
     ment, to the heights of wonder raised,
Our delicious words, our dalliance, our delight that sudden
     blazed!

In the splendor of the ballroom as your slender form sur-
    rendered, did you hear Time's curtain rend?
Hear the cymbals and the anthems mingling with responsive
    resonance, hear the people's voice ascend?
Did you not avow the sleep of separation at an end!

Once before we knew such passion, this our bliss is a remem-
    brance, now the past is in full flower,
For the grave is transitory, unextinguished our desire burns
    once more with its old power,
As when near the Nile we trysted, in that brief, that fateful
    hour!

                                 [*1906–07*]

St. Sebastian

In slow and smoky fires thou burn'st and art consumèd,
    Oh, thou, my soul.
In slow and smoky fires thou burn'st and art consumèd—
    With wordless dole.

Thou standest like Sebastian, pierced with pointed arrows,
    Harassed and spent.
Thou standest like Sebastian, pierced with pointed arrows,
    His young breast rent.

Thy foes encircle thee and watch with gleeful laughter
    And bended bow.
Thy foes encircle thee and watch with gleeful laughter
    Thy torments slow.

The embers burn and gentle is the arrow's stinging
    As night descends.
The embers burn and gentle is the arrow's stinging:
    Thy trial ends.

Why hastens not thy dream unto thy lips, now pallid
    With deathy drouth?
Why hastens not thy dream unto thy lips, now pallid,
    To kiss thy mouth?

                                   [*1907*]

Benediction

"Que tes mains soient bénies, car elles sont impures."
—REMY DE GOURMONT

The shining of your golden eyes I bless!
It broke my dark delirium with light.

The smile that wavers on your lips I bless!
Like wine it held me with its subtle might.

The poison in your kisses hid I bless!
All thoughts, all dreams are poisoned by your kiss.

The scythe that sings in your embrace I bless!
All my past years you have mown down with this.

The kindling fire of your love I bless!
I wrapped its flame about me joyfully.

The darkness of your spirit, lo, I bless!
For that its wings were outstretched over me.

Blessed all you gave, blessed what your soul denies;
I bless you for the fears, the agonies,

That after you I strove toward paradise,
That here, without its gates, I stand and freeze!

[1908]

GEORGY CHULKOV

Autumnal Love

Purple Autumn unloosed her tresses and flung them
On the heavens and over the dew-heavy fields.
She came as a guest to the old, silent manor,
Singeing the grasses with red;
Through the garden she sauntered,
Then she climbed up the balcony, barely
Touching the fragile old rails.
She pushed the door softly,
Softly she entered the room,
Sprinkling the rug with her yellowish sand,
Dropped a red leaf upon the piano.
From that hour on, we heard her unceasing rustle,
Rustle and stir and soft whisper.

And our hands suddenly met
With no new words, new and forever false:
As though we had hung a wreath of red roses
On a black wrought-iron door
Leading into a vault
Where rotted the dear remains
Of a beloved dream.

Autumnal days were upon us,
Days of inscrutable longing;
We were treading the stairs
Of autumnal passion.
In my heart a wound, like an icon lamp,
Burned and would not be quenched.
The cup of autumnal poison
We pressed to our lips.

By the serpentine garden path Autumn had led us
To the pond lilies,
To the pool edged with worn sands.
And over the lilied waters and in the roses of evening,
We made love, more superstitiously.

And through the dark night,
On the langorous bed,
At the feet of my love,
I loved death anew.
The minutes rang tinkling like crystals
At the brink of an autumn grave:
Autumn and Death drunkenly clinked their glasses.

I pressed my thirsty lips
To the feet the icon lamp ruddied,
I drank the cup of love.
Scorched by the fires of crimes,
Stretched on the cross of lusts,
Filled with shame at needless betrayals,
I drank the cup of love.
In the hour of ineffable dalliance
I sensed the whisper
Of autumnal, of deathbed passion.
And kisses like keen needles
Burned and pierced,
Weaving a wreath of thorns.

VIKTOR HOFMAN

Summer Ball

The evening of the ball was hushed,
The summer ball, with scarce a quiver
In the dark lindens where they brushed
The sharpest curve of that still river.

Where, on the river's very brink,
The willows drooped like drowsy dreamers,
There it seemed beautiful to link
The banners and the colored streamers.

A singing waltz that dreamed and sighed,
And many glances, meeting, swerving,
Soft clouds that, tenderly enskied,
Seemed women's shoulders, softly curving.

The river looked a sculptured stream,
Or else the heavens' still reflection,
Their miracle's exultant gleam
Revived in fading recollection.

The clouds were hemmed with broader gold
Where, faint, a crimson gleam was clinging.
Serene the dream that thus could hold
The waltz, still summoning and singing.

A waltz, with linden boughs above,
And many glances, meeting, swerving,
And near, ah, near, the wonder of
Someone's long lashes softly curving.

                    1905

MIKHAIL KUZMIN

From This Summer's Love

4 "Night Was Done"

Night was done; we rose and after
Washing, dressing, kissed with laughter.
Past was all the sweet night knows.
Lilac breakfast cups were clinking
While we sat like mere friends drinking
Tea—and kept our dominoes.

And our dominoes smiled greeting,
And our eyes avoided meeting,
Like our lips, they gave no clue.
We sang *Faust*, we played, defying
All night held, as though denying
Night had ever known us two.

[1906]

From Alexandrian Songs

WISDOM

3 "How I Love the World"

How I love the world in all its beauty,
O eternal gods!
The sun, how I love it, the reeds,
and the greenish glitter of the sea
through the slender acacia branches!
How I love books (those of my friends),
the hush of my lonely house,
and the view from the window
overlooking the melon patches!

How I love the bright crowds in the square,
the shouting voices, the singing, and the sun,
the lively laughter of boys playing ball,
the return home
after a pleasant stroll,
in the evening
when the first stars are out,
past the inns with windows already alight,
companioned by a friend who has become remote!
O eternal gods, how I delight
in serene melancholy,
in love that is brief,
in death that does not regret the passing of a life
whose every feature is cherished,
and which, I swear by Dionysos, I love
with all the strength of my heart
and of the flesh that is so dear to me!

4 *"Dying Is Sweet"*

Dying is sweet
on the battlefield
in the hissing of arrows and spears,
when the trumpet sounds
and the sun of noon
is shining,
dying for country's glory
and hearing around you:
"Hero, farewell!"
Dying is sweet
for an old, venerable man
in the house
on the bed
where his forebears were born and died—
surrounded by children
grown men,
and hearing around him:
"Father, farewell!"
But sweeter,
wiser,

having spent the last obol,
having sold the last mill
for a woman
who the next day is forgotten,
having come
from a gay promenade
to the mansion already sold,
to sup
and, having read the tale of Apuleius
for the hundred and first time,
to open your veins
in the warm, fragrant bath,
hearing no farewell;
and through the high slit of a window
must come the scent of stock,
dawn must be glowing,
and flutes be heard in the distance.

1908

LOVE

1 "My Faulty Memory"

My faulty memory cannot tell me
when I first met you:
if it was morning, or by day at all,
at evening, or late in the night.
I recall only rather pale cheeks,
gray eyes beneath dark brows,
the swarthy neck with the blue collar,
and it seems I saw this in my early childhood,
although my years are many more than yours.

4 "People See Gardens"

People see gardens with houses in them,
and the ocean purple in the sunset,
people see gulls over the waters,
and women on flat roofs;
people see soldiers in battle dress,
and, on the square, vendors with trays of small cakes;

people see the sun and the stars,
streams and flashing brooks;
but I see everywhere and only
pale, swarthy cheeks,
gray eyes under dark brows,
and that incomparably graceful figure—
thus the eyes of lovers see
what the wise heart bids them see.

Fujiyama in a Saucer

Through the tea vapor I discern Mount Fuji:
Upon a yellow sky, a golden cone.
Strange, how a saucer can foreshorten Nature!
But that fine ripple pierces to the bone.

The sun, no bigger than an ant's eye, lances
The dangling cobweb of the clouds, and black
Tea leaves: winged fish, upon the wavering topaz
Of the high heavens trace a shifting crack.

Within this tiny world, spring's world is lying:
The horn will hollo, the almond's fragrance ride
Upon the air, the porcelain rim enclosing
The entire bay, though it were twice as wide.

But now a twig of unforeseen mimosa,
Slicing the heavens, rests on them and glows—
As, sometimes, an enchanted verse will dazzle,
Beaming from pages of pedantic prose.

[*1917*]

VYACHESLAV IVANOV

Nomads of Beauty

"You are artists, nomads of Beauty."
                    —TORCHES

For you—ancestral acres,
And, choked, the graveyard waits.
For us, the free forsakers—
The prairies Beauty fates.

For us—the daily treason,
The camps we daily flee,
Who break with each new season
A false captivity.

Trust distance for its marvels,
All veils as sheer disguise,
The springtide's emerald carvels,
The breadth of all the skies.

Oh, vagrant artists, shepherd
Your droves of dreams unbound;
And sow, although you jeopard
The soon-abandoned ground.

And from your open spaces
Rush down, a whirling horde,
Where slaves tamed to the traces
Adore their overlord.

Destroy their Eden's bowers!
Where bare and virgin lies
The land, where your steppe flowers,
And there your stars will rise.

                                1904

"The Holy Rose"

The holy rose her leaves will soon unfold.
The tender bud of dawn already lies
Reddening on the wide, transparent skies.
Love's star is a white sail the still seas hold.
Here in the light-soaked space above the wold,
Through the descending dew the arches rise
Of the unseen cathedral, filled with cries
From the winged weavers threading it with gold.
Here on the hill the cypress, in accord
With me, stands praying, a cowled Eremite.
And on the rose's cheeks the tears fall light.
My cell is festive where bright rays are poured.
And in the east the purple vines bleed bright
And seething, overflow. . . . Hosanna, Lord!

From Vespers

III *"Clear the Fountain Waters"*

Clear the fountain waters glowing,
Living streams, the wellsprings flowing,
Cold, in darkling woods, a spring.
In the shed, cool stillness streaming,
O'er the well, a candle gleaming
On Christ's crown its gilding flings.

In the Eden field—a bower,
And a fountain, and a flower.
Christ, star-voiced, the spirit stills:
"Come, before my wellspring stooping,
Of my quiet waters scooping—
For the stintless bucket fills."

V *"Now the Golden Leafage"*

Now the golden leafage is beggared.
Shining through the porches of autumn
Shows the cool, blue stillness of heaven.

Lo, the thin-trunked grove is transcended:
Carved in stone, a columned cathedral.
Smoke scrolls wind about the white pillars.

Hung above the portal are curtains—
Openwork: like nets of God's fishers
That the catch has slipped through and broken,
Like thy tatters, humble and sacred,
At the entrance to a white temple,
Oh, thou golden, mendicant music!

1908

Funeral

Of funerals, the saddest
Is love's that dies unanswered.
The soul has two to bury:
The soul of the beloved
And its own other selfhood.
And a third enters, living,
The funeral flame that wraps them;
His wings a yoke has weighted:
Him the wise lips of lovers
Call in their kisses Eros,
And gods, the Resurrector.

The Balance

Sadness and stillness. What a bright transparency!
Enskied a woman seems to stand invisibly
Holding a crystal balance and intently poring
Over the instant, its frail equipoise adoring.

But every yellow leaf that from the branches sails,
Laying its little weight of gold upon the scales,
May force the pan ripe summer's bounty freighted
Toward the grave whereto the world of light is fated.

[*1913*]

The Euxine

Beneath the window swallows build their nest;
A finch flies to the scattered crumbs below
In our refectory, a radiant guest.
Roses are burning where not long ago
The garden was all white with plum and cherry;
Alone the swarthy cypresses asway
Perform their ritual as is customary.
What diamond-blue expanse sends ray on ray,
Cusped by wisteria's mauve clusters there?
The plane trees fringe the Euxine's azure gaze,
Nurse of Medea's strong allure. I sink
Beneath a tree in drowsy dreams, to stare
After a sail, and wave it toward the haze
Of myth, toward distant vapors turning pink.

[*1917*]

From Winter Sonnets

III "The Winter of the Soul"

The winter of the soul. . . . The living sun
Warms it obliquely and from far away.
But the dumb drifts rise up to blind and stun
A spirit lulled by the lone blizzard's lay.

Come, place the firewood, and the hearth flame leaps
To cook your sup of porridge busily;
The hour suffices; then, with all that sleeps,
Sleep, too. Oh, deep grave of Eternity!

Ice-choked, life's wellspring lies beneath a cloud,
The fount of fire is no longer brave. . . .
Oh, do not seek me under my close shroud.
My double drags his coffin, a meek slave;
But I, the true self, flesh cannot command,
Toil at the temple builded by no hand.

1920

VIII *"Threadbare Roof"*

The threadbare roof is shaken by the wind,
In the half-dark iron clangs, a groan sounds, low.
The vacant land is wrapped in winter's shroud,
The alley is a graveyard built of snow.

Midnight is not the hour for strolling through
Streets where the spirit of the plague seems risen
To haunt the city; life's withdrawn and hides
In a secret corner of its barren prison.

I dragged my feet to the hovel, where the storm
Blows through the chinks, yet whose frail walls have got
A nook safe from the wind that whips and whines.
Within the magic circle it is warm;
Upon the hearth bubbles a boiling pot,
And, like the smile of a friend, Fire shines.

1920

MAXIMILIAN VOLOSHIN

From Cimmerian* Twilight

I *"The Evening Light"*

The evening light has soaked with ancient gold
And gall the hills. Like strips of tawny fur,
The tufts of shaggy grass glow ruddier;
Past fiery bushes metal waves unfold;
Piled boulders, naked cliffs the sea has holed
Show enigmatic fronts that lour and blur.

* The reference is to the Crimea, which in ancient times was inhabited by
people known as Cimmerians.

In the winged twilight figures seem to stir:
A huge paw looms, a jowl grins stark and bold,
Like swelling ribs the dubious hillocks show;
On what bent back, like wool, does savory grow?
What brute, what titan, to this region cleaves?
The dark is strange . . . and yonder, space is clean.
And there the weary ocean, panting, heaves,
And rotting grasses breathe of iodine.

II "Here Stood a Sacred Forest"

Here stood a sacred forest. Here moved the divine
Wing-footed messenger, whose passing brushed the glades.
Cities stood here: their ruin's mere remembrance fades,
Where now only the sheep graze on the burnt incline.
Sharp-etched the peaks! Their toothed crowns catch the shine
As the green dusk, eerily sad, invades.
Whose timeless anguish stings my soul as with edged blades?
Who knows the road of gods? The start and the decline?
The churning rubble grinds and groans as long before;
Against the sandbanks of the wide and echoing shore,
Lifting its heavy crests, the troubled ocean fumes;
And starry nights drop their slow tears into the sea. . . .
While outcast gods, whose faces light no more illumes,
Gaze and demand and summon inescapably.

III "Above the Rocking Waters' Ripples"

Above the rocking waters' ripples fiercely stand
Deep-rooted crests: a desert ridge of craggy stubble;
Black precipices frown on torrents of red rubble—
The grievous reaches of an inscrutable land.
In the sad, solemn dreams that haunt me I have found
A lost land's echoing bays where, as late dusk is falling,
More sorrowfully and more musically calling,
Forsaken waves in waste hexameters resound.
And gliding on that pathlessness as on a river
Of darkness, a sail floats with the mysterious quiver
Of anguished winds and of the deep that heaves and fails.
Thrust by the seas' blind push, my fated skiff is going
Forth where the road of daring and of penance hails,
While lamplike in the sky the Seven Stars are glowing.

From Lunaria

XV *"Pure Pearl of Silence"**

Pure pearl of silence brooding on the sky,
Presider o'er conception, lamp of dreams,
Love's crystal, altar where night's mystery gleams,
Queen of the waters where thou lov'st to lie,
From the damp depths, with what a plaintive sigh,
Through my dark crucifixions toward thy beams,
O Dian, O fierce Hecate, there streams
Vision on vision, unlived, snakelike, shy.

How sweet yet weirdly joyless are the folds
And caves thy diamond delirium holds.
The flashing mica of thy empty seas
In listless ether shows like horror's face,
Thou frozen cry that nothing can appease,
Thou dead world's avid corpse, cast out on space.

1913

Terror

They worked at night, they went through
Reports, dockets, depositions.
They signed sentences hurriedly.
They yawned. And drank.
In the morning they served out vodka to the soldiers.
In the evening, by candlelight,
Those listed, men and women, were summoned,
And driven into a dark courtyard.
Their clothing, shoes, linen, were removed
And tied into bundles
That were loaded onto trucks and carted off.
The rings and watches they shared among themselves.

* This concludes a cycle of fifteen sonnets, so written that the last line of
each forms the first line of the next, the final sonnet being composed of
the first lines of the preceding fourteen.

At night they drove the barefoot and the hungry
Over icy ground,
With a northeaster blowing,
To the vacant outskirts of the city.
With rifle butts they pushed them to the gully's edge,
Snapping on their flashlights.
The machine guns worked half a minute.
Those not mown down they did for with bayonets.
Some were thrown into the pit alive.
Earth was flung in hastily.
Then, marching to a spacious Russian song,
They returned to town.
At dawn wives, mothers, dogs
Made their way to the gully.
They dug up the earth, they quarreled over bones,
They kissed the beloved flesh.

1920

Under Sail

Five days we have been cruising, nor once have furled
The bellying sails.
Nights have been spent in bays,
In coves and estuaries,
Where a full moon blossomed above the dunes.
By day the wind drives us along the shallow
And lonely sandbanks,
Seething with white foam.
Stayed by the carven rudder,
I watch
From the high prow
The dance of the deck;
The massed seas shimmer, and beyond,
The interlacing rigging frames
The untenanted ocean.
A balked wave's splash,

A taut mast's creak,
A gurgling underneath the prow—
And one still sail. . . .
Behind—the city,
All a red ecstasy
Of spilling flags,
Inflamed with fear and anger,
Chill with rumors,
Quivering with hope,
Tortured by hunger,
Plagues and blood—
City where tardy Spring glides stealthily,
In a lace veil of flowers and acacias.
But here—only the windless, soundless, unplumbed deep.
The sky, the water, are two valves
Of a vast pearl shell.
The sun is caught in cobweb rays.
The ship in cloudy spaces hangs,
In blunt and smoky splendor.
Yonder is seen the shore of your bare land
Of wormwood, drought, and stone—
Your land fatigued
With being the thoroughfare of tribes and peoples.
I shall set you as a witness to their madness,
And I shall lead you by a bladelike path,
That you may bear within you the immense
Silence of the twilit, shimmering sea.

1923

ANDREY BELYI

"Once More I Pray"

Once more I pray, as doubt torments me and appalls;
The saints with bony fingers threaten from the walls.

Stern faces like black spots upon the icons show,
And, dark with centuries, the gilt has lost its glow.

But now the window is aflood with streaming rays,
And in the molten sun all is alive, ablaze.

"Thou gentle light," the choir is chanting, and behold,
The saints' dark faces gleam with a puce-colored gold.

And, incense-wreathed, the priest moves altarward as one
Who as a nimbus wears this ecstasy of sun.

1903

Fields

It is a wolf's hunched back that bristles
And flashes there along the rise.
Upon the azured snow the shadow
With what light leaps in silence flies.

Now it is dropping down an incline,
Below a fir now shrinks away.
A dog cries in the wintry distance,
Getting the scent, and hugs the sleigh.

What power is theirs: the night, the mournful
Expanse, and panic fantasy,
This thunder-throated icy powder,
The heavens' austere finery.

1907

"Enough"

Enough. Wait no more, hope no longer.
My pitiful people, erase
Yourselves, flee! Years of torment,
Break up, fall away into space!

These ages of want, of enslavement. . . .
O motherland, into your vast
Allow me to sob out my heart now,
Out into your damp, empty vast.

Beyond, on the rough, hunchbacked meadow,
Where a flock of green oaks lifts its head,
The crowns lightly, loftily swaying
Beneath massive clouds' shaggy lead;

Where Astoundment appalls, in the open:
A bush, paralytic, with thin
Arms failing, the branchy rag whistles
How piercingly into the wind;

Where, surmounting the network of hillocks,
As night overshadows the pole,
The fell, yellow eyes of your taverns,
Demented, peer into my soul;

There, there, where dread deaths and diseases
Have furrowed a track you can trace,
Go, vanish, Russia, my Russia,
Vanish away into space!

1909

From Christ Is Risen

22

And the news
Pealed:
A hosanna.

A strange
Flame
Is revealed
In the cave of unfaith.

And behold!
The murk,
Irradiate, owns
It is dawn,
And our bodies
Are rolled
Away from us—

Even as stones.

23

Russia,
My country—

Thou art
That Woman clothed with the sun
To whom
All eyes
Are lifted. . . .

I see clearly:

Russia,
My Russia,
Is the God-bearer
Overcoming
The Serpent. . . .

The peoples
Inhabiting Thee
Have stretched out
Their hands
Through the smoke
To Thy spaces
That are filled with song,
Filled with the fire
Of a descending seraph.

And my throat
Locks with emotion.

24

I know:
An airy vast
Is shed
Round each of us
Like a nimbus;

Each man's head
Glows
With lightnings raying from
This age's
Embered woes.

And the Word that now
Stands midmost of the heart,
Of the storm-trumpeted
Spring,
Swelling the voiceful depths
Of its fiery throat,
Breaks prison:

Dearly beloved
Sons—
Christ is Risen.

1918

ALEXANDER BLOK

"I Have Foreknown Thee"

"Longing and loving, you shall yet slough off
The heavy sleep of earthly consciousness."
—**VLADIMIR SOLOVYOV**

I have foreknown Thee! Oh, I have foreknown Thee. Going,
The years have shown me Thy unalterable face.

Intolerably clear, the farthest sky is glowing.
I wait in silence Thy longed-for and worshiped grace.

The farthest sky is glowing: soon Thou wilt be nearing.
Yet terror clings to me: Thy image will be strange,

And insolent suspicion will rouse at Thy appearing;
The features long foreknown, beheld at last, will change.

How shall I then be fallen, undone by the surrender
Unto my deathy dream, bowing to bitter change!

The farthest sky is glowing; nearer looms the splendor!
Yet terror clings to me: Thy image will be strange.

[*1901*]

"A Little Black Man"

A little black man ran through the town.
He extinguished the street lamps, high on his ladder.

Dawn was approaching, white and slow.
With the strange little man it climbed the ladder.

Where soft, silent shadows, black and brown,
Where the lamplight's yellow stripes had been sleeping,

Morning twilight upon the steps lay down,
Into the curtains, into the door cracks creeping.

Ah, how pale is the city when night has died!
The little black man is crying now, outside.

[*1903*]

Little Catkins*

Little boys and little maidens
Little candles, little catkins
  Homeward bring.

Little lights are burning softly,
People cross themselves in passing—
  Scent of spring.

Little wind so bold and merry,
Little raindrops, don't extinguish
  These flames, pray!

I will rise tomorrow early,
Rise to greet you, Willow Sunday,
  Holy day.

                    1906

The Unknown Woman

Of evenings now above the restaurants
Heavily hangs the thick and troubled air;
The spirit of spring, brooding, pestilent,
Governs the drunken outcries rising there.

Beyond the dusty alleys and beyond
The boredom of the summer villas gleams
The faint gold sign over the bakery,
And in the distance sound the children's screams.

* On the eve of Palm Sunday, which the Russians call Willow Sunday,
consecrated sprigs of pussy willow and lighted candles are carried home
from church. The poem was intended for a primer sponsored by The
Most Holy Synod.

This is the hour when the practiced wags,
Their derbies cocked, stroll beyond the town
And with the ladies by the sad canals
Go promenading slowly up and down.

Thinly upon the lake the oarlocks creak,
The women shriek, and in its usual place
Up in the heavens the indifferent moon,
Bored with it all, pulls a stupid face.

Reflected every evening in my glass,
The sole companion of my solitude,
I see one friend, by the strange acrid wine,
Even as I, befuddled and subdued.

And at the neighboring tables, wearily
The drowsy waiters watch the hours pass
As pass they must, while drunks with rabbits' eyes,
Blinking, cry out: *"In vino veritas!"*

And every evening at the appointed hour
(Or is it but a dream I dream again?)
The figure of a girl in shining silks
Is seen to move across the foggy pane.

Slowly she picks her way among the drunks,
And always uncompanioned, all alone,
Breathing of fragrance as of mist, she comes
To sit beside the window, the Unknown.

From her resilient silks and mournful plumes
And from her narrow hands with their great rings
Legends are wafted: the air round her stirs
With wordless whispers of mysterious things.

By her strange nearness held as by a spell,
I peer behind her somber veil and see
The fairy gleam of an enchanted shore,
And an enchanted vista beckons me.

I am made master of unspoken things,
Another's sun is given me to keep,
Into the secret places of my soul
The acrid wine has found a way to creep.

And in my brain the ostrich feathers toss
Their plumy curves, and sink and sway and rise,
And on the distant shore mysteriously
Flower two wide and fathomless blue eyes.

Deep in my soul a secret treasure lies,
The key to it is mine and only mine!
Yes, drunken monster, you made no mistake!
I know, I know: truth lies in wine.

[1906]

"When Mountain Ash"

When mountain ash in clusters reddens,
Its leafage wet and stained with rust,
When through my palm the nail that deadens
By bony hands is shrewdly thrust,

When o'er the rippling, leaden river,
Nailed to the cross, in agony,
Upon the wet gray height I quiver,
While, stern, my country watches me,

Then far and wide in anguish staring
My eyes, grown stiff with tears, will see
Down the broad river slowly faring,
Christ in a skiff approaching me.

And in his eyes the same hopes biding,
And the same rags from Him will trail,
His garment piteously hiding
The palm pierced by the final nail.

Christ! saddened are the native reaches.
The cross tugs at my failing might.
Thy skiff—will it achieve these beaches,
And land here at my cruciate height?

1907

"She Came out of the Frost"

She came out of the frost,
Her cheeks glowing,
And filled the room with
Freshness of air and perfume,
A ringing voice
And chatter
Utterly disrespectful
Of serious pursuits.

She proceeded to drop
A fat volume of an art review
On the floor,
And suddenly
My room
Began to look fearfully crowded.

All this was somewhat annoying
And rather absurd.
She asked me, however,
To read *Macbeth* to her.
When I came to: "The earth hath bubbles . . ."
(I cannot say it without agitation),
I noticed she too was agitated
And was staring out of the window.

It appears that a large spotted tomcat
Was cautiously crawling
Along the edge of the roof
After two doves that were billing.

I got angry, chiefly
Because the doves, not we, were kissing,
And the days of Paolo and Francesca were gone.

1908

"Your Landscape"

Your landscape, O my North, enchants me!
The desolate expanse I see
Extends as far as the horizon,
As empty as my reverie!

My stubborn, vicious spirit vexes
The silence with its laughter—sign
For a dour raven with his echo
To shake the boughs of a dead pine.

Below, boil waterfalls that gnaw through
Granite, oak tree, root and limb;
And on the rocks are naiads, singing
The unmarried virgins' sexless hymn.

And in this din of icy waters,
The ravens' caw that racks the day,
Where barren virgins goggle, fish-eyed,
My life rots languidly away.

                                        1909

"Beside the Unwashed Window"

Beside the unwashed window the spring day
Passed unemployed. Behind the wall I heard
A voice singing, my wife's, as restlessly
Rehearsing tedium as a caged bird.

Dispassionate, unhurried, I reviewed
My memories, now sapped of all concern.
Truth's countenance was pitilessly plain:
Life has roared past me, it will not return.

Thoughts will recur, yes, old debates resume,
Only bleak dullness will not be in doubt.
Why draw the window shade? Within the soul
The day's last embers long ago burned out.

                                        1909

"What Pain"

There a man was burned to death.
                    —AFANASY FET

What pain it is, when death invades the heart,
To make pretense of living, and for those
Who have not lived rehearse the tragic play
Of passions that still wrestle with repose.

And peering at one's nightmare, in the wild
Turmoil of feeling find an order, tame
By art's reflection life's consuming fire,
That the unravaged thus may taste the flame.

                              [*1910*]

"How Narrow Is the Circle"

How narrow is the circle of our being:
As all roads lead to Rome, we can foresee
The past stretching ahead into a future
That will repeat the pattern slavishly.

I, like all others, know what lot awaits me
As I proceed upon my darkening way:
Again to love Her where She reigns in heaven
Whom here on earth I shall again betray.

                              1914

"Yes. Thus the Poet"

Yes. Thus the poet hears his Dæmon speak:
My freeborn dream returns again, again,
To cling to darkness and to poverty
Where the insulted dwell in filth and pain.
Down, down, go plumb the meekest misery,
Another world is visible from there.
Have you seen children on the Paris streets,
Or beggars on the bridge in winter air?

Open your eyes, be quick to open them
To life's bottomless horror, see it clear
Before your land is swept by the whirlwind
That will lay waste whatever tenants here.
Let righteous anger thicken and grow ripe;
Make ready for the work: you dare not turn
Away. . . . If you are helpless, let despair
And anguish gather in your breast and burn.
At least do this: wipe from a life of lies
The oily rouge that suits its face so ill;
Go play the frightened mole and dig yourself
A place deep underground and there be still,
Alone, morose, bitterly hating life,
Despising this black world and all its ways,
And if not glimpsing what the future holds,
Stern in denial of these present days.

[1911–14]

"To Sin, Unshamed"

To sin, unashamed, to lose, unthinking,
The count of careless nights and days,
And then, while the head aches with drinking,
Steal to God's house, with eyes that glaze;

Thrice to bow down to earth, and seven
Times cross oneself, and then once more
With the hot brow, in hope of heaven,
To touch the spittle-covered floor;

With a brass penny's gift dismissing
The offering, the holy Name
To mutter with loose lips, in kissing
The ancient, kiss-worn icon frame;

And to come home, then, and be tricking
Some wretch out of the same small coin,
And with a hiccup to be kicking
A trembling cur in his lean groin;

And where the icon's flame is quaking
Drink tea, and reckon loss and gain,
From the fat chest of drawers taking
The coupons marked with spittle stain;

And sunk in feather beds to smother
In slumber such as bears may know—
Dearer to me than every other
Are you, my Russia, even so.

1914

"Those Nurtured in the Stagnant Years"

Those nurtured in the stagnant years cannot
Recall what path they took. We pay our debt
To Russia's frightful years when we were born,
For there is nothing that we can forget.

Years that burnt all to ashes! If you bode
Madness or presage hope, how can we know?
The days of war, of freedom, both alike
Branded our faces with a blood-red glow.

We are struck dumb: it was the tocsin's clang
Shut fast these lips of ours that can nor bless
Nor curse. Our hearts, that swelled with fervor once,
Are filled now with a fateful emptiness.

Let croaking ravens beat their wings above
The bed where we lie down with death, alone—
Unto those worthier be, O God, O God,
Thy Kingdom shown!

[1914]

The Hawk

Over the empty fields a black hawk hovers,
   And circle after circle smoothly weaves.
In the poor hut, over her son in the cradle,
   A mother grieves:
"There, suck my breast: there, grow and eat our bread,
And learn to bear your cross and bow your head."

Time passes. War returns. Rebellion rages.
   The farms and villages go up in flame,
And Russia in her ancient tear-stained beauty,
   Is yet the same,
Unchanged through all the ages. How long will
The mother grieve, and the hawk circle still?

1916

The Twelve

1

   Black night.
   White snow.
   The wind, the wind!
It all but lays you low.
   The wind, the wind,
Across God's world it blows!

   The wind is weaving
   The white snow.
There is ice below.
   Stumbling and tumbling,
   Folk slip and fall—
God pity all!

   From house to house
   A rope is strung,
   A sagging placard on it hung:

All power to the Constituent Assembly!
A bent old woman, tearful, trembly,
Stares at the placard in despair.
　Her blear eyes see
　How many fine foot-clouts could be
Cut from the canvas wasted there,
　While the children's feet go bare. . . .

Like a hen she picks her way
Across the snow-blocked thoroughfare.
　"Oh, Mother of God, look down and see!
　Those Bolsheviks will be the death of me!"

The wind lashes at the crossing
And the frost stings to the bone.
With his nose stuck in his collar
A bourzhooy* stands all alone.

And who is this? He has long hair
And mutters with a wrathful air:
　"Renegades!
　Russia is dead!"
A writer chap, no doubt, who has
　A glib tongue in his head. . . .

And here, slinking through the snow
Comes a cassock, black and bulky. . . .
Comrade priest,
　Why so sulky?

You used to strut—
Do you recall?
Your belly with its pendent cross
Shining on one and all.

A lady wrapped in caracul
　Turns to confide
To a companion: "Oh, we cried and cried. . . ."
　She slips—and smack!
She's flat upon her back!

* A colloquial form of *"bourgeois"*; it is used disparagingly of a member
of the exploiting middle class.

Oh, oh, oh!
Lift her up, so!

The restive wind flirts,
A gay, cruel clown,
Wringing the skirts,
Mowing men down.

Fierce-fisted, it kneads
The big placard that reads:
All power to the Constituent Assembly.
A gust wafts the words:

". . . Sure, we had a meeting too . . .
. . . In that building just ahead . . .
. . . We were divided,
But we decided:
Ten for a spell, twenty-five for the night,
A kopek less wouldn't be right . . .
. . . Let's go to bed . . ."

It's getting late.
An empty street.
Only an old deadbeat
Goes past with shuffling gait.
And the wind wails.

"Come here,
Poor dear,
Give us a kiss!"

"Bread!
What's ahead?
Get along!"

Darkness, darkness overhead.

Hate, sorrowful hate
Bursts the heart . . .
Black, holy hate . . .

Hey, comrade,
Look sharp!

2

The wind is romping, the snowflakes dance.
In the night twelve men advance.

Black, narrow rifle straps,
Cigarettes, crumpled caps.

A convict's stripes would fit their backs,
Fires, fires mark their tracks. . . .

 Freedom, ho, freedom,
 Unhallowed, unblessed!

 Rat-tat-tat!

It's freezing, comrades, freezing!

"Now Vanka's off with Katya, on a spree. . . ."
"The tart, her stocking's stuffed with *kerenki!*"*

"And Vanka's got into a game that pays."
"He's ditched us, he's in uniform these days."

"Well, Vanka, you bourzhooy bastard, you!"
"Just try and kiss my girl—you'll see who's who!"

 Freedom, ho, freedom,
 Unhallowed, unblessed!
 Vanka's with Katya. . . .
  You know the rest.

 Rat-tat-tat!

Fires, fires mark their track,
Their rifle straps are gleaming black.

March to the revolution's pace!
We've a grim enemy to face!

Comrades, show spunk, take aim, the lot!
At Holy Russia let's fire a shot,

* Bills issued in 1917 while Kerensky headed the Provisional Government.

At hutted Russia,
Fat-rumped and solid,
Russia the stolid!

Eh, eh, unhallowed, unblessed!

3

Our boys, they marched away
To serve in the Red Army,
To serve in the Red Army—
It's do or die today!

Eh, what bitter sorrow,
A sweet life we've won!
A ragged overcoat,
An Austrian gun!

It's all up with exploiters now.
We'll set the world on fire, we vow,
Flaming, flaming amidst blood—
Bless us, Lord God!

4

The driver shouts, the snow's awhirl.
Vanka's scudding with his girl,
Two electric lanterns winking
On the sleigh's trim shafts. . . .
Hey, make way!

Uniformed, the dandy dashes,
Silly fool whom nothing fashes,
How he twirls his black mustaches,
Twirls, and teases,
Sure he pleases. . . .

Look at Vanka: he's got shoulders!
Listen: Vanka knows the game!
He is grabbing hold of Katya,
Trying to get round the dame.

Now she lifts her face, the girl's
Parted lips show teeth like pearls.
"Ho, Katya, my Katya,
Chubby mug!"

5

"On your neck, my little Katya,
The knife scored a mark still fresh.
There are scratches on the flesh
Under your left breast, my Katya!

Eh, eh, dance for me!
You've a pair of legs, I see!

You used to go a pretty pace,
Wearing linen trimmed with lace!
You used to whore with the gold-braid crew—
Whore then, and get along with you!
Eh, eh, whore all you wish—
You make my heart leap like a fish!

Say, recall that officer,
Katya—how I knifed the cur?
Don't tell me your memory's vague,
Just refresh your wits, you plague.

Eh, eh, refresh me, too,
Come and let me sleep with you!

In gray gaiters you went round,
Gobbled chocolates by the pound,
Whooped it up with the cadets—
Now plain troopers are your pets?

Eh, eh, little tart,
Sin away and ease your heart!"

6

. . . The stallion gallops past again,
The driver, shouting, gives him rein.

"Andrukha, stop them, hold the horse!"
"Run back, Petrukha! Cut their course!"

Crrack-crack-crack! Crrack-crack-crack!
The snow leaps up and eddies back.

The sleigh and Vanka are out of sight.
"Now cock the gun again, wheel right!"

Crrack! "You'd better watch your game:
. . . .
Stealing another fellow's dame!"

"The rat is gone. But I know who
Tomorrow will be quits with you."

And where is Katya? "Dead. She's dead!
The pretty slut shot through the head!

Happy, Katya? Don't you crow?
You carrion, lie there in the snow!"

March to the Revolution's pace!
We've a grim enemy to face!

7

And again the twelve go marching,
Shoulders back and guns in place,
Only he, the poor assassin,
Marching, does not show his face.

Forward, forward, stepping faster,
Marching with a reckless tread,
Like a dog without a master,
Muffled up, he strides ahead.

"Comrade, what on earth has got you?
Why is it you act so dumb?"
"Spill it, Pyotr, is it Katya
Makes you look so God-dam' glum?"

"Well, comrades, you know the story.
Katya was my girl by rights.
Yes, I loved her. God, our roaring
Black and drunken summer nights. . . .

Her bright eyes—they drove me to it—
How they dared you, black as coal!
And her shoulder, well I knew it
With its poppy-colored mole. . . .
I, mad fool, I had to do it,
Went and killed her . . . damn my soul. . . ."

"Listen to the bastard's patter!
Pyotr, are you a woman? Pooh!
Is your spirit soft as batter?
Got no guts, you donkey, you?
Come, friend, cut this silly chatter.
Take yourself in hand, man, do!"

"Comrade, we cannot be nursing
You or anyone just now.
Quit your glooming and your cursing.
Bigger loads won't make us bow!"

Pyotr moves at a slower pace
And he shows a careless face,

Once again he lifts his head,
And his eyes grow bright.

  Hi! Hi! What a din!
Sure, a bit of fun's no sin!

Lock your doors and windows tight!
There are looters out tonight!

Burst the cellars—wine is free!
Tonight the rabble's on a spree!

8

  Oh, the bitter sorrow!
    Dullness, wearying,
      Deadly!

My time
  I will pass, I will pass.

My pate
  I will scratch, I will scratch.

Sunflower seeds
  I will crack.

With my knife
  I will rip, I will rip.

Fly like a sparrow, bourzhooy!
I'll drink to my dead little dove,
To my black-browed love
In your blood. . . .

God rest the soul of thy servant, Katerina. . . .

Ugh! I'm fed up!

9

The city's roar has died away,
All's quiet on the Neva's brink.*
No more police. We can be gay,
Fellows, without a drop to drink.

A bourzhooy, standing at the crossing,
Nose in his collar, does not stir,
While, tail between his legs, beside him
Shivers a cringing, mangy cur.

The bourzhooy like a silent question
Stands there, starved: a dog that begs—
The old world like a kinless mongrel
Behind him, tail between its legs.

10

How it's blowing! How it's snowing!
  The flakes blind you as they fly.
You can't see where you are going
  Through the blizzard whistling by.

Funnel-shaped, the snow swirls high,
Pillar-like against the sky.

"Savior, here's a blizzard!" "What!
Pyotr, you're a dunderhead—
Did your Savior and His kin
Save you from committing sin?
Pyotr, you are talking rot!
Whose fault is it Katya's dead?"

* The two lines are a variant of the opening of a popular song based on
a poem by Fyodor Glinka (1788–1880), uncle of Mikhail Glinka, the
composer.

You're a murderer—understand?
There is blood upon your hand!"
March to the Revolution's pace!
We've a grim enemy to face!

On and on the steady beat
Of the workers' marching feet!*

11

. . . And the twelve, unblessed, unhallowed,
Still go marching on,
Ready for what chance may offer,
Pitying none. . . .

On, with rifles lifted
At the unseen enemy.
Through dead alleys where the snow has sifted,
Where the blizzard tosses free.
Onward, where the snow has drifted
Clutching at the marcher's knee.

The red flag
Whips their faces.

Creaking snow,
Measured paces.

The grim foe
Marks their traces.

Day and night the blizzard flings
Snow that stings
In their faces.

On, the steady beat
Of the workers' marching feet!

12

. . . Onward as a haughty host they march.
"Hey! Who else is there? Come out!"
Only wind, wind bellying the flag,
Tossing the red flag about.

* Variant of the refrain of a revolutionary song popular at the turn of
the century.

Up ahead a snowdrift towers sheer.
"Who is hiding in the drift? Come out!"
A starved mongrel shambles in the rear,
Limping off as though it feared a clout.

"Skip! D'you want your mangy fur
Tickled by this bayonet?
The old world is a mongrel cur. . . .
Beatings are the best you'll get."

. . . Teeth bared, gleaming in a wolfish grin,
Furtively it follows on behind,
A chilled mongrel, without friend or kin. . . .
"Hey! Who goes there? Answer quickly, mind!"

"Who's waving the red flag?" "Just try and see.
Lord, what darkness, and what blinding snow!"
"Who are those that run there stealthily,
Clinging to the houses as they go?"

"We will get you and your comrades too!
Best surrender while you're breathing still."
"Comrade . . . it will be the worse for you.
Come out, or we'll shoot to kill!"
Crrack-crack-crack! A solitary
Echo answers, from the houses thrown,
While the blizzard, wild and merry,
Laughs among the snows alone.

Crrack-crack-crack!
Crrack-crack-crack!

. . . Forward as a haughty host they tread.
A starved mongrel shambles in the rear.
Bearing high the banner, bloody red,
That He holds in hands no bullets sear—
Hidden as the flying snow veils veer,
Lightly walking on the wind, as though
He Himself were diamonded snow,
With mist-white roses garlanded:
Jesus Christ is marching at their head.

1918

The Scythians

Panmongolism—a slogan quite bizarre,
But nonetheless like music to my ear.
                    —VLADIMIR SOLOVYOV

You are the millions, we are multitude
And multitude and multitude.
Come, fight! Yea, we are Scythians,
Yea, Asians, a slant-eyed, greedy brood.

For you—the centuries, for us—one hour.
Like slaves, obeying and abhorred,
We were the shield between the breeds
Of Europe and the raging Mongol horde.

For centuries the hammers of your forge
Drowned out the avalanche's boom;
You heard like wild, fantastic tales
Of Lisbon's and Messina's sudden doom.

For centuries your eyes were toward the East.
Our pearls you hoarded in your chests
And mockingly you bode the day
When you could aim your cannon at our breasts.

The time has come. Disaster beats its wings.
Each day the insults grow apace.
The hour will strike, and it may chance
Your Paestums will go down and leave no trace.

Oh, pause, old world, while life still beats in you,
Oh, weary one, oh, worn, oh, wise!
Halt here, as once did Oedipus
Before the Sphinx's enigmatic eyes.

Yea, Russia is a Sphinx. Exulting, grieving,
And sweating blood, she cannot sate
Her eyes that gaze and gaze and gaze
At you with stone-lipped love for you, and hate.

Yea, you have long since ceased to love
As our hot blood can love; the taste
You have forgotten of a love
That burns like fire and like fire lays waste.

All things we love: pure numbers' burning chill,
The visions that divinely bloom;
All things we know: the Gallic light
And the parturient Germanic gloom.

And we remember all: Parisian hells,
The cool of Venice's lagoons,
Far fragrance of green lemon groves,
And Cologne's masses that the smoke festoons.

And flesh we love, its color and its taste,
Its deathy odor, heavy, raw.
And is it our guilt if your bones
May crack beneath our powerful supple paw?

It is our wont to seize wild colts at play:
They rear and impotently shake
Wild manes—we crush their mighty croups.
And shrewish women slaves we tame—or break.

Come unto us from the black ways of war,
Come to our peaceful arms and rest.
Comrades, before it is too late,
Sheathe the old sword; may brotherhood be blest.

If not, we have not anything to lose.
We too can practice perfidies.
By sick descendants you will be
Accursed for centuries and centuries.

To welcome pretty Europe, we shall spread
And scatter in the tangled space
Of our broad thickets. We shall turn
To you our alien Asiatic face.

Go, all of you, to Ural fastnesses;
We clear the ground for the appalling scenes
Of war between the savage Mongol hordes
And pitiless science with its massed machines.

Know that we will no longer be your shield
But, careless of the battle cries,
We'll watch the deadly duel seethe,
Aloof, with indurate and narrow eyes.

We will not move when the ferocious Hun
Despoils the corpse and leaves it bare,
Burns towns, herds cattle in the church,
And smell of white flesh roasting fills the air.

For the last time, old world, we bid you rouse,
For the last time the barbarous lyre sounds
That calls you to our bright fraternal feast
Where labor beckons and where peace abounds.

[1918]

VLADISLAV KHODASEVICH

The Seed's Way

The sower strides along the furrows, true
As those his father, his grandfather, knew.

There in his hand the seed glimmers like gold—
To sink into the dark beneath the mold.

And, where the blind worm carves a passageway,
Fated to perish, it will sprout one day.

Thus, like the seed, my soul, once having lain
In darkness, dead, will come to life again.

You, too, my country, my people, you will give
Yourselves to this dark year, die, and so, live.

For the sole truth vouchsafed us is our stay:
Whatever lives must follow the seed's way.

[1917]

The Monkey

The day was hot. The forests were on fire.
Time dragged. Behind the country house next door
A cock was crowing. The gate swung behind me.
There on a bench, leaning against the fence,
A wandering Serb, lean, swarthy, had dozed off.
A heavy cross, fashioned of silver, hung
On his half-naked breast, down which great drops
Of sweat were rolling. On the fence, close by,
A small red-skirted monkey crouched, and chewed
The dusty leaves of lilac overhead.
A leather collar on a heavy chain
That pulled her back pressed hard against her throat.
The Serb, roused by my step, awoke and wiped
His sweat, and begged some water for the creature.
He tasted it, to test how cold it was,
Then placed the saucer on the bench. At once
The monkey, wetting eager fingers, seized
The saucer in both hands. She leaned her elbows
Upon the bench, and crouching thus, she drank.
Her chin was almost resting on the boards,
And her back arched above her half-bald pate.
Even so Darius, centuries ago,
Fleeing the phalanxes of Alexander,
Must have leaned to a puddle in the road.
When she had drunk her water, casually
The monkey brushed the saucer off the bench,
And standing up, with an immortal gesture
She offered me her small black horny hand
The moisture had left cool. . . .

Though I have pressed the hands of lovely women,
Of poets, and of men who led a nation,
Yet there was not one hand among them all
Had such a noble shape. Not any hand
Ever touched mine in such full comradeship!
I swear by God that no one ever looked
Into my eyes so wisely and so deeply;
Her soft gaze pierced me. That indigent creature
Revived for me the sweetest lore bequeathed
By far antiquity to human hearts.
And in that moment life appeared so full,
It seemed to me the sun and moon, the waves
Of all the seas, the winds, the heavenly spheres,
Were choiring together, organ music
That rang as wonderfully in my ears
As in the days beyond man's memory.
And then the Serb, knuckling his tambourine,
Went off, the monkey perched on his left shoulder:
A maharajah on an elephant.
And in the heavens, wreathed in opal smoke,
A swollen, raspberry-colored sun was hanging.
Heat, with no hope of thunder, lay upon
The wheat fields that were wilting in the blaze.
That was the very day war was declared.

1919

The Cork

O cork that stoppered the strong iodine,
How rapidly you rotted quite away!
Thus is the body quietly consumed,
Burnt by the soul, unseen, day after day.

1921

"It Scarcely Seems Worth-While"

It scarcely seems worth-while to sing, to live:
Uncouth, unsafe, the days through which we crawl.
The tailor sews, the builder rears his beams;
The seams will come apart, the house will fall.

But then through this corruption suddenly
I hear sometimes, how moved to feel it true,
Astir and throbbing in that rotten frame,
A different life, one altogether new.

Just so, enduring her routine dull days,
A woman restlessly will lift and press
Her hand against her belly's swelling weight
With what a swift astonished tenderness.

1922

IVAN BUNIN

"The Hops"

The hops already have sere leaves to show
Along the fences, and beyond the farms
In gardens where the light, its heat now spent,
Lies mellow-bright, the great bronze melons glow.

The grain has all been hauled away. You catch
A glimpse, above a hut out on the steppe,
Of a gray windmill with a lifted wing
That shines against the sky, a golden patch.

[1903]

Russian Spring

In the valley the birches are bored.
On the meadows, a dingy fog.
Sodden, with horse dung floored,
The highroad is bleak as a bog.

From the village asleep on the plains
Comes the odor of fresh-baked bread.
Two tramps with their packs are at pains
To limp on till they come to a bed.

Spring mud is thick on the streets
Where puddles gleam in the sun.
Steam drifts from damp earthen seats;
The fumes from the oven stun.

The sheep dog, dragging his chain,
Yawns on the barn-door sill.
Indoors there is reek and stain.
The haze-wrapped steppe is still.

The carefree cocks perform
For spring, till the day is spent.
The meadow is drowsy and warm,
The glad heart indolent.

[*1905*]

A Song

I'm a plain girl whose hands are stained with earth,
He is a fisherman—he's gay and keen.
His far white sail is sinking in the firth.
Many the seas and rivers he has seen.

The women of the Bosporus, they say,
Are good-looking . . . and I—I'm lean and black.
The white sail sinks far out beyond the bay.
It may be that he never will come back.

I will wait on in good and evil weather.
If vainly, take my wage, go to the sea
And cast the ring and hope away together.
And my black braid will serve to strangle me.

1906

Daghestan

Watch out, plant your feet firmly in the stirrups.
The gorge is darkening, loudening waterfalls
Crowd closer; where the gorge ends, rocky masses
Thrust at the sky like an aggressive wall.

Above its brow, stars diamond the distance;
Upon its chest, in ominous darkness lies
A mountain village: an else-hidden dragon
Peering downward with a thousand eyes.

190?

Flax

She sits upon the tumulus and stares,
Old woman Death, down at the crowded road.
Like a blue flame the small flax-flower flares,
Thick through the meadows sowed.
And says old woman Death: "Hey, traveler!
Does anyone want linen, linen fit
For funeral wear? A shroud, madam or sir,
I'll take cheap coin for it."

The mound remains serene: "Don't crow so loud!"
It says, "The winding sheet is dust and cracks
And crumbles into earth, that from the shroud
May spring the sky-blue flax."

[1907]

The New Church

A fresh spring gust blew down upon us
Across the altars, new and clean,
And someone overhead dripped whitewash
Upon the golden icon screen.

Sonorous noise roamed round the columns.
In smocks, our brushes lifted high,
We climbed the scaffolding, and upward
Into the cupola, the sky.

The plasterers would sing together
With us. Not in the common way
We painted Christ, Who listened to us
In the new church, so bright and gay.

Our simple songs, we thought, would take Him
Back to the sunlight on the floor
At Nazareth, back to the workbench,
And the blue tunic that He wore.

[1907]

In an Empty House

The blue wallpaper has lost its hue,
Gone daguerreotypes and icons, too—
Only where they hung for many years
The old blue in patches now appears.

Now forgotten, now forgotten quite
Much that once was all the heart's delight.
Those alone who will not come again,
Those have left a trace that will remain.

[1916]

"Early, a Sunrise"

Early, a sunrise that is slow to start,
The beating of a sixteen-year-old heart.

Once more the morning murk stirs drowsily,
Warmed by the blossoms of the linden tree.

Hushed and mysterious, the house below,
With the one window that I cherish so.

The sun that lights my cosmos is behind
That window blind.

1917

NIKOLAY GUMILYOV

Evening

With heaviness this wingless wind is cursed,
The sunset is a melon that has burst.

You ache to give the clouds a gentle shove,
They float so indolently up above.

Upon such languid evenings you will see
Coachmen whip up their horses savagely,

And fishers tear the waters with the oar,
And woodsmen batter at the oaks they floor. . . .

While those who in their being must rehearse
The movement of the throbbing universe,

Who house within them, slumbering or astir,
Rhythms to come and all that ever were,

Write winged verses whose resistless sweep
Rouses the sluggard elements from sleep.

1915

Nature

The little lake is quiet, motionless
As water in a brimming bowl.

Bamboos resemble huts undoubtedly,
The trees are but a sea of roofs.

And like pagodas rocks jut spikily
Above the shrubs and flowers there.

It gladdens me to find eternal Nature
Apprenticing herself to us.

1918

The Sixth Sense

Fine is the wine in love with us, and the goodly
Bread that goes into the oven for our sake,
And the woman, whom, after teasing and torment,
At last, how deliciously, we take.

But what shall we do with the rosy sunset
Where already a chill is in the sky,
The unearthly serenity and silence,
And with those verses that refuse to die?

You cannot eat them or drink them, you cannot kiss them. . . .
The moment evades us, and we wring our hands,
Hands that would hold it, but we are helpless:
We were not framed to answer their demands.

Just as a boy forgets his games as he watches
Girls bathing, and suddenly catches fire,
Still ignorant of love, yet now awakening
To the mysterious motions of desire;

As in the early world the slippery creature,
Feeling his back throb with the unformed wings,
Screamed in the primal thicket, helpless to counter
The will to soar that works in creeping things—

So while centuries pass—how long, O Lord?—the spirit
Cries out, flesh faints, being without defense
Under the scalpel of art, of nature, bearing
The organ fit to enable a sixth sense.

1921

Persian Miniature

The game of hide-and-seek I play
With sullen death cannot endure—
Then the Creator will transform me
Into a Persian miniature.

A turquoise sky. A Prince who scarce
Raises his almond eyes to note
The upward motion of a swing
Where a girl's airily afloat.

A Shah, grasping a bloody spear,
Mounts rapidly a perilous slope,
Daring vermilion cliffs, to climb
After a fleeing antelope.

And tuberoses, that none awake
Or in a dream's imagining
Has seen, and grassward trailing vines,
All on a honied evening.

Verso, I shall rejoice to bear,
As clean as clouds above Tibet,
The mark that there a master's hand
Has, how indubitably, set.

A fragrant, aged man, perhaps
A merchant or a courtier, will
Love me at sight, and with a love,
Sharp, stubborn, that time cannot kill.

Thus I shall be the lodestar of
Long days whose sameness never ends,
And shall replace for him, in turn,
His wine, his mistresses, his friends.

And then, in truth, will come to pass—
Delight denied, as is despair—
My immemorial dream: to rouse
Adoration everywhere.

1921

Second Canzone

We are not in the world at all, but somewhere
Out in the world's backyard, amid a maze
Of shadowy nothings. Drowsily the summer
Leafs through the broad blue pages of clear days.

The pendulum, callous and conscientious,
Time's fiancé, still undiscomfited
Though unacknowledged, takes the scheming seconds
And deftly slices off each pretty head.

So parched lies every road here and so dusty,
And so does every shrub for dryness strain,
That a white seraph will not meet us, leading
A unicorn sedately by the rein.

And only in your secret sorrow, darling,
Is there a fiery opiate to stay
The curse of this sad place of desolation,
Like a fair wind from countries far away.

Where all is brilliance, all is movement, singing,
And soft enchantment to the eye and ear—
There is it that we live! A stagnant cistern
Has prisoned only our reflection here.

1921

MIKHAIL ZENKEVICH

"Belated Sunflowers"

Belated sunflowers smoldered in the meadow,
And, in the sapphire of the sky inlaid,
The curve of a hawk's wing luxuriated
In the mild heat and glittered like a blade.

And setting bounds to mortal man's desiring,
Above the stubble of the fields Fate sped
Behind us like a disembodied shadow
Of the sharp wing that glided overhead.

Magnificent and languid as this noonday,
Taming the rising heat, you strode with ease.
Alone your skirts frothed in a foam of laces,
Beating against your proud and stately knees.

And in your wide eyes that were faintly misted,
Ready to swoop upon the doomed, a mite
Of sultriness immobile on the azure,
Passion showed hawklike, gleaming dark and bright.

1916

ANNA AKHMATOVA

Confession

Silence: now he has shriven me.
In lilac dusk the taper smolders;
The stole's concealing drapery
Falls darkly over head and shoulders.

"Talitha kumi": is it He
Once more? How fast the heart is beating. . . .
A touch: a hand moves absently
The customary cross repeating.

[1911]

"Broad Gold"

Broad gold, the evening heavens glow,
The April air is cool and tender.
You should have come ten years ago,
And yet in welcome I surrender.

Come here, sit closer to me, look
With eyes that twinkle, mouth that purses,
Into the little blue-bound book
That holds my awkward childish verses.

Forgive me that I long forsook
Joy's sunny paths, nor glanced toward any;
Forgive me those whom I mistook
For you—alas, they were too many.

[1915]

Prayer

Make me feverish, sleepless, and breathless,
Let the years of prostration be long,
O Lord, take my child, my companion,
The mysterious power of song.

Thus I pray at each matins, each vespers,
After these many wearying days,
That the storm cloud which lours over Russia
May be changed to a nimbus ablaze.

[1915]

"Upon the Hard Crest"

Upon the hard crest of a snowdrift
We tread, and grown quiet, we walk
On toward my house, white, enchanted;
Our mood is too tender for talk.

And sweeter than song is this dream now
Come true, the low boughs of the firs
That sway as we brush them in passing,
The slight silver clink of your spurs.

[1917]

"All Is Sold"

All is sold, all is lost, all is plundered,
Death's wing has flashed black on our sight,
All's gnawed bare with sore want and sick longing—
Then how are we graced with this light?

By day there's a breath of wild cherry
In the city, from woods none descries;
At night new and strange constellations
Shine forth in the pale summer skies.

And these houses, this dirt, these mean ruins,
Are touched by the miracle, too;
It is close, the desired, the despaired of,
That all longed for, but none ever knew.

[1921]

"An Unparalleled Autumn"

An unparalleled autumn erected a glorious dome;
All the clouds were commanded to leave it undarkened and
pure.
And men marveled: September is gone, and yet where are the
days
Shot with dampness and chill? How long can this wonder
endure?
In the turbid canals the mild waters shone emerald-clear,
And the nettles had fragrance more rich than the roses to give;
And the sunsets that laid on the air their unbearable weight
Of demoniac crimson, we shall not forget while we live.
Like a rebel who enters the capital, thus the proud sun,
Which this autumn, so springlike, was hungry to smile at and
woo,
Till it seemed any moment a snowdrop, transparent, would
gleam—
Then I saw, on the path to my door, stepping quietly, you.

[1922]

"Reject the Burden"

Reject the burden of all earthly solace,
Put from your heart the claims of home and wife;
Does your child hunger? Give unto a stranger
The bread that else would feed that little life.

Humble yourself to be the meanest servant
Of your worst enemy, and learn to call
The brute beast of the forest ways your brother,
And ask of God nothing, nothing at all.

1923

"Not with Deserters"

Not with deserters from the battle
That tears my land do I belong.
To their coarse praise I do not listen.
They shall not have from me one song.

Poor exile, you are like a prisoner
To me, or one upon the bed
Of sickness. Dark your road, O wanderer,
There's wormwood in an alien's bread.

Here, into smoking fires that blacken
Our lives, the last of youth we throw,
Who in the years behind us never
Sought to evade a single blow.

We know that in the final reckoning
No hour will need apology;
No people in the world are prouder,
Simpler, less given to tears, than we.

1923

Lot's Wife

And he who was righteous loomed radiant, striding
Behind the Lord's messenger up the black hill.
But she walked reluctant—alarm spoke within her:
"It is not too late, you may look on it still,

Upon the vermilion-stained towers of Sodom;
You spun in that court, and you sang on that square;
That house whose tall windows confront you with blankness
Once knew you, a bride; you bore your sons there."

She turned to behold it, and pain was her master;
Her eyes yearning toward it could no longer see;
Abruptly her body grew salt-white, translucent;
Firm earth held her feet that would never go free.

And is there not one who would weep for this woman,
Or one who would find her loss bitter to brook?
Alone in my heart, uneclipsed, unforgotten,
Is she who gave over her life for one look.

1924

"Oh, How Good"

Oh, how good the snapping and the crackle
Of the frost that daily grows more keen!
Laden with its dazzling icy roses,
The white-flaming bush is forced to lean.

On the snows in all their pomp and splendor
There are ski tracks, and it seems that they
Are a token of those distant ages
When we two together passed this way.

1940

From Requiem, *a Cycle* [1957] 1963

Proem

This was when no one smiled, none but the dead,
Glad of peace, of final immunity,
And, like a useless appendage, Leningrad
Swung around its prisons hopelessly.

This was when they were moving regiments
Of the condemned, each with his load of pain,
And the song of separation sounded
Curtly in the whistle of the train.

Stars of death, the stars that hung over us,
Where guiltless Russia lay in filth and mud,
Writhing under the Black Maria's tires,
Writhing under boots that had trodden in blood.

1935

7 *The Verdict*

And so the word of stone
Dropped on my still living breast.
No matter—somehow I shall cope
With what, after all, I had guessed.

Today I have much to do:
I must first put memory to death,
Must petrify my soul,
Must learn again how to draw breath.

If not . . . summer's hot rustle
Outdoors makes holiday.
I had foreseen this empty house
On such a brilliant day.

[1939]

10 *Crucifixion*

A choir of angels glorified the hour,
In fire the heavens melted. To the Father He
Cried loudly: "Why hast Thou forsaken me?"
But to the mother: "Do not weep for me."

Magdalene wept, threshed, sobbed in helpless torment;
The beloved disciple, as one who petrifies,
Watched; and where the mother stood, in silence,
None dared to turn his eyes.

1940–43 ?

Epilogue I

I learned how faces that were fresh grow gaunt,
How dread peers out from under half-shut lids,
How suffering covers cheeks with line on line
Of cuneiform's rough arrowheads and grids;

How hair, ash blond or black, suddenly turns
Gray; how on obedient lips a smile but half
Formed fades away, and witheringly
Fear quivers in a little arid laugh;

And I pray, not for myself alone,
But for everyone who stood with me, all, all
Who stood in the bitter cold, in the July heat,
Beneath the red, blinded wall.

Epilogue II

Once more the hard hour of remembrance is near.
I see you, I feel you, it's you whom I hear:

The one who could barely be suffered to move,
The one who no more walks this earth that we love,

And the one who, shaking her beautiful head,
Said, "I come here as if it were home." So she said.

I would I could name every one, but how know,
When the list is removed and there's nowhere to go.

But I've woven their shroud, wide enough, from each word,
Each poor whisper of theirs that I overheard.

And if they should stop my hurt mouth, from which streams
A hundred million else unuttered screams,

Let me be remembered in that very way
On the eve of my memorial day.

And if in this country in years to be,
A monument were to be raised to me,

I should consent, provided only
It be not erected near the lonely

Seashore beside which I was born—
My last link with the sea is long outworn,

Nor in the czars' park near the stump that's hidden
And a sad ghost seeks me, the tryst forbidden,

But here, where for three hundred hours I stood,
And the door was bolted to me for good.

For blessèd death may make me forget
The thunders that Black Marias jet,

Forget the dread door whose clang never ceased,
And an old woman's howl of a wounded beast.

Let the melting snow flow down like tears
From shut bronze lids through the countless years,

And the prison pigeons coo far off,
While Neva's ships float with a gentle sough.

1940

Start of Long-Range Bombing

Abruptly all was changed: the hurrying crowd
Could not accommodate its daily round
To what it heard, knew only that it heard
Neither a city nor a country sound.
True, it was like a brother to the roll
Of distant thunder, but the thunder spends
The moisture and the freshness of high clouds,
Its mutterings are promises—a friend's.
It brings the rumor of the gaiety
Of showers that the fields are avid for;
But this noise was an arid one: it scorched;
The anguished ear could not believe the roar
Would mount, would swell, would spread
Until my child was numbered with the dead.

[1941]

"From the Stern Squares"

From the stern squares of Leningrad blowing,
Or from Lethe's blest fields, thanks to you
What a whiff of cool freshness is flowing;
By the fences you've set poplars growing;
Asian stars, by the myriad, are glowing,
That over my sadness you drew.

[1942]

Courage

What hangs in the balance is nowise in doubt;
We know the event and we brave what we know;
Our clocks are all striking the hour of courage—
That sound travels with us wherever we go.
To die of a bullet is nothing to dread,
To find you are roofless is easy to bear;

And all is endured, O great language we love:
It is you, Russian tongue, we must save, and we swear
We will give you unstained to the sons of our sons;
You shall live on our lips, and we promise you—never
A prison shall know you, but you shall be free
Forever.

[1942]

From an Airplane

Versts by the hundred, miles by hundreds, hundreds
Of dim kilometers beneath our track:
Reaches of salt marsh, feather grass that billowed;
Beyond, the somber cedar groves showed black.

As though for the first time I saw my country,
And, with a pang of recognition, knew:
It is all mine—and nothing can divide us,
It is my soul, it is my body, too.

[*1944*]

The Mistress of the House

Once, before I came, a witch
Lived alone here in this room.
On the eve of the new moon
You may see her shadow loom.

Still her shadow falls across
The high threshold crookedly,
And, evasive but intent,
She looks sternly in at me.

I myself am not of those
By another's witchcraft caught.
I myself. . . . But I do not
Give my secrets up for naught.

1946

From Sweetbrier Is Blossoming, *a Cycle (1946–1956)*

5 Nameless

The strange no-meeting issued
In desolation: dead
Silence crushing utterance,
Words that remained unsaid.
Glances that failed of meeting
Do not know where to go,
And only tears are happy
That they can flow and flow.

Somehow a Moscow suburb's
Sweetbrier is parcel of
This story—and they'll call this
A deathless love.

Epilogue 1

"Again you are with me, dear Autumn"
        —INNOKENTY ANNENSKY

Let one who would bask in the South, paradisal
And palmy, rest there to the end,
But here it is northerly, and I have chosen
The autumn this year for a friend.

I live in a house not my own, I have dreamed it,
The house, it may be, where I died,
Whose mirrors are filled through the langorous evening
With strangeness they half seem to hide.

The fir trees are stubby and black where I ramble,
The heather's like wind when it's swayed,
And like an old knife gleams the moon's pallid splinter,
A knife with a thin, jagged blade.

The precious remembrance of our last no-meeting
Is here with me early and late—
The flame, cool, ethereal, pure, of the triumph
I won over fate.

From The Secrets of the Trade, *a Cycle*

2 *Poet*

And this you call work—it's a carefree
Existence! To catch, ere it's flown,
What music has privately hinted,
And jestingly call it my own.

And using another's blithe scherzo
For lines far too languid to run,
To swear your poor heart is lamenting
In fields that smile back at the sun.

And later, when pinewoods play trappist,
To do what bold eavesdroppers dare,
While the fog's impalpable curtain
Hangs vaguely as smoke on the air.

Not feeling one qualm of conscience,
I take things from left and right.
Life is sly, but I take something from it,
And all from the stillness of night.

                                    1959

4 Last Poem

It is bounding with life and arrives with a roar
Like a thunderclap startled; it bursts through the door,
Throat shaken with laughter, it spins without pause,
Declaring delight in boisterous applause.

Another, the child of the hush at midnight,
Steals toward me from nowhere as if by some sleight;
From a mirror not mine that nameless one gazes,
And mutters harsh, half-comprehensible phrases.

Then too there are some that will come in broad day,
Ignoring me quite as if I were away,
And across the white paper flow lightly, flow fully,
As pure as a stream in an untrodden gully.

And here is a secret one, gliding around,
No sound yet no color, nor color nor sound,
It sharpens and shines, then eludes you; contrive
To seize it, yet you will not take it alive.

But this! . . . It drank blood from my veins with less ruth
Than love, cruel girl, showed me in my youth,
And abruptly retreated into unbroken
Silence, as though it never had spoken.

Here is the bitterest grief I have known:
It vanished, whose traces, this thing that has flown,
Reached the brink of that uttermost none can descry,
And lacking it, what is my lot but to die?

                                    1959

From the Oriental Notebook

How drunk we were, each with the other, that marvelous night,
when only the Asian darkness gave us light,
and the irrigation canals were murmuring
and the black carnations' scent pierced like a sting.

And we walked alone through a city not ours, through a savage
        song
and midnight heat—the Serpent coiled among
the constellations in the thick-starred skies,
and we did not dare to turn and meet one another's eyes.

And it seemed as if ages walked with us, unseen,
and as if an invisible hand were striking a tambourine,
and there were stranger sounds, like something we must mark:
secret signals that whirled about us there in the dark.

Thus once, and only once, we walked together, as though
we had got into no human story, and, of a sudden, the glow
of the moon like a diamond sailboat swam into view
over our parting meeting, the single encounter we knew.

And should that night return to you also, mind
my wish, however belated, oh, be kind
and send me, waking or dreaming, by my choice
this: an Asian reed pipe's slender voice.

                                    1960

"I Did Not Laugh"

I did not laugh, I did not sing
Or speak the whole day through,
But all we once had shared I longed
To share once more with you:

Our first light-hearted difference,
Absurd, serene, unreal;
And then, hasty, inedible,
Our final wordless meal.

                1962

Early Spring Elegy

The blizzard had ceased in the pinewoods,
But, drunk without liquor, how clear
The song that all night, like Ophelia,
Elate silence intoned for our ear.

And he, who but seemed, to that silence
Had promised unwavering faith;
His leave taken, he generously lingered,
He lingered with me until death.

[1964]

OSIP MANDELSHTAM

"On Every Still Suburban Street"

On every still suburban street
The gatekeepers are shoveling snow;
A passer-by, I do not know
The bearded peasants whom I meet.

The kerchiefed women come and go,
There's yelping from some crazy tyke;
In teahouse and in home alike
The samovars' red roses glow.

1913

"Valkyries Are Flying"

Valkyries are flying, the violins sing,
The bulky opera's finale nears;
Flunkies, burdened with heavy furs,
Await their masters on marble stairs.

In the gallery a ninny still applauds;
The curtain is ready to descend.
Cabbies stomp, dancing round bonfires.
"Prince So-and-so's carriage!" The audience leaves. End.

[*1913*]

"The Hooves of Horses"

The hooves of horses speak to us of times
When life is coarse and simple, and on hard
Benches, hunched in their heavy coats,
You see the porters sleeping in the yards.

Roused by a knocking at the iron gates,
With regal sloth one gets up on his feet
And gives a feral yawn; beholding him,
It is your image, Scythian, that I meet—

When Ovid, love now on the wane, in verse
That mingled Rome and snow in one sad strain,
Sang of the two-wheeled oxcart lumbering
Along in the barbaric wagon train.

[*1914*]

"The Woods Have Orioles"

The woods have orioles; there is no other measure
For classic verse save this: the vowels' quantity.
In every year but once alone does Nature proffer
Duration, as in Homer's metric, palpably.

The day is yawning, say that it is a caesura;
An early indolence grows heavy by slow stealth;
The oxen graze, and you, lulled by a golden langor,
Can draw forth from your reed no single whole note's wealth.

1914

"Hours of Sleeplessness"

Hours of sleeplessness. Homer. Taut sails. Tonight
I've read half through the catalogue of ships, that spreading
Clamorous brood which rose up over Hellas, heading
For Troy, those ships that are a troop of cranes in flight—

A wedge of cranes that flies toward lands hidden from view.
Divine the foam asperging the heads of kings. Ah, tell us
Where do you sail, Achæans? What takes you forth from Hellas?
Were it not for Helen, what would Troy be to you?

The sea, and Homer—all is moved by love. I wonder,
Which should I listen to? Homer is hushed. The roar
Of the black sea goes gnashing on, a furious orator,
And near my pillow now looses its ponderous thunder.

1915

"The Droves"

The droves pause in their grazing, gaily neighing,
Now Roman rust is staining everything;
As time's transparent stream bears off in silence
The dry gold that belongs to classic spring.

Treading on autumn oak leaves which so thickly
Carpet the paths that lately all forsook,
I shall recall the countenance of Caesar,
This feminine profile with the crafty hook!

Far from the Capitoline and the Forum,
Here Nature quietly consents to dim;
I hear Augustus, hear, too, the years rolling
Like imperial apples on earth's rim.

May old age yet make luminous my sorrow:
The Rome that bore me has now finally
Returned to me; kind autumn was my she-wolf,
And August, month of Caesars, smiled at me.

1915

"The Air Strikes Chill"

The air strikes chill. Although transparent spring
Has clothed Petropolis in pale-green down,
The Neva's waves are faintly sickening
As if they were Medusa's coiling crown.
On the embankment of our northern stream
The fireflies of hurrying motors gleam.
Steel dragonflies and beetles flit and whirr,
And stars are pins of gold whose glitter pricks,
But stars can never mortally transfix
The heavy emerald of the sea water.

[*1916*]

The Twilight of Liberty

Come, brothers, hail this great and twilight year,
Come, celebrate the dusk of liberty.
The nets, a forest of them, are let down
Into a savage, dark, nocturnal sea.
Bleak is the season in which you arise,
O sun, O people in your sovereignty.

Come, celebrate the fateful burden that
The people's leader now assumes with tears;
Exalt and hail the dark burden of power;
Weighted with black oppression through the years,
O time, your ship is splitting and it sinks—
There is no one who has a heart but hears.

We have pressed swallows into service, birds
Battle for us in winged legions, so
The sun cannot be seen, the whole air heaves,
It twitters, trembles, stirs with life; below,
The nets—dense dusk—obliterate the sun,
And earth is swimming on the turgid flow.

Well, then, let's try it, give the rudder one
Huge, clumsy, creaking turn. For all you're worth,
Pull! Earth swims forward. Courage, men! Come, part
The waves as with a plow, to harvest dearth.
We'll yet recall when Lethe chills our bones
The price we paid: ten heavens for the earth.

1918

From Armenia, *a Cycle*

VII "Not Ruins"

Not ruins—no—but mighty cylinders of trees cut down,
Anchors—stumps of felled oaks, of a feral and fabulous
      Christendom,
On capitals, rolls of stone cloth like goods from a plundered
      pagan store,
Grapes big as pigeons' eggs, curls that are rams' horns,
And sullen eagles with the wings of owls, not yet defiled by
      Byzantium.

[*1930*]

"For the Sake of the Thundrous Valor"

For the sake of the thundrous valor of coming ages,
And the towering tribe of man, I paid the cost,
Forfeited more than my place at the feast of my fathers,
Too, my gaiety fled, my repute was lost.

Horribly, a wolfhound leapt on my shoulders,
But the blood of a wolf does not run in my veins.
Rather tuck me away, like a cap in the sleeve of
A heavy greatcoat fit for Siberia's plains.

Then I'll not see the squelching filth nor the cowards,
Nor on the wheel the bloodied bones of the strong,
Broken; instead, in their primal beauty,
The blue foxes will shine for me all night long.

Lead me into the dark where the Yenisei rushes,
Where, grazing the dawn, the fir trees rear,
For the blood of a wolf does not run in my body,
And none shall kill me who is not my peer.

[1931] 1955

"Lady, Past Mistress, You"

Lady, past mistress, you, of guilty glances,
Lady of little shoulders, you who frowned
Upon male wickedness, see—it is tamed now,
No sound is heard when utterance is drowned.

Fish swim, fins glowing redly through the water,
Their gills agape. Here, watch them oafishly
Opening their mouths, and feed the foolish creatures
The poor half-bread of mere carnality.

We are no goldfish swimming in the pond there.
Our custom is most sisterly: how lean
Is the warm body—palpable and fragile,
The ribs, and futile, the moist pupils' sheen.

The eyebrow's risky path's marked by a poppy;
A Janissary, what is it that grips
My heart, viselike, seeing this flight of slender
Red, this pitiful crescent of the lips?

Do not be angry, darling Turk, I'm ready
To sew myself into a sack with you,
To swallow your dark words, follow you, drunken
On crooked waters that make you drunk, too. . . .

Help for the perishing—your gift, Maria!
Forestall death: fall asleep, to give it trial.
Here I am standing on your very threshold.
Go, go away—oh, stay on yet awhile.

[1934] 1961

VELEMIR KHLEBNIKOV

Incantation by Laughter

O you laughniks, laugh it out!
O you laughniks, laugh it forth!
You who laugh it up and down,
Laugh along so laughily,
Laugh it off belaughingly!
Laughters of the laughing laughniks, overlaugh the laughathons!
Laughiness of the languish laughers, counterlaugh the laugh-
dom's laughs!
Laughio! Laughio!
Unlaugh, relaugh, laughlets, laughlets,
Laughulets, laughulets.
O you laughniks, laugh it out!
O you laughniks, laugh it forth!

[1910]

"Elephants So Fought"

Elephants so fought with their tusks
That they looked like white stone
Under the sculptor's hand.
Reindeer so twined their antlers
That they seemed linked by an old marriage,
With infatuations and infidelities on both sides.
Rivers so flowed into the sea
That the hand of one seemed to choke the throat of the other.

1911

"On This Day"

On this day that belongs to blue bears
Who went capering on quiet lashes,
Far beyond the blue waves I foresee
In the cup of the eyes the command to awaken.

On the silver spoon of the offered eyes,
Proffered to me is the sea and on it a stormy petrel,
And birdy Russia, I see, will fly
To the noisy sea between the unknown eyelashes.

Yet, overturned by the sea wind of love,
Someone's sail lies in the blue-curved water,
But then the first thunder and the farther path of spring
Will sink and be drowned in the hopeless.

1918

Asia

A slave girl always, yet with the birthmark of kings on her
        swarthy breast,
And a State seal at her ear where an earring should be swinging,
Now a virgin holding a sword, and now
A midwife—old woman who'd long been bringing rebellions to
        birth.

You turn the pages of that mighty book
Where the writing shows the pressure of the seas' hand.
At night people shone there, dazzling as ink,
The killing of kings was a fierce exclamation mark,
Victories served as a comma—look
At the battlefield: points, whose rage is not shy, for this
Is the wrath of the people, plain before your eyes,
And the cracks of centuries, a parenthesis.

1921

From Zangezi

"I Am a Butterfly"

I am a butterfly who flew
Into the room of human life,
To leave a trace of my wings' dust
On the obdurate windows: a prisoner's signature
On the stern panes of Fate.
So humdrum and gray
Is life's wallpaper!
Is the transparent windows' "no"!
My blue glow is worn away, and the design of dots,
The sky-blue storm of my wing, the first freshness,
The pollen, are gone, my wings have turned transparent and
            withered;
Wearily I beat against man's window.
Eternal numbers knock from beyond
Like a call to one's birthplace,
A number is summoned to return to the numbers.

1922

VLADIMIR MAYAKOVSKY

From A Cloud in Pants

I am to the present-day tribe
just a long dirty joke, but I
see him crossing the mountains of time,
him whom nobody sees.

Where bobtailed eyes fall short—
at the head of hungry hordes,
revolutions its crown of thorns,
the year 'sixteen draweth nigh.

And I
prepare the way.
I am wherever there's pain;
and where tears rain,
on every drop I crucify
myself.
It's too late now to forgive.
I've scorched the souls
where tenderness could live,
and that's a tougher job than capturing
a thousand thousand Bastilles.

And when,
announcing its arrival
by revolt,
you go to meet the savior,
I will bolt
ahead, drag out my soul for you,
trample it,

flatten it to a big rag!
And give it to you,
bleeding, for your flag.

1915

Moonlit Night

A Landscape

There'll be a moon.
Already there's
a bit of it,
and now, in the air, a full moon is hanging.
Must be God
poking around
in the star chowder
with a marvelous silver spoon.

1916

Spring

The city's taken off her winter things,
And the snows' mouth is watering.
Sappy and gabby, just like a cadet,
Comes Spring.

1918

Our March

Slog the squares with rebel tramping!
Higher, crags of haughty heads!
We will wash the worlds' cities
With the surge of a second flood.

Brindled, the ox of days.
Slow, the dray of years.
Our god's Speed.
Our hearts—drums.

What heavenlier than our golds?
What bullet wasp can sting us?
Our weapons are our song.
Our gold—our roaring voices.

Meadow, gather your greens,
Line the lair of days.
Rainbow, furnish yokes
For the swift steeds of the years.

The starry sky is bored:
We have shut it out from our songs.
Hey, Great Dipper, demand
That they hoist us to heaven alive.

Drink to joy! Sing!
Spring has flooded our blood.
Heart, beat, leap!
Our breasts are crashing brass.

                                        1918

A Most Extraordinary Adventure

That Befell Vladimir Mayakovsky in the summer,
at the Rumyantzov Cottage, Mount Akula, Pushkino,
on the Yaroslavl Railway

The sunset flamed: a hundred suns,
summer had wheeled into July,
the heavens stirred and blurred
with heat,
and it was in the country this occurred.
Pushkino sat
on Mount Akula's hump,
and at its foot
a village writhed, its clump

of roofs as warped as bark.
Now off beyond the village was
a hole,
and every day
the sun dropped down into that hole,
as slow as sure.
And every morrow,
the sun, as red
as ever, raised his head
to flood the world.
Dawn after dawn
it was the same,
till it began to pall upon
me, till
I just got sore.
One day, in such a rage
that everything grew pale and shook with fear,
I shouted right in the sun's face:
"Climb down! D'you hear?
Stop it—haunting that lousy pit!"
I yelled, right at the sun:
"You loafer!
You've a soft berth in the clouds,
while I must sit,
not knowing if it's winter, if it's summer,
just painting posters!"
I yelled to the sun:
"You wait!
Listen to me, you golden-browed,
instead of setting as you always do,
why don't you come around," I cried out loud,
"and have a glass of tea
with me?"
What have I done!
Now I'm a goner!
Here's the sun
coming to call on me
himself,
and of his own free will!

His beamy legs flung wide,
the sun strides right across the hill.
Pretending I'm not scared,
I beat retreat.
His eyes are in the garden now,
he's tramping through the garden now.
Filling
the windows,
filling
doors and cracks,
the burly sun walked in,
just so—dropped in,
and having got his breath,
spoke in a great bass voice:
"I have to hold my fires in check
the first time since creation.
You've invited me?
Then, poet, get the tea!
And don't forget the jam."
And though I wept with heat
and dripped a flood of sweat,
I got the samovar.
"Well, have a seat,
friend luminary."
The devil must have made me shout
my impudences at the sun.
Abashed,
I sat on the chair's edge,
afraid of what was going to happen next!
But from the sun
a strange light flowed—
he didn't seem too vexed—
and I, forgetting my embarrassment,
no longer scary,
sat—
talking to the luminary!
I chat
of this and that,

saying Rosta* has got me down,
and the sun says:
"Oh, well,
don't fret,
Just take it in your stride.
Do you believe
that it's a cinch for me
to shine?
You go and try!
But I—
I undertook the job
to light the earth:
well then, I shine for all I'm worth."
And so we chat until it's dark—
that is, till when night used to come.
What kind of darkness can there be,
when the sun's there?
Now, having become chummy, we
address each other quite familiarly.
And soon,
in open friendship, just like that,
I pat him on the back.
And then the sun says—not to be outdone:
"Well, comrade, I declare,
we are a pair!
Let's go, poet,
let's soar,
and sing to scare
the drabness of the world.
I'll pour out light,
you'll do no worse
in pouring forth your verse."
At that the sun lets fly a cannon ball:
the prison wall
of nights falls flat.
Rays and words,
shine for all you're worth!

* Russian Telegraph Agency.

And when the sun gets tired,
and night, the stupid sleepyhead,
wants to drop off,
suddenly I am fired
with zeal, and shine for all I'm worth,
and day rings forth again.
Always to shine,
and to the very last
to shine,
and let the rest go hang;
thus runs
my motto and the sun's!

1920

Heinesque

Her eyes flashed lightning:
"I saw you
with another woman.
You're the lowest,
the vilest. . . ."
And she went on
and on,
and on, railing.
I'm a learned chap, darling,
quit your thundering.
If lightning didn't strike me dead,
then, by God, thunder
won't scare me.

1920

From The Tale of How Fadey Learned of the Law Protecting Workingmen*

Fadey had fought on every front
And helped the Commune as a soldier can.
He'd shed
   whole bucketfuls
      of blood.
And now
   he's home again,
       a working man.
He looked at Moscow,
      and at all the folk.
And then he scratched his pate and spoke:
"I've got to earn my bread," says he,
"But here is NEP—†
     what will become of me?
Once more I'll have to stand,
       waiting, hat in hand.
And then the boss
     will hire another, to my loss.
Oh, damn it all to hell!
The goose hangs high—
     and all I get's the smell!"
Prov cut him short:
     "Come, that's enough.
Why are you handing out such stuff?
Today
   we manage things another way;
You can't just hire
     whom you like—then fire.

* This piece was written to order for the Moscow local of the Printers' Union. The contract called for the composition of "a poem in verse popularizing the Code of Labor Laws," and it was stipulated that Comrade Mayakovsky "convey in a poetic and artistic form the exact meaning of the articles of the Code indicated by the Union." The end product was the result of collective effort, Mayakovsky collaborating with several fellow poets.
†New Economic Policy, which partly reinstated private enterprise.

You cannot pick
                    workmen out of the air.
Go to the Labor Exchange, get them there."
"Good heavens!"
                    growls Fadey.
And Prov says: "Scratch your pate!" and grins:
"Today it is the workingman who wins.
It's not the boss who hires and fires—
                                        times change:
The cur has got to bow
                    to the Exchange!"

                                        1924

From Going Home!*

I don't want
                    to be plucked like a flower
in a meadow
                    after working hours.
I want
        the Gosplan†
                    to sweat, debating
my production quota
                    for the year.
I want
        the commissar of the times
                                    to lean
over my thought with an order.
I want
        my heart's ration of love
to be the extra one
                    allotted to specialists.

---

* The poem was written just after Mayakovsky's return from the United
States, at the end of 1925. The Fourteenth Congress of the Communist
Party was then in session. The political report of the Central Committee
was presented by Stalin.
† State Planning Commission.

I want
    the shop committee
                   when my work is done
to secure my lips
           with a padlock.
I want
    the pen to be equal
               to the bayonet.
I want
    Stalin
        representing the Politbureau
to report
      on the output of verse
as he does
      on the output
             of pig iron and steel:
"Out of workingmen's
          hovels
we've climbed
         to the top;
in the Union
      of Republics
          the appreciation of poetry
has surpassed
      the prewar level. . . ."

                      1925

So What?

I made the newssheets rustle, opening
Their eyes that blinked.
              And suddenly
From every frontier
          the gunpowder smell
Came stinging home to me.
For those past twenty
            it is nothing new
To grow where tempests rage.

                              We are not glad,
Of course, but then what cause
Have we got to be sad?
The seas of history
                    are rough.
These threats,
                these wars, we'll brave,
And break into the open,
                        cutting them
As a keel cleaves
            the wave.

                                            1927

From At the Top of My Voice

1 "My Voice Will Reach You"

I too
    am fed up
            with agitprop,*
I too would like
            to scribble ballads about you—
there's more dough in it
                    and it's nicer.
But I
    curbed
        myself,
            treading
on the throat
        of my own song.
Listen,
    comrade descendants,
to an agitator,
        a bigmouth ringleader.
Shouting down
        the torrents of poetry,

---

* The section of the Central Committee of the Communist Party in charge of agitation, propaganda, and Party education.

I will step
          across the slim volumes of lyrics,
speaking like a live man
                    to the living.
I will enter
          the communist future
but not like
          a Yeseninny prophet-paladin.
My verse will reach you
                    across the range of ages
and over the heads
          of poets and premiers.
My verse will reach you,
                    but not in this wise:
not like an arrow
          in lyrical venery,
not the way a worn coin
          reaches a numismatist,
not like the light from a dead star.
My verse
          by its labor
                    will pierce the mountain of years,
and appear
          visible,
                    tangible,
                              hefty,
as an aqueduct
          built by Roman slaves
enters
          our days.
Finding by chance,
                    in barrows of books
where verse lies buried,
the iron lines,
touch them
          with respect
like old,
          but terrible weapons.

2 *"Let Fame"*

Let fame,
          like a comfortless
                         widow,
Walk behind geniuses
                    in funeral processions;
You, my verse, die,
                die like a common soldier,
As in an attack our men
                       died their anonymous deaths.
I spit
     on tons of bronze,
I spit
     on marble slime.
As for fame,
          we'll square accounts amicably—
Sharing one monument:
Socialism
         built
             in battle.

                                        1930

"It's Two O'Clock"*

It's two o'clock. You are in bed, I take it.
A silvery Oká: the Milky Way.
I'm in no hurry; why wake and disturb you
With telegrams' electrical display?
The incident is closed now, and the vessel
Of love smashed on existence, if you please.
We've settled our accounts, and there's no reason
In listing mutual pains, griefs, injuries.

* Mayakovsky's last poem, unfinished. Lines 1, 3, 4, are jotted down in the poet's notebook for 1928. He inserted lines 5–8 in his suicide note, changing "We've settled our accounts" to "I have settled accounts with life." The Oká is a tributary of the Volga. There are no punctuation marks in the original text.

Just see how still it is. Night lays a starry
Tax on the sky. You get up and converse,
At such an hour as this, with all the ages,
With history, and with the universe.

[1930] 1934

BORIS PASTERNAK

"The Drowsy Garden"

The drowsy garden scatters insects
Bronze as the ash from braziers blown.
Level with me and with my candle,
Hang flowering worlds, their leaves full-grown.

As into some unheard-of dogma
I move across into this night,
Where a worn poplar age has grizzled
Screens the moon's strip of fallow light,

Where the pond lies, an open secret,
Where apple bloom is surf and sigh,
And where the garden, a lake dwelling,
Holds out in front of it the sky.

1913

Improvisation

A flock of keys I had feeding out of my hand,
To clapping of wings and croaking and feathery fight;
On tiptoe I stood and stretched out my arm, and the sleeve
Rolled up, so I felt at my elbow the nudging of night.

And the dark. And a pond in the dark, and the lapping of
    waves.
And the birds of the species I-love-you that others deny
Would be killed, so it seemed, before the savage black beaks,
The strong and the strident, were ever to falter and die.

And a pond. And the dark. And festive the palpitant flares
From pipkins of midnight pitch. And the boat's keel gnawed
By the wave. And always the greedy noise of the birds
Who fighting over the elbow fluttered and cawed.

The gullets of dams were agurgle, gulping the night.
And the mother birds, if the fledglings on whom they dote
Were not to be fed, would kill, so it seemed, before
The roulades would die in the strident, the crooked throat.

1915

The Urals for the First Time

Without an accoucheuse, in darkness, pushing her
Blind hands against the night, the Ural fastness, torn and
Half-dead with agony, was screaming in a blur
Of mindless pain, as she was giving birth to morning.

And brushed by chance, tall ranges far and wide
Loosed toppling bronze pell-mell in thunder-colored rumbling.
The train panted and coughed, clutching the mountainside,
And at that sound the ghosts of fir trees shied and stumbled.

The smoky dawn was a narcotic for the peaks,
A drug with which the fire-breathing dragon plied them,
As when a specious thief upon a journey seeks
To lull his fellow travelers with opium slipped them slyly.

They woke on fire. The skies were poppy-colored flame,
Whence Asiatics skied like hunters after quarry;
To kiss the forests' feet the eager strangers came
And thrust upon the firs the regal crowns they carried.

Arrayed in majesty, by rank the firs arose,
Those shaggy dynasts, their grave glory clamant,
And trod the orange velvet of the frozen snows
Spread on a tinseled cloth and richly damasked.

1917

From Spring, *a Cycle*

I *"How Many Buds"*

How many buds, how many sticky butts
Of candles, April kindled, now are glued
Fast to the boughs! The park is redolent
Of puberty. The woods' retorts are rude.

The forest's throat is caught fast in a noose
Of feathered throats: a lassoed buffalo
Bellowing in the nets as organs pant:
Wrestlers who groan sonatas, deep and slow.

Oh, poetry, be a Greek sponge supplied
With suction pads, so it soaks up and cleaves.
Then I would lay you on the wet green bench
Out in the garden, among sticky leaves.

Grow sumptuous frills, fabulous hoopskirts, swell,
And suck in clouds, roulades, ravines, until
Night comes; then, poetry, I'll squeeze you out
And let the thirsty paper drink its fill.

1917

Three Variations

I *"When Consummate the Day"*

When consummate the day hangs before you,
Each detail to be scanned at your ease,
Just the sultry chatter of squirrels
Resounds in the resinous trees.

And storing up strength in their langor,
The ranked piney heights are adrowse,
While the freckled sweat is pouring
From the peeling forest's boughs.

2 *"Miles Thick with Torpor"*

Miles thick with torpor nauseate the gardens.
The catalepsy of the valley's rage
Is weightier, more threatening than a tempest,
Fiercer than hurricane's most savage raid.

The storm is near. The dry mouth of the garden
Gives off the smell of nettles, roofs, and fear,
And of corruption; and the cattle's bellow
Rises columnar in the static air.

3 *"Now Tatters"*

Now tatters of denuded clouds
Grow on each bush in tasseled groves.
Damp nettles fill the garden's mouth.
It smells of storms and treasure troves.

The shrubs are tired of lament.
In heaven arched prospects multiply.
Like web-toed birds on swampy ground
The barefoot azure treads the sky.

And willow branches and the leaves
Of oaks, and tracks beside the spring,
Like lips the hand has not wiped dry,
Are glistening, are glistening.

1917

From Rupture, *a Cycle*

9 *"The Piano, Aquiver"*

The piano, aquiver, will lick the foam from its lips.
The frenzy will wrench you, fell you, and you, undone,
Will whisper: "Darling!" "No," I shall cry, "what's this?
In the presence of music!" But nearness there is none

Like twilight's, with the chords tossed into the fireplace
Like fluttering diaries, for one year, and two, and three.
O marvelous insight, nod, only nod—you may
Well be astonished. For—look—you are free.

I do not hold you. Go, yes, go elsewhere,
Do good. *Werther* cannot be written again,
And in our time death's odor is in the air:
To open a window is to open a vein.

[*1918*]

"I've Come from the Street, Spring"

I've come from the street, Spring, where the poplar stands
Amazed, where distance quails, and the house fears it will fall,
Where the air is blue, like the bundle of wash in the hands
Of the convalescent leaving the hospital.

Where evening is empty: a tale begun by a star
And interrupted, to the confusion of rank
On rank of clamorous eyes, waiting for what they are
Never to know, their bottomless gaze blank.

[*1918*]

"Here the Trace"

Here the trace of enigma's strange fingernail shows.
"It is late. Let me sleep, and at dawn I'll reread
And then all will be clear. Till they wake me, there's none
Who can move the beloved as I do!" Indeed,

How I moved you! You bent to the brass of my lips
As an audience stirred by a tragedy thrills.
Ah, that kiss was like summer. It lingered, delayed,
Swelling slow to a storm as it topples and spills.

As the birds drink, I drank. Till I swooned, still I sucked.
As they flow through the gullet, the stars seem to stop.
But the nightingales shuddering roll their bright eyes,
As they drain the vast vault of the night, drop by drop.

1918

"Waving a Bough"

Waving a bough full of fragrance,
In the dark, with pure good to sup,
The water the storm had made giddy
Went running from cup to cup.

From chalice to chalice rolling,
It slid along two and hung,
One drop of agate, within them,
Shining and shy it clung.

Over the meadowsweet blowing,
The wind may torture and tear
At that drop—it will never divide it,
Nor the kissing, the drinking pair.

They laugh and try to shake free and
Stand up, each straight as a dart,
But the drop will not leave the stigmas,
Wild horses won't tear them apart.

1920

"We're Few"

We're few, perhaps three, hellish fellows
Who hail from the flaming Donetz,
With a fluid gray bark for our cover
Made of rain clouds and soldiers' soviets
And verses and endless debates
About art or, it may be, freight rates.

We used to be people. We're epochs.
Pell-mell we rush caravanwise
As the tundra to groans of the tender
And tension of pistons and ties.
Together we'll rip through your prose,
We'll whirl, a tornado of crows,

And be off! But you'll not understand it
Till late. So the wind in the dawn
Hits the thatch on the roof—for a moment—
But puts immortality on
At trees' stormy sessions, in speech
Of boughs the roof's shingles can't reach.

[*1921*]

"Fresh Paint"

I should have seen the sign: "Fresh paint,"
    But useless to advise
The careless soul, and memory's stained
    With cheeks, calves, hands, lips, eyes.

More than all failure, all success,
    I loved you, for your skill
In whitening the yellowed world
    As white cosmetics will.

Listen, my dark, my friend: by God,
    All will grow white somehow,
Whiter than madness or lamp shades
    Or bandage on a brow.

1922

Out of Superstition

The cubbyhole I live in is a box
    Of candied orange peel.
Soiled by hotel rooms till I reach the morgue—
    That's not for me, I feel.

Out of pure superstition I have come
    And settled here once more.
The wallpaper is brown as any oak,
    And there's a singing door.

I kept one hand upon the latch, you tried
    To fight free of the nets,
And forelock touched enchanted forelock, and
    Then lips touched violets.

O softly, in the name of times long gone,
    You play the old encore:
Your costume like a primrose chirps "Hello"
    To April as before.

It's wrong to think—you are no vestal: you
    Brought in a chair one day,
Stood on it, took my life down from the shelf
    And blew the dust away.

                                    1922

Definition of the Soul

To fly off, a ripe pear in a storm,
With one leaf clinging on as it must.
Mad devotion! It quitted the branch!
It will choke with its throat full of dust!

A ripe pear, more aslant than the wind.
What devotion! "You'll bray me? You're brash!"
Look! In beauty the thunder-spent storm
Has blazed out, crumbled down—sunk to ash.

And our birthplace is burned to a crisp.
Say, fledgling, where now is your nest?
O my leaf, with the fears of a finch!
My shy silk, why still fight and protest?

Do not fear, song, grown like a graft.
And what goal is there yet to be sought?
Ah, "here"—fatal adverb, of you
The shudder of the graft never thought!

1922

"You Pictures Flying"

You pictures flying slantwise in a shower
From the highway that blew the candle out,
I can't wean you away from rhyme and measure,
Deserting hooks and walls in your skew rout.

Suppose the universe goes masked? Or even
That every latitude breeds some of those
Who are on hand to stop its mouth with putty
And seal it for the winter: just suppose!

Yet objects tear their masks off, all their power
Leaks out, they leave their honor where it lies,
Should there be any reason for their singing,
Should the occasion for a shower arise.

[*1922*]

Roosters

Nightlong the water labored breathlessly.
Till morning came, the rain burned linseed oil.
Now vapor from beneath the lilac lid
Pours forth: earth streams like *shchee* that's near the boil.

And when the grass, shaking itself, leaps up,
Oh, who will tell the dew how scared I am—
The moment the first cock begins to yawp,
And then one more, and then—the lot of them?

They name the years as these roll by in turn,
And on each darkness, as it goes, they call,
Foretelling thus the change that is to come
To rain, to earth, to love—to each and all.

[1923]

Dame's Violet

Not long ago the rain walked through this clearing
Like a surveyor. Now with tinsel bait
The lily of the valley's leaves are weighted,
And water got into the mullein's ears.

These are the frigid fir trees' quondam nurslings,
Their ear lobes stretched with dew; they shun the day,
And grow apart, single and solitary,
Even their odors separately disbursed.

When it is teatime in the summer villas,
The fog fills the mosquito's sail, and night,
Plucking the strings of a guitar but lightly,
Stands among pansies in a mistlike milk.

Then with dame's violet everything is scented.
Faces and years. And thoughts. Every event
That from the thievish past can be commanded
And in the future taken from Fate's hand.

[1927]

From Waves, *a Cycle*

I *"We Were in Georgia"*

We were in Georgia. You can get this land
If hell is multiplied by paradise,
Bare indigence by tenderness, and if
A hothouse serves as pedestal for ice.

And then you'll know what subtle doses of
Success and labor, duty, mountain air
Make the right mixture with the earth and sky
For man to be the way we found him there.

So that he grew, in famine and defeat
And bondage, to this stature, without fault,
Becoming thus a model and a mold,
Something as stable and as plain as salt.

ll "The Caucasus Lay Spread"

The Caucasus lay spread before our gaze,
An unmade bed, it seemed, with tousled sheets;
The blue ice of the peaks more fathomless
Than the warmed chasms with their harbored heats.

Massed in the mist and out of sorts, it reared
The steady malice of its icy crests
As regularly as the salvos spat
In an engagement from machine-gun nests.

And staring at this beauty with the eyes
Of the brigades whose task it was to seize
The region, how I envied those who had
Palpable obstacles to face like these.

O if we had their luck! If, out of time,
As though it peered through fog, this day of ours,
Our program, were of such substantial stuff,
And frowned down at us as this rough steep lours!

Then day and night our program would march on,
Setting its heel upon my prophecies,
Kneading their downpour with the very sole
Of its straight backbone into verities.

There would be no one I could quarrel with,
And not another hour would I give
To making verses: unbeknown to all,
No poet's life, but poems I would live.

1931

To a Friend

Come, don't I know that, stumbling against shadows,
Darkness could never have arrived at light?
Do I rate happy hundreds over millions
Of happy men? Am I a monster quite?

Isn't the Five-Year Plan a yardstick for me,
Its rise and fall my own? But I don't quiz
In asking: What shall I do with my thorax
And with what's slower than inertia is?

The great Soviet gives to the highest passions
In these brave days each one its rightful place,
Yet vainly leaves one vacant for the poet.
When that's not empty, look for danger's face.

1931

"If Only, When I Made My Debut"

If only, when I made my debut,
There might have been a way to tell
That lines with blood in them can murder,
That they can flood the throat and kill,

I certainly would have rejected
A jest on such a sour note,
So bashful was that early interest,
The start was something so remote.

But age is pagan Rome, demanding
No balderdash, no measured breath,
No fine feigned parody of dying,
But really being done to death.

A line that feeling sternly dictates
Sends on the stage a slave, and, faith,
It is good-bye to art forever
Then; then things smack of soil and Fate.

1932

March

Blazing sun that fairly makes you swelter,
Crazed, the whole ravine is rampaging.
Like the labors of a sturdy milkmaid,
Spring's incessant chores are in full swing.

Snow is wasting, feeble with anemia,
Branchlets of blue veins betray decline.
But the cow barn seethes: there life is smoking,
Health glows radiant on the pitchforks' tines.

Oh, these days, these days and nights! At midday,
Drops are drumming, while the driblets spill
From the eaves where icicles are failing;
Chatter of those never-resting rills!

Flung wide open—stable, shed, and cow barn.
Pigeons peck oats from the snow, and there:
Giver of life, answerable for all this—
Dung, fresh fallen, smells of the fresh air.

                                                    1948

Night Wind

The singing, the drunken clamor have died down.
Tomorrow it's early to rise for everyone.
Lights go out in the huts. The boys and girls
Have made their way home now, the junketing done.

Only the wind saunters haphazardly
Along the same overgrown path it took before
With a crowd of lads returning from the party.
He hangs his head, hiding behind a door.

He has no liking for these nocturnal wrangles,
For angry assessments of wrong and right.
He would prefer a peaceful settlement
Of the differences in his quarrel with the night.

Before him—row on row of garden fences.
The two argue, as if compelled by a goad;
While they dispute the sources of their quarrel,
The trees draw closer together on the road.

1961

MARINA TSVETAYEVA

"No Longer Now"

No longer now the same God-given bounties
Where now no longer the same waters glide.
Then fly, and hasten, doves of Aphrodite,
Through the great gates that sunset has swung wide!

And on the chill sands I shall lie, withdrawing
Into the dimness of unnumbered days. . . .
Like the shed skin the snake is coldly eyeing—
My youth, outgrown, has shrunk under my gaze.

1921

From Good News

"Alive And Well"

Alive and well!
Louder than thunder—
The blow of an axe—
Joy!

No, an axe
Is too small:
A hammer to stun
An ox—joy!

Dumbstruck,
In terror.
What tax
Will they lay, what ask
In exchange?

From the knees
That bend
To the roots of the
Hair standing on end—
Terror!

You are alive?
Your eyes closed (appalled!)
But you breathe,
When called—
You hear?

Saved by the boat?!
Oh, my crane,
The youngest of the white flock
Afloat in the blue!

Dead—come to life??!
A half-uttered sigh,
A stone from the sky,
A crowbar, a loy
Piercing the head—
No, a blade
Up to the hilt in the chest—
Joy!

1921

From Disciple, *a Cycle*

VI "All the Magnificence"

All the magnificence
Of trumpets—only the whisper
Of grasses—before Thee.

All the magnificence
Of tempests—only the twitter
Of birds—before Thee.

All the magnificence
Of pinions—only the tremor
Of eyelids—before Thee.

[*1921*]

Love

A yataghan? Or fire?
Too grand! Don't make so wild a claim
For just a pain,
That you know like the shape of your hand,
Or your own child's name.

EDUARD BAGRITZKY

"My Honeyed Languor"

My honeyed languor comes
                            of silence and of dreams
And boredom long-drawn-out
                            and songs that gauchely yearn;
The cocks embroidered on white towels give me joy,
I like the soot that clings to icons old and stern.

To the hot buzz of flies
                            day after day goes by,

And a meek piety on each its blessing lays;
Beneath the eaves a quail
                              is mumbling sleepily;
The smell of raspberry jam pervades the holidays.

At night the billowing
                              soft goose down wearies me,
The stuffy icon lamp blinking is said to view,
And as he cranes his neck
                              the gay embroidered bird
Commences his long chant
                              of cock-a-doodle-doo.

Here you have granted me
                              a modest refuge, Lord,
Beneath a blissful roof
                              where turmoil cannot grow,
Where clotted days like jam
                              that from a teaspoon drips
In heavy drops
             perpetually flow, flow, flow.

                                                  1919

Spring, the Vet, and I

The sign says HOSPITAL—a blue haze wraps it now.
The veterinary goes over a cow.

The hand painted with manganese
Feels first the udders, then the strong butt of
The tail, and soon the cow
Beneath the bull will stretch and howl with love.
They clear the nuptial circle with their spades,
The starling sings the epithalamy.
The zodiac has come to earth: Pisces
Is in the pond, and on the grass Taurus is plain to see.

(The world of wet boughs swells
To fill the sky.
The orange wasp casts spells
In the wet arbors. Why,
Even the caged larks try
Their voices: there's so much to tell!)

The sign says HOSPITAL; above, blue haze expands.
With quiet zest the vet washes his hands.

A noise behind the gates.
Let's see what's doing.
Swelling their flanks, the cows
Drift dimly, mooing;
Like spotted smoke they move,
Misty with milk and grassy memories
Of meadow haze. Dew hangs like bells
Upon their horns. Blue vapor seethes
About those steady feet.
Well, vet, what are you thinking of?
Now it is time for you to lay your hands
Upon these beasts: to bless alike repose and movement and
Death, and the aching howl of love.

(The household of the April world:
The bugs and lizards, tiny things,
Parcel this earth among them, take
And split it into bits:
Ah, boys on swings,
How the boughs shake!)

The sign says HOSPITAL—a blue haze wraps it yet.
I'm here! I'm near! Old vet!

I stand above you like your conscience, vet.
I make the rounds of all your days like death!
Don't stop!
Work till you drop!
Fight with your wife!
Get drunk!
But keep your faith with life! Don't fail!
Into the crock of milk a warm star falls.

The world lies seamless,
Ironed-out and clean.
It bursts with green,
It shines like water,
Like a maple leaf
Washed by the rain!
It's close! It flutters at your elbow! Seize it and
Squeeze it like a quick bird in your hand!

    (A star stands on the doorsill—
    Do not scare it!
    Woods, roads, ravines—
    Oh, life unplumbed!
    A star stands on the sill—
    Don't scare it now, keep still!)

Above the sign blue haze coils lazily.
Off in the distance the vet bows to me.

Upon his perch the starling tries his best.
Earth steams as though fresh from a Turkish bath. No wind.
Above the birds in space that's thinned
To emptiness the planets knock
One on another with a cobbled sound.
Wild geese have a date
With rivery countries.
And the attendants make
For town, with huge stars tête-à-tête.
Earth flows with semen.

    (Child of labor, rise,
    Barefooted, stirred;
    This world is yours to seize
    As though it were a honeycomb
    Sparkling with dew for you!
    Oh, whirl of vernal suns,
    Young surf of seas!)

1930

NIKOLAY TIKHONOV

"Fire, the Rope"

Fire, the rope, the bullet and the axe,
Like servants bowed and followed where we went,
And in each drop that fell a deluge slept,
Pebbles turned into mountains where they lay,
And in a small twig trodden underfoot
Whole forests rustled, their black arms outspread.

At table falsehood ate and drank with us,
Bells tolled out of mere habit stupidly,
Our coins lost weight and rang a thinner chime,
And children looked on corpses without fear.
Those were the days when first it was we learned
Words bitter, beautiful and harsh.

1921

"Our Rooms"

Our rooms are turned to rolling wagons
With wheels that creak on roads of air;
And down below, the moony water
Is playing gently with green hair.

We travel over crystal bridges,
Across the earth, across the sky.
Its red cheek pressed against our windows,
The sun sings out as we roll by.

And every heart's a summer beehive
Blazing with a dark honeyed gleam,
As though we were the lucky first ones
To bend our heads above the stream.

We do not know who leads us onward,
What end our hurrying wheels will find,
But, like a bird set free, the spirit
Darts on a wing that rips the wind.

1921

"We Have Unlearned"

We have unlearned how to give alms, forgotten
How to breathe the salt air above the sea,
And how to meet the dawn, and in the market
Buy golden lemons for two coins or three.
Ships call on us only by chance, and freight trains
Bring cargoes out of habit, that is all;
Just count the men belonging to my country—
How many dead will answer to the call!
But we have no occasion to be solemn—
A broken knife's no good to work with, but
With the same knife that is all black and broken
Know that immortal pages have been cut.

1922

SERGEY YESENIN

"Where Dawn Is Sprinkling"

Where dawn is sprinkling her red waters on
The cabbages and beets,
A little nuzzling maple reaches up
To suck its dam's green teats.

1910

Autumn

How still it is among the junipers!
Autumn—a bay mare—cleans her mane of burrs.

Her hoofs' blue clatter sounds above the bank
Of the still river where the reeds are rank.

The monkish wind steps gingerly, his tread
Kneads the heaped leaves with which the road is spread,

And at the rowan clusters he will lean
To kiss the red wounds of the Christ unseen.

1914

"In the Clear Cold"

In the clear cold the dales grow blue and tremble;
The iron hoofs beat sharply, knock on knock.
The faded grasses in wide skirts assemble
Flung copper where the wind-blown willows rock.

From empty glens, a slender arch ascending,
Fog curls upon the air and mosswise grows,
While evening, low above the river bending,
In its white waters washes his blue toes.

1915

Droves

Upon green hills in droves the horses graze
And blow the golden bloom off passing days.

From the high slope into the azure bay
Tumbles the pitch of heavy manes asway.

They toss their heads above the still lagoon,
Caught with a silver bridle by the moon.

Snorting in fear of their own shadows, they,
Whose manes will screen it, wait the coming day.

1915

"Hopes, Painted"

Hopes, painted by the autumn cold, are shining;
My steady horse plods on as calm as Fate;
His dun lip twitches moistly at the lining
Of my blown coat: he does not change his gait.

On a far road the unseen traces, leading
Neither to rest nor battle, lure and fade;
The golden heels of day will flash, receding,
And labors in the chest of years be laid.

1915

"First Snow"

First snow—it calls me: lilies of the valley
Flare in my heart, so strong I feel, so gay.
There is an early star like a blue candle
Evening has kindled so it lights my way.

I do not know if there is light or darkness.
Is that the wind or cock crow? As I stare,
I think instead of winter in the meadows
A flock of swans has softly settled there.

How marvelous you are, you velvet whiteness!
The light frost stings my blood to sweet unrest.
How much I long to press against my body
One of the birches that has bared its breast!

Oh, the mysterious murk of the dense forest!
Oh, snowy fields' enchantment and surprise!
How my arms ache with the delicious longing
To close about a willow's woody thighs.

1917

From Transfiguration, *a Cycle*

III *"Ho, Russians"*

Ho, Russians,
Fishers of the universe,
You who scooped heaven with the net of dawn,
Blow your trumpets!

Beneath the plow of storm
The earth roars.
Golden-tusked, the colter breaks
The cliffs.

A new sower roams the fields;
New seeds
He casts into the furrows.

A radiant guest drives toward you
In a coach.
Across the clouds
A mare races.

The breeching on the mare:
The blue;
The bells on the breeching:
The stars.

1918

From The Jordan Dove, *a Cycle*

2 *"The Moon"*

The moon is the tongue
In the bell of the sky;
My country's my mother,
A Bolshevik, I.

That all may be brothers
Is cause for me
To rejoice in your death,
My own country.

Sturdily, loudly
I ring the blue bell,
And make the moon swing
For your passing knell.

Yours, world of brothers,
The song I raise.
I hear glad tidings
Float through the haze.

1918

"Oh, Listen"

Oh, listen—the sleigh's rushing on, the sleigh's rushing on,
        do you hear?
It is good to be lost in the hushed snowy fields with my dear.

The gay wind is bashful—advancing and shyly retreating again.
And a bell goes on rolling and rolling across the bare plain.

Then it's hey, my sleigh! Hey, my sleigh! Yes, and it's ho, my
        dun horse in the snows!
In a clearing a drunken young maple twirls round on her toes.

We will drive up and ask: What's the matter? And then in a
        twink there will be
An accordion playing, and we'll dance together all three.

1925

"A Moony Thin Desolation"

A moony thin desolation,
Vast plains in anguish immersed—
My carefree youth once knew this,
I loved it, like others, and cursed.

The roads with their dusty willows,
And the tune that the cartwheels play. . . .
Not for aught that I might be offered
Would I listen to it today.

I am weary of huts and hearthstones,
Spring storming the apple trees
I can love no longer for thinking
Of the fields in their poverty.

Now my heart is given elsewhere—
In the moon's consumptive light
I see stone and steel as the secret
Of my country's coming might.

Oh, Russia, give over dragging
Your wooden plow through the fields!
The birches ache, and the poplars,
When they see what the harvest yields.

Perhaps the new life will reject me,
My future is blank, but I feel
A longing to see beggared Russia
Become a Russia of steel.

And hearing the bark of the motors
Through the blizzards, shrill and strong,
I have no wish at all to listen
To the cartwheels' creaking song.

1925

NIKOLAY KLYUYEV

A Cottage Song

The stove is orphaned now; the old housewife has died,
The trivet tells the pot with tears; their talk is harried.
Behind the pane two trustful magpies, side by side,
Chirp: "May is near, today the finches will be married,
Smith Woodpecker with busy knocking has stripped his throat,
The mole—that sullen miner—creeps sunward, meekly leaving
His tunneled dark estate to bugs without a groat;
The cranes are homing now, the sparrow, pert and thieving,
Has heard the jackdaw blurt the secret of her egg."
The tangled mop awaits the bucket, limp and tired;
She thinks the unwashed porch for spuming suds must beg.
How gay would be the splash of water, how desired
A window full of sunray tow, an endless fairy tale. . . .
Behind the stove the house sprite gabbles, quick and clever,
Of the new tenant's stillness within the churchyard's pale,
Of crosses listening to things nameless forever,
Of how the dark church entry lulls the lingering dream.
The house sprite gabbles on above the bleak hour's starkness.
The peasant hut is scowling; a pewter eye agleam,
The lonely window stares out at the thaw and darkness.

1920

ANATOLY MARIENHOF

"Savage Nomad Hordes"

Savage nomad hordes
Of Asia
Spilled fire out of the tubs!
Razin's execution is avenged,
And the piece of Pugachov's* beard
Torn out by the roots.
Hoofs
Have trampled
The scruff of the earth,
Chill with centuries,
And the angelic sky, like a stocking
With a hole in its heel,
Has been taken out of the laundry trough
Clean.

1918?

October †

We trample filial obedience,
We have gone and sat down saucily,
Keeping our hats on,
Crossing our legs.

---

* Stepan (Stenka) Razin, celebrated in folk balladry, led a popular rising in southeastern Russia in 1670–71. Yemelyan Pugachov, a pretender to the Russian throne, headed a similar rebellion of malcontents a century later in the reign of Catherine II.
† The month of the Bolshevik Revolution.

You don't like it that we guffaw with blood,
That we don't wash rags washed millions of times,
That we suddenly dared
Earsplittingly to bark: Wow!

Yes, sir, the spine
Is as straight as a telephone pole,
Not mine only, but the spines of all Russians,
For centuries hunched.

Who on earth is noisier now than we?
You say: Bedlam—
No mileposts—no landmarks—
Straight to the devil: on the church porch our red cancan is
      glorious.

You don't believe? Here are hordes,
Droves of clouds at men's beck and call,
And the sky like an old wife's cloak,
And the sun has no eyelashes. . . .

Jesus is on the cross again, and Barabbas
We escort, arm in arm, down Tverskoy Boulevard. . . .
Who will break in, who? The gallop of Scythian horses?
Violins bowing the Marseillaise?

Has it ever before been heard of, that the forger
Of rails braceleting the globe
Should smoke his cheap tobacco as importantly
As the officer used to clink his spurs?

You ask: and then?
And then dancing centuries.
We will knock at all doors
And no one shall say: Goddamyou, get out!

We! We! We are everywhere:
Before the footlights, on the proscenium,
Not gentle lyricists,
But flaming buffoons.

Pile rubbish, all the rubbish in a heap,
And like Savonarola, to the sound of hymns,
Hurl it into the fire. . . . Whom should we fear?
When the mundiculi of puny souls have become—worlds.

Each day of ours is a new chapter of the Bible.
Every page will be Great to thousands of generations.
We are those about whom they will say:
The lucky ones lived in 1917!
And you still shout: They are lost!

You are still whimpering lavishly!
Dunderheads,
Isn't yesterday crushed, like a dove
By a motor
Dashing madly from the garage?

1918?

DEMYAN BEDNYI

The Young Forest

A landowner, some years ago,
Went driving through his woods, which made a splendid show.
   His coachman, Filka, on his perch
   Looked strong of sinew and of bone.
The landowner admired the woods he called his own.
"Just see my saplings, Filka: pine and birch!
My boy, this is a forest, eh? Look round a bit:
This used to be a waste, but now just look at it!

That's where good switches grow—hop down and fetch a few;
The peasants need their drubbings—rods will come in pat."
"Mm, yes," drawled Filka, "yes . . . the very thing for that. . . .
Just let them grow . . . they'll make stout clubs, I promise you."
    The moral of this tale is clear to any cub:
    Years passed, and every switch became a club.

1915

Nepman*

Just watch them, comrade . . . with an owner's eye. . . .
    And let them pasture on the busy street,
These cattle; let them batten and feed high,
    And so make rich and juicy meat.
Let their fleece grow. But do not let your wits
    Go gathering wool, or they'll give you the slip.
And threaten, not with knives, just with a whip.
    And when the time is ripe, then we'll be quits,
And the whole flock's thick pelts be ours to clip.

1922

No One Knew

(April 22, 1870)

It was a day like any other,
The same dull sky, the same drab street.
There was the usual angry pother
From the policeman on his beat.
Proud of his fine new miter's luster,
The archpriest strutted down the nave;
And the pub rocked with brawl and bluster,
Where scamps gulped down what fortune gave.

---

* A private entrepreneur permitted to engage in business under the New Economic Policy inaugurated in 1921, who was later expropriated.

The market women buzzed and bickered
Like flies above the honeypots.
The burghers' wives bustled and dickered,
Eyeing the drapers' latest lots.
An awestruck peasant stared and stuttered,
Regarding an official door
Where yellow rags of paper fluttered:
A dead ukase of months before.
The fireman ranged his tower, surveying
The roofs, like the chained bears one sees;
And soldiers shouldered arms, obeying
The drill sergeant's obscenities.
Slow carts in caravans went winding
Dockward, where floury stevedores moiled;
And, under convoy, in the blinding
Dust of the road, a student toiled,
And won some pity, thus forlorn,
From the drunk hand who poured his scorn
In curses on some pal and brother. . . .
Russia was aching with the thorn
And bearing her old cross, poor mother,
That day, a day like any other,
And not a soul knew that—*Lenin was born!*

1927

VASILY KAZIN

The Bricklayer

I make my way home at evening,
Fatigue is a comrade who sticks;
And my apron sings for the darkness
A strong red song of bricks.

It sings of my ruddy burden
That I carried so high, high
Up to the very housetop,
The roof that they call the sky.

My eyes were a carousel turning,
The wind had a foggy tone,
And morning, too, like a worker,
Carried up a red brick of its own.

I make my way home at evening,
Fatigue is a comrade who sticks;
And my apron sings for the darkness
A strong red song of bricks.

1920

The Carpenter's Plane

Smoothly riding,
Bravely gliding,
Like a swan my plane swims by.

Now she hurries
Through the flurries
Of the shavings as they fly.

Sail, unbowed one,
Proud one, proud one,
Though the river road be rough.

Warmth is streaming
Through the creaming
Waves of shavings that you slough.

Now she's sweeping
Past the leaping
Swishing waterfalls with ease—

Ah, my beauty,
Do your duty,
While the foam seethes round my knees.

1922

ALEXANDER BEZYMENSKY

Village and Factory

Huts that stand like plaited baskets.
Birds. Green forest. Space. And heat.
Cobwebs in the dark soul's corners.
Thought's slow whisper. Peace. Retreat.

Dirt and soot. Thick sweaty odors.
Crisp steel shavings. Whistles. Noise.
Straight bold thinking. Heavy labor.
Life's pulse throbbing like a boy's.

1920

STEPAN SHCHIPACHEV

On the Boulevard

Oh, what a night! The hoarfrost flies
From every bough in ashen flecks.
The old man with the telescope
Looks like a parrot in his specs.

The others hurry to get warm,
But he is not as others are.
Immune to cold, he sells the sky
To passers-by: a dime a star.

Sunflower

The sunflower has nowhere
to shelter from the rain—
his feet in mud, the water
between the beds won't drain.

Capped, carroty and freckled,
you see the chap remain
fast in the bed—why should he
run? He likes the rain.

1938

"Here Sorrow Had No Limit"

Here sorrow had no limit and no bottom,
Here poverty tramped the bleak road alone,
Where clasping to their breasts their unweaned babies,
Polish madonnas stood, carved out of stone.

They stared far off into the country distance
Where the thin soil crumbles as it is plowed,
Stood quietly and stared, the only mothers
Whose eyes the tears of sorrow did not cloud.

1939

"Agreed That I Shall Die"

Agreed that I shall die and that I must
Turn, as time passes, to a little dust.

A barefoot girl will cross the field, and I
Will stir, beyond corruption, and will seize
Tenderly with hot dust those legs of hers
That smell of daisies to her very knees.

1940

"They Never See Themselves"

They never see themselves, the great blue spaces,
And, clear and pure in the eternal cold,
The snowy mountains never see their glory,
The flower cannot watch itself unfold.

So it is sweet to know that if you wander
Through woods, or if you climb a craggy rise,
Nature delights, discovering her beauties
With your insatiable eyes.

1945

"A Gust of Supple Wind"

A gust of supple wind springs up,
Tousles her hair until it flies,
Then closely drapes her dress across
Her almost girlish breasts, her thighs.

Beyond the foaming foliage
Of plum and apple tree she stands—
Surely the wind knows what it is
To have a sculptor's happy hands.

"Hour on Hour"

Hour on hour it rains and rains.
It will be raining hour on hour—
         through the wet pane
         the sky shows gray:
this is no summer shower, autumn spins
         the long gray yarn
                  of rain.

She'll spin and spin and spin until
the puddles in the fields begin
      to wear a thin
      if hazy glaze,
until the early frost turns earth to steel
      that rings beneath
         the heel,

till finally the spinster comes to feel
—from the clear cold—that she must leave her wheel,
      must turn and go,
yielding her place to winter, who will weave
      the shining sheets
         of snow.

1964

SEMYON KIRSANOV

This Will Pass

If you were to die
a hundred years from now,
I should know the painstaking possibilities of science.
I should know
that the fantastic surgeon of the future
out of the first willing
girl
could make me a you.

The skin and the voice
having been figured out
with the aid of precision instruments,

the Institute of Similars
would produce
an absolute you.

At first the memories would not coincide,
but that too the fantastic surgeon of the future
could correct.
The childhood of the deceased
is suggested to her,
and for complete resemblance
a safe little tuberculosis
is planted in her lungs.

I am sure that given
my means,
a willing girl would be found,
she would come in a stranger
and go out an absolute you.

And maybe really
in the fantastic future
not I, but someone else
will marry
an absolute you.

I'm not such an egoist,
as long as it's you.

1940

This Will Remain

But look: the water
that she lifted in her palms to wash with
is now
in the curve of a cloud
or in a subterranean stream
or in a blade of grass.

And that earth
she walked on,
who loved the May Day square,
that earth either sparkles in the dew
or is coated with tar
or is in the window box where Aunt Motya grows
geranium and aloe.

And the air
she exhaled
also serves a needy blade of grass
somewhere!

I know—
she is
no more.
But the world has somehow been touched by her?

I kiss the pink ticket
with its emblem,
which admitted you
to the speakers' platform
on our first,
your last
May Day.

1940

KONSTANTIN SIMONOV

"Just Wait for Me"

Just wait for me and I'll return.
But wait, oh, wait with all your might. . . .
Wait when your heart is saddened by
The pouring rains, the sallow light.

Wait when the wind heaps up the snow,
Wait when the air is dry and hot.
Wait when the rest no longer wait
For those whom they too soon forgot.
Wait when the letters fail to come,
Wait on, through dread and through despair,
When those who wait together end
Their waiting and turn otherwhere.

Just wait for me and I'll return.
And show no kindliness to such
As know by heart that it is time
To cease from grieving overmuch.
Let both my mother and my son
Believe me lost, let friends who tire
Of waiting longer sit them down
Barren of hope beside the fire,
And let them toast my memory
In bitter wine as friends will do.
Wait. While they drink, be waiting still,
Nor lift the glass they pour for you.

Just wait for me and I'll return,
To spite all deaths that men can die.
Let those who gave up waiting say:
"It was his luck"—that is a lie.
It is not theirs to understand
Who gave up waiting, wearily,
How under fire I was safe,
Since, waiting, you protected me.
And none but you and I will know
How I escaped the thrust of fate—
Simply because, better than all
The others, you knew how to wait.

1941

SERGEY ORLOV

Pause on the March

The blazing sun has made the armor hot,
Thick on our clothes the dust of the campaign.
Oh, to pull off the coveralls, and sink
Into the shady grass, but first it's plain

We've got to check the motor, lift the hatch;
Let her cool down. No matter how we feel,
Sure you and I can stand up to the worst:
We're human beings, but she's only steel.

1944

MIKHAIL MATUSOVSKY

Happiness

When wisps of smoke from the guns were flying
Between the sky and the shaken land,
And men alone could endure the pounding
That was too much for the stones to stand;

When, swathed in flame and in smoky tatters,
The world careened like a ship in churned
Tempestuous seas; when to live was painful
And only dead men were unconcerned;

When, to the creaking of ice in springtime,
I looked about me, a human speck
Alone there, deep in the snow, preparing
To die—the Germans on my neck;

When gunfire woke me and deathy tremors
Convulsed the forest at night, it brought
No dread, no envy of others' fortunes;
I kept revolving a single thought:

To live, not stealthily, not abjectly,
But swoop, an avalanche as it flies!
The happiness I demand is total,
Not on half will I compromise.

                                        1945

Long Roads

It was a German town that we awoke in,
With unfamiliar quiet everywhere.
These pyramidal roofs are alien to me,
These mean and narrow streets I cannot bear.

I keep on dreaming that I'm done with dreaming
And that I really wake again in sight
Of my foredestined city, of my Moscow,
Airy and buoyant and suffused with light.

What's fame to me, mountains of golden treasure,
Rivers of wine? I'd give it all away
If I could see, spread out before my window,
The Russian spaces on a summer's day;

If I could hear, beyond the homely timbers
That wall my cottage, the wet pine trees sough
When autumn comes to bring us gifts of pasties
Bursting with mushrooms—that would be enough;

Only to stub bare feet on the harsh stubble,
Grow tired with walking, day-long on the go,
And on the road in winter note a fox's
Faint tracks, half blotted by the wind-blown snow;

Only to hear the thin chirp of a cricket
Hidden in a dry rick of dusty hay,
To look into a Russian stream for pebbles
That the clear shallows struck with sun display.

The challenge of the town patrol is sterner.
It rains as always from a sky of lead.
Endless the long, long roads that stretch behind me,
And only alien cities lie ahead.

1945

ILYA SELVINSKY

Landscape

A white, white cottage,
A day sea-blue and still.
Chicks in an upturned helmet
Peck at the trash it spills.

An ordinary helmet
With swastikas and all.
The farmer turns: "Paraska!
Hi, you old hag!" he bawls.

So four-year-old Paraska
Trots to the chicks at food.
Perched on a log,
                    the farmer,
Eyeing the helmet, broods.

"See it? The chickens got it."
He is still young, but gray.
"A smoke?" "Sure."
                    Matches. Amber.
A pouch that smells of hay.

Bluish the smoke. We're silent,
More thoughtful than our wont.
He fought near Moscow. I was
On the Crimean front.

                              1945

YEVGENY DOLMATOVSKY

Frost

I wish you'd write me a letter about the frost
(You can't be warm unless there's a frost, you know),
And about the little birch tree, the bashful one,
White as white can be in its cloak of snow.

Write me about the drifts that are piled up
To a giant's shoulders, and tell me everything
About the blizzards that strike so savagely
And kiss so hotly, every kiss a sting.

Write me how thick the ice is in the stream,
And how it sparkles in moonlight; write me all
About the stove, how it crackles cosily,
And how the cricket chirps in a crack in the wall.

Be good and write me about the fire on the hearth,
All the small homely things beyond belief;
I remember how I would hold my wrist to the flame
And it looked translucent as a maple leaf.

. . . Oh, far and far away is my Russia, dressed
In silver, bridal in her bright array.
Here rains run over the sidewalks slantingly,
Spring-fashion, on a January day.

Don't look for blizzards here, don't hope to see
Fresh fallen snow. There is no winter here,
Where men wear rubbers and not thick felt boots,
And capes not overcoats at the end of the year,

Where they have radiators in every room,
Hot baths at any hour, day and night.
But I am lost with nothing to keep me warm.
Send me a snowstorm and I'll be all right.

1946

YELENA SEREBROVSKAYA

Mines

An orchard will be planted here, you say,
And deep into the earth your spade is thrust.
But battles were fought here: you cannot trust
This ground, a mine may lurk beneath the clay.

Perhaps the sapper missed a single one;
There lies a stupid end, you understand.
A careless step, a movement of the hand—
A blast, and joys and arguments are done.

But here in the old flat I cannot find
A corner that bears touching: everywhere
Letters, belongings, things they used to wear
Who'll not return. Oh, house that grief has mined!

Dumb objects speak, needing nor words nor wits,
Of the misfortune that is hard to brook.
A movement of the hand, a careless look—
And all at once the heart is blown to bits.

1946

MIKHAIL LVOV

"I Trod Upon the Age's Heels"

I trod upon the age's heels, pressed closer
And felt its very breath, but never turned;
Upon its chilly iron I was bedded
And where I walked its scorching fires burned.

We moved together to the bounds of courage,
It holds my eyes, my soul: they'd pay the cost
In blood if I should try to tear them from it,
Like hands soldered to iron by the frost.

1947

FYODOR BELKIN

Rooster

His feathers are burnished gold;
On tiptoe he crows, debonair;
He claws up roots in the garden
And sorts his booty with care.

A worthy paterfamilias,
He surveys his chicks with a tingle
Of pride; struts the yard like a warrior—
A pity his spurs never jingle!

His life is battles and flights;
Like an eagle he'll dart and be gone;
He fights with the neighbor's cock
Day-long until blood is drawn.

He pulls his frayed cloak close,
Deep in thought on his perch; he thrives
Like the Mongols of old: a hundred
Fights, and a score of wives.

1946

ALEXEY MARKOV

At the Market

I'll ask how much the woodsy mushrooms are,
And price the milk that shines in a cold jar,
The grapes, too, that a hawker has piled high,
The flowers a girl holds out to catch the eye;
I'll price the multicolored wealth of wares. . . .
A pity that my pocket is quite bare. . . .
I'll ask the price of what's on every stall
And take away with me nothing at all.
And yet I'll carry off the lot, you'll see,
Even the girl's good looks will go with me.

1946

LYUDMILA TATYANICHEVA

"The Snowstorms Sleep"

The snowstorms sleep, grown weary of pursuit,
The chase was long and they have had their fill.
You barely touched my mouth as you bent to it,
And when you brushed my hand your palm was chill.

But not for naught the winds sang in the dark:
The storm's white horse will rear to its full height,
And suddenly midnight will strike a spark
From the immobile fir tree's malachite.

1946

"The Bear Has Shifted"

The bear has shifted—lies on his left side now.
Winter will soon be leaving at a trot.
Why must I still keep staring at the window
And wait—oh, will he come or not?

The January night is dark, is bitter.
I do not hear your horse come galloping
Up to the porch. Here on my palm a snowflake
Alights like a wee moon upon the wing.

But I believe in joy. Streams will be ringing
Like bells. And we shall meet, come time and tide.
Let winter rage! Deep in his lair, it's certain,
The bear has shifted—he lies on his left side.

1946

July

Now ripened berries fill
The forest clearing's lap.
Sternly the fir trees watch
Over the valley's nap.

Bright scarlet strawberry juice
Has stained the reindeer's lips;
While, in his antlers caught,
A bluebell swings and dips.

1960

PYOTR KOMAROV

Goat

A Taiga Etching

A she-goat comes to drink,
Only an osier moves;
Upon a stone she sets
Her tiny chiseled hooves.

She stoops toward the stream
And pricks her ears in brief
Panic, then shyly plucks
A little willow leaf.

1944-45

Oak

It stands, a sentinel, on the broad floodland,
Guarding the rye; from root to tip
The tree is stanch; and not for naught each acorn
Looks like a cartridge in its clip.

1949

NIKOLAY RYLENKOV

"Get Up"

Get up—a kerchief thrown across your shoulders,
Go out into the meadows: overhead,
Above the surging flood of the white buckwheat,
See where the sails of a great dawn are spread.

The blame will lie with us and that entirely
If, as we watch it riding there on high,
Happiness, slowing slightly as it nears us,
Under such sails as these should pass us by.

1946

"Thin Ice—Transparent Mica"

Thin ice—transparent mica—in the fields
Glazed the rain puddles overnight. I go
Outdoors into the cold, but why I make
For winter's threshold now, I scarcely know.

I like to wander where the summer paths
Are lost; drawing a breath deep as a sigh,
I break the ice—transparent mica—and
Scoop from a puddle a handful of sky.

1957

YAROSLAV SMELYAKOV

The Kremlin Firs

It was truly a happy
idea,
this bringing
to Red Square
not the tearful wake
of willows,
nor the silvery fairy tale
of birches.

Let the somber
Kremlin fir trees
stand quietly, quietly,
at dawn,
sharp-crested
children of snowstorms,
our memorial
to that January day.*

Their austere attire
is after our heart,
and so is their silent
beauty,
the constancy
of their stern branches,
the unbending line
of the Siberian trunks.

1953

* Lenin died on January 21, 1924.

NIKOLAY YEGOROV

After the Rain

Generous and clean, it watered the warm earth;
now the tongue's still that wagged so loud and free,
and its departing gesture is to hang
a lucent necklace on the linden tree.

But, all indifferent to such costly gifts,
she lets the diamonds on her branches go,
and does not even watch them as they fall
into the small blue puddle there below.

1955

VIKTOR BOKOV

Winter

Roofs are white beads upon a little string.
A kolkhoz village. January. Days
Like this are plunged in such a quietude;
And everywhere frost pours its misted glaze.

Columns of smoke aligned against the sky
As straight as soldiers on parade: a frieze.
In rapid counterpart to those stiff ranks
The flicker of schoolboys racing by on skis.

Upon the river, sand bars, deeps, and shoals,
Lying as stilled as if beneath a spell,
Ice thrones it in the manner of a prince,
Having robbed the stream of every tinkling bell.

Among humped contours blunted by the snow,
Like the first flecks of crimson that one marks
When dawn is breaking, bullfinches at play
Glow here, glow there, a flock of burning sparks.

There is a snowdrift swimming toward the river
To drink from a black ice hole if it may.
Then, in the sky beyond, a sudden glitter
Where pigeons flash from somewhere far away.

They drown in silvery dust in the pure blue.
Now there is only blue, pallid and still,
Where chill, filling the air, bites to the bone,
Where the whole universe is blank with chill.

Spread smoothly over meadow, roof, and road,
That white felt blanket makes a sparkling throw.
Winter has this for dowry, that is like
A fairy tale of long and long ago.

Snow underfoot. Snow underneath the runners.
The world is walled in snow, faceless and deep.
The winter crops are breathing quietly.
The hayricks are all fast asleep.

1956

VADIM KOROSTYLEV

Baby Camel

Leaning against the long legs of a camel
Stands, not a baby camel, but a marvel.

He has not lived more than a little while—
This yellow hump on downy matchstick legs.

He has not lived more than an hour perhaps,
Yet he can yell, and in a haughty bass.

What dignity is in the little head
That reaches out toward the saksaul* twigs.

The nose is a black patch that, twitching, sniffs
The thick sweet smell, the homely smell of milk.

He totters off. If he walks clumsily,
In every movement there is camel pride,

Declaring: I will be a richer yellow,
Carry a grander hump than all my brothers.

1956

* A small leafless tree growing in the deserts of Central Asia.

MARGARITA ALIGER

Two

And so once more they quarrel in the trolley;
Their anger, flaring, will not let them see
That they stand stripped before a crowd of strangers.
Helpless and hurt, I watch them enviously.

They do not know their happiness; there's no one
To show it to them, tell them what is plain:
Think! You are next each other, breathing, speaking,
And it can still come right for you again.

1956

"I Keep On Paying"

I keep on paying, pay and pay,
For every step I pay,
But then it happens!—Oh, to live
Just one unpaid-for day.
And life is friendly, bountiful,
But slyly keeps account,
So in a month, or in a year,
I'm billed twice the amount.

1961

Third Spring

The tree, storm-struck a fortnight since:
a stump half dead, color of soot,
denies decapitation
and puts forth a green shoot.

Oh, how inevitably life
returns, by ways we do not know.
Within me a new tenderness,
if timidly, attempts to grow.

Confusion will not let me speak;
I shield it from rough winds of spring,
but dare not put a name to it,
and cannot help the nameless thing.

1961

VERONICA TUSHNOVA

"Tonight Sleep Will Be Slow"

Tonight sleep will be slow
in coming, and when it comes will bring
bad dreams: I said no
when you wanted to give me
spring—I refused the spring.

But all night long
it sings and sings and keeps
at its little song
that will not
let me sleep;
how can you command it to go,
say: "Be still!"
You wanted so
to give me spring,
the bitter wind that blows,
dawn in the woods, the small drops strung below
the boughs, the snow's turquoise tinge,
the icicles' brittle fringe,
ask me again—
I'll not say no.

1964

VASILY FYODOROV

Art

We talked of beauty, debated
What it means.
With infant naïveté, he said,
"I'm for a left art. You?"
"For a left art, yes,
But not left of the heart."

1958

ALEXANDER TVARDOVSKY

The Starling

On the porch a trooper marvels
At a starling: "Take my word,
There is something to that fellow,
Yes, a starling's quite a bird.

"In this scorched and blistered garden
That's attached to our new base,
All day long the chap is busy,
Keeps at work about the place;

"He's rebuilding, he's repairing,
Just as if to signify:
War or no war, still the thing is
To increase and multiply."

1945

To My Critics

Teach me, would you, my critics, give me a facile
Lesson: yes, according to you
I must be deaf, blind, shape my verses
By what I may and what I may not do.
But forgive me if I foresee a future
Hour, oh, not near, when you'll hector me,
You yourselves, questioning, insisting:
Poet, where were you? What was it you did see?

1958

NIKOLAY ASEYEV

Honey and Venom

July is commencing to breathe and to flower
with blossoms that hang from the branches of lime,
and the numerous murmurous bees should be named as
the poets that each of them is—it is time;

for these bees raise as one bee a simmering music
that neither pauses nor ceases nor slows,
filling the hives' common coziness featly
with a sweet store, as the swarm comes and goes.

And he who dares to disturb their long labor
or jar the hum of that honey-smooth strain,
feeling the fiery sting will discover
the pleasure of honey brings venomous pain.

1960

LEONID MARTYNOV

"A Snake in Passing"

A snake in passing slipped me this remark:
To each his Fate! But I'm not in the dark
About how wrong it is to live this way—
To twist and turn, always to supplely stray.

1949

"Around Us Sounds Abound"

Around us sounds abound—you'd seize
And alter them by force? Pursue them
With letters, with piano keys:
They will escape—you'll not subdue them.

> One thing is certain—there are tales
> That we do hear—but no endeavor
> To trap them in trite words avails,
> That way is sealed to you forever.

Speech turns refractory and shreds
Discourse: the gamut's order shatters.
Notes capsize, walk upon their heads,
To catch the real voice of real matters.

> And for long years somewhere someone
> Has worked to smooth, emend, erase.
> Well, then . . . God grant that on soft stone
> He yet may leave a fish's trace.

"The Apple's Frozen"

The apple's frozen:
Sticks to the peddler's tray;
And not one kiosk shows a flower today;
The skating rink is open, and the way
Up to the ski run is knee-deep in snow;
The skies are cloud-swept—can the snow delay?
A pine log crackles where the stove's aglow. . . .
All this adds up: spring isn't far away.

"And Once Again"

And once again
The birds
Wheel in the sky:
Doves reeling,
Titmice, swifts, pewees.

Still, there are limits, there's a ceiling,
There are landmarks and boundaries.

Eh, you,
Don't rush about inanely!
Shoulder to shoulder, fall in line;
Choose any order, show it plainly:
Fly in formation, by design!

And yet
The fleet ones turn
And, sheering
In dizzy motion, whirl and round,
As if they were beyond all steering
By anyone upon the ground.

How reprehensible!
How painful!
No one to check them: there they fly,
Disdainful of control, or heedless,
As in millenniums gone by!

Enough!
I will step in:
I'll radio orders, discipline them, scotch
Their antic flight.

And yet,
I can't resolve to intervene.
I stand
And watch.

Ovidiopolis

Yes, Ovid,
I had a view of it:
Your little Ovidiopolis.
It was quiet, except for the wind banging the wickets;
Hard to say which was more trying, the quiet, or the wind,
Flying from the Euxine over the Dniester estuary.

I know, Ovid,
It was not very merry
Sitting at those smoky fires with the Getae in sheepskins,
You so badly wanting to talk,
Balked by their uncouth language.

Talk about what?
The Parrhasian Virgin, Callisto.
She twined her icy breath with what little heat remained
Under this moon, that waxes and wanes
Above a land that for you was the bleak end of the world.
For us, seeing that winters here, if sharp, are short,
This is the South, the gate beyond which an eternal summer
        waits.
But more than half converted to your view,
I gave a bitter laugh,
And echoed your lament:
"Here, alone and lonely, cast on the shores of the seven-
        mouthed Dniester,
I have come under the spell of the Parrhasian Virgin. . . ."

Perhaps we can toy with the name
And lay claim to it as par-Russian?
Perhaps she'd a bit of the look of those Russian virgins to come,
One of the sisters now traipsing along the estuary,
Snaring the songs of the world on their pocket transistors,
Hanging about the ferry,
Trying to catch a taxi to Odessa. And this Odessa screams
As noisily as the city of your dreams, your Rome.

But you, crouched at your fire with the ancient Getae,
So homesick, you would just as soon be dead,
My poor old Ovid,
This never entered your head!

1963

ARSENY TARKOVSKY

Field Hospital

The table faced the light. I lay
Head down, lay like a carcass being weighed,
My throbbing soul was hanging by a thread,
And I beheld myself as from a distance.
I did not need a makeweight there to match
A greasy market counterbalance.

                                This
Took place in the middle of a shield of snow,
That showed some chips along its western margin,
A region of unfreezing marshes, of
Trees that stood awkwardly with their legs broken,
And helpless little railroad stations: wreckage
Like battered skulls now tenantless and black
Beneath the snow that capped them more than once,
Yes, even thrice.

                        That day time was suspended,
All watches stopped, then, and the souls of trains
No longer flew along the low embankments,
Lanterns unlit, on gray flippers of steam,
And raven weddings were not celebrated,

There were no blizzards, no thaws in the limbo
Where I lay in my shame, in nakedness,
In blood, outside the gravitation field
Of any future.

                    But now the shield of blinding snow
Started to move and turn upon its axis,
And flying low came seven blaring planes,
And on my body, like the bark of trees,

Gauze stiffened, and blood, the blood of another
Flowed slowly from a flask into my veins,
And like a fish flung upon sand I breathed,
Swallowing the micaceous, earthy, hard,
Cold, blessed air.

My lips were blistered, dry with fever sores,
I still had to be spoon-fed, and even yet
I was unable to recall my name.
But on my tongue spontaneously King David's
Vocabulary came to life.

                    And then
The snow melted away, and early spring,
Reaching up delicately on tiptoe
Swathed the wakening trees with her green kerchief.

                              1964

BORIS SLUTZKY

Housing Construction

A roof overhead. In the corner a stove that smokes.
But then, there are three more corners, all for you.
Two square windows. At night you will see the dark,
And the sun by day,
                    if you haven't too much to do.
A roof overhead!
              Off with the right boot! Off
With the left!
            Into the corner's cozy paradise!
A roof overhead!
A roof overhead!
When there's a roof overhead, oh, but it's nice!

                           1960

NIKOLAY ZABOLOTZKY

The Face of the Horse

Animals do not sleep. In the darkness of night
They stand like a stone wall above the world.

The sloping head of a cow with its smooth horns
Makes a noise in the straw.
The rocky forehead draws
The primeval cheekbones apart, weighing the head down,
And the inarticulate eyes
Heavily roll round.

The face of a horse is beautiful and aware.
He listens to the talk of leaves and of stones.
He is all attention! Understands the beasts' howls
And the nightingales' undertones in the tattered grove.

And knowing everything, with whom can he share
His marvelous visions?
The night is deep. In the dark firmament
The constellations rise.
And the horse stands sentry—a knight,
The wind plays with his fine hair;
His eyes burn: two vast worlds, his mane
Is spread like the cloak of a king.

And if man could truly see the horse's marvelous face,
He would tear out his own helpless tongue
And give it to the horse.
Of course, the horse deserves speech!

What words we would hear:
Words big as apples. Thick, like honey or curds.

Words that pierce like flame,
And that winging into the soul, like fire into a hovel,
Light up its mean furnishings.
Words that do not die,
Words that nourish songs.

But now the stable is empty.
The trees, too, have vanished.
Stingy morning has furled the mountains,
And opened the fields for work.
And the horse, caged in shafts,
Pulling a covered cart,
Looks with submissive eyes
At the stock-still mysterious world.

[1926] 1961

"All That the Soul Had Known"

All that the soul had known seemed dispersed, forgotten,
And I lay on the grass like a lump, sorry and bored,
And a flower arose above me, its beautiful body plain,
And a grasshopper stood beside it, tinily keeping ward.

And then I opened my book, a large, well-bound volume,
To the frontispiece: a sketch of a plant that, black and dead
As it was, from the silent page held out to Nature
The truth of the flower or its lie, not to be gainsaid.

And, astonished, the living flower looked at its presentment
As if it would understand that alien wisdom, till
Its leaves trembled with thought's unfamiliar effort
And with the inexpressible thrust of the will.

And the grasshopper lifted his trumpet and abruptly Nature
        wakened,
And sad Creation intoned a paean to Mind that was heard
Abroad, and in my old book the flower's printed image
Stirred, so that my heart in answer stirred.

1936

"Nature That Bred Me"

Nature that bred me taught me austerity.
It is enough if I find at my feet the rayed
Downy ball of a seeding dandelion,
Or come on a plaintain lifting its tough blade.

The commonest plants are the dearest, every one;
These, more than the rest, reach into and sting
The heart as you watch their leaves start to unfurl
When the dawn light awakens in the spring.

In the country of daisies, where, at the edge,
The stream, choking, sings, I would choose to lie
All night long until morning, hour on hour,
With my face upturned to greet the sky.

Life in a torrent of luminous dust would flow,
Flow through the foliage, and from the heavens' height
The misty stars would unloose their radiance,
Flooding the shrubs with an unearthly light.

And, listening to noises of spring among
The enchanted grasses, joyfully sleepless,
I would lie through the night alone, and think long thoughts
Of fields and forests in their boundlessness.

1953

From Spring at Miskhor*

1 Judas Tree

When, suffering from a chill, old Mount Ay-Petri
Towers, its flanks and summit hoar,
The crooked little Judas tree is blooming
Redly along the southern shore.

* Crimean seaside resort.

Spring wanders in the neighborhood, already
The valleys know that she is near,
Where, filled with perfidy's familiar poison,
And grief and loss, the flowers peer.

1953

At the Seashore

The scent of savory, acrid, dry, is mingled
With the Crimea's sleepy noons for me,
And with this cypress, with this house that presses
Close to the rock face, and will always be.

The sea conducts the concert that the billows
Perform by heart; space is a sounding board;
Brushing the cliff, sound soars, while echo, dancing
Among the stones, flings her bright song abroad.

Upon the heights are traps set by acoustics:
The lisp of distant streams here gains in power;
The boisterous storms boom with cannons' thunder,
And here a girl's kiss opens like a flower.

Dawn, and the whistling of a throng of titmice;
The scarlet on the heavy grapes gleams sharp.
Time loiters here. And children gather savory,
Grass of the steppe, near the immobile scarp.

1956

From Last Love

1 Thistles

Someone, it seems, brought in a bunch of thistles
And set it on the table there for me.
A conflagration rages there, a crimson
Round dance of fires spinning boisterously.

These stars surrounded by their bladed prickles,
These splashes of a northern dawn amaze
The room, like bells that moan and fling out thunder,
And deep within, how lanternlike they blaze!
This also is an image of the cosmos,
An organism built of rays, the glare
Of an unfinished battle, the sharp glitter
Of lifted swords that thrust into the air.
This is a tower of fury and of glory,
Where blade strikes blade, where, with what savage art,
A bunch of bristling flowers, bloody-headed,
Are cut indelibly into my heart.
Into my breast, wedgelike, a thorn is reaching;
Her beautiful sad gaze in vain denies
The hour of parting we await together,
While all my light comes from her quenchless eyes.

1956

VIKTOR KOCHETKOV

"The Battle Raged"

The battle raged. Earth seethed
With fires, fiercely bright.
The world was narrowed to
The groove of the gun sight.
But we,
Resolved, armed with strong faith, we hurled
Forward, and gave back its old
Dimensions to the world.

1960

Quatrain

Posted where all alarms converge, how vainly
I look for respite that the times deny.
As if one man alone were answerable
For the whole planet, and that man were I.

1960

NIKOLAY PANCHENKO

From A Soldier's Poems

4 *"We Who Went"*

We who went, leaving no offspring,
were out of luck, you may well say:
old men snatched our girls like helpless
captives, who could not tell them nay.
Boys with evil minds were the ones
to take the women and have their fun,
called them old hags and quickly dropped them,
picked up the young, as if they were tarts;
no defenders came to the rescue,
there were no guards to take their part.
The guards lie quiet under the turf,
their bones are for the roots to devour.
Little girls fathered by other men
take them songs and flags and flowers.

1961

7 *"There Are Long-lived Generations"*

There are long-lived generations.
Not my own. Before it was full-grown

It got a soldier's ration,
Shouldered a pack and a rifle,
Heaved, like a sack, the country on its back,
And stepped, abruptly adult,
Into war!
Behind it lay a past it had not built,
A future that it would not build—before.
But if my generation had not been,
What, then, would you be,
History?

1961

ANTONINA BAYEVA

Meadowsweet Is Blossoming

No sooner did the birch half open its buds
than hasty marsh tea
                began to blossom in the taigá,
and purple willows grew stalks
                  for clusters gray with pollen.
A little later
         in the floodlands of the Tobol
meadowsweet, too, rose, slightly, on tiptoe,
to be taller
         if by half an inch only.
Autumnal rains
         had drenched the roots;
all through the winter it was under snow,
ferocious blizzards whipped it,
long frosts chilled it to the marrow. . . .

It bore all that,
            perked up,
and it is dandling
                on resilient thin twigs
flowers that look like birdcherry blossoms.

1962

YURY SKORODUMOV

Rain

The day began with a good-humored sunrise,
And wore on cheerfully;
The weather was
Now clear and windless,
Now showers coming down in bucketfuls.

Straight,
Without the swank of lightnings and of rainbows,
They burst out of the massive clouds,
Descended on the kolkhoz orchard vertically,
And minutes later ceased abruptly.

Then again horizons brightened,
And up above the dimming waters—
Colors:
Orange and yellow,
And, a bit higher,
Pale blue.

And in the sunset glow,
Like gold-flecked nets,
Winds are hung out to dry
On maples and on telegraph wires.

1962

YEVGENY VINOKUROV

"The Goths Were Being Baptized"

The Goths were being baptized.
                              Like men doomed
They waded in, till they stood shoulder-deep,
Their swords held high in their unchristian fists:
Those fists, at least, unbaptized they would keep.

Whatever the commandments preach to us,
Meekness that knows no limits must be wrong.
I am resolved to hold my fist as high.
I shall be generous. But may it be strong.

1961

"I Feel Essential Reason"

I feel essential reason lies in b e i n g,
I sense, I know, I fully fathom it,
Shouting with all my fervent flesh in protest
Against non-being: I do not submit.

My organism is, as it were, an organ
Whose resonance tells life's glory. How possibly
Can I not be? An age is mine, unbounded—
Not anything can ever destroy me.

I am prepared to probe all, to endure all.
The speech of things my very blood receives.
My faith is limitless, my feeling—truth.
The body irrefutably believes.

1961

"Out in the World"

Out in the world, alone, a man went walking,
Wrapped his coat round him, raised his collar, set
His back against the wind upon the corner,
And, hunching himself, lit a cigarette.

Entered the park. A pond, little and greenish.
In freshly painted boats, the moorings lay.
Whistling, he broke a long twig from a willow,
Slapped it against his leg as if in play.

Spat from the wooden dock into the water,
Spat lazily, without malice, for a whim.
Indeed, nothing had happened, just, abruptly
He knew, you see, that life was done, for him.

[*1963*]

"I've Always Understood"

I've always understood eternity
Is a bad business, very, very bad.
You joke with it, and then, my boy, you're sunk.
Maybe it's better not to think of it?

No matter how you try to handle it,
No matter how you twist or measure it,
Split it or bray it, stretch or crumple it,
You can do nothing with it, that's for sure.

All right, then, let it stare in at the window.
Well, there's an eyeful for you—a big deal?!
In whose way is it, eh? Out there, far off,
And all alone.

1964

"I'm A Human Being"

I'm a human being. I ask you to love me.
Here are my two eyes. The light in them is fed
From within. Each moves in its orbit.
And here's my nose. Freckles, more than one blackhead.

I'm a human being. My image is God's.
Here He is. Here I am. Which is which you can't tell on a bet.
Now the mouth smiles. Now it is torn by an outcry.
Again, the teeth are clamping a cigarette.

I'm a human being. For that reason only
I ask you to love me. My life is a guarding of
A source of light, deep down, in nether darkness.
I'm a human being. I ask for your love.

1964

"No Matter"

No matter how it was,
I'm sure, I'm sure, I'm sure,
Although I know that this
Can never be—and yet!

Long years will pass, and then
One day the door will creak,
And, standing back of me,
Breathless, you'll blindfold me
With your soft hands.

1964

"It's Over"

It's over. I've recovered. Gaiters.
The knapsack holds a loaf. A clout
Is wrapped about some salt. By grasping
The doorjamb lightly, I've walked out.

All that I needed was a fortnight
For these plain features to acquire
Refinement that perhaps has power
Before which beauty must retire.

Fierce suffering has touched my forehead
With thoughtfulness that mocks the wise,
Drawn lines beside my mouth, and swollen
The weary bags beneath my eyes.

I hardly kept my feet—a shadow.
Where were you, soul, before? No doubt
Now of your presence in my body—
As the loaf's in the knapsack, the salt in the clout.

1964

"Spring"

Spring. I'm fifteen.
I write verse.
I'm preparing to bus to the suburb where the pine woods are.
To tramp the damp paths
With a notebook.

From the front door I emerge
Into the brick-walled yard.
I lift my eyes:
There, far off, in the ice hole
The blue infinite
Shimmers like water.
But I see something else.
Through every window I see girlish legs.
Window-cleaning. Spring house-cleaning, washing
Is under way.
Spring scrubbing of floors!
Like Greek festivals
When they harvest the grapes!
Bare arms.
Hair pinned in a topknot.
Skirts tucked up.
Knees and elbows glisten.

I meditate the mystery of the curve.
Oh, the curves of the human body!
I lower my eyes.
I cross the yard.
It is thick with clotheslines hung with laundry.
A huge exhibition of intimate things.
A giant profanation of femininity.
Here two colors triumph:
Sky-blue and pink.
Carnality, rioting shamelessly,
Has raised these two as a banner,
Having craftily stolen them from naïveté.
I make an effort
To fight my way to the street.
Having dodged a bed sheet,
I dive under a chemise,
I surface.
I lift my eyes.
There, far off, in the ice hole,
Shimmers, like water, the sky-blue
Infinite.

I heave a sigh of relief,
But I see there, too, a floating cloud,
Curved
Like a woman.

1964

"Sometimes"

Sometimes, with friends, while I'm tormenting
The lemon in my cup of tea,
I startle, too abruptly sensing
Time's flight, immense eternity.

Then well I know that we all orbit
In boundlessness. Oh, could we flit
Beyond the humdrum daily cycle,
And soaring, rise up over it!

Launched on the universe's mid-stream,
To swing in boundlessness—to give
Yourself to air too rare for breathing,
But where you'd *live*.

1964

She

She sits down for a bite; halving the slice, she
Commands: "Eat!" I obey! It's tyranny!
She rattles pots, the goddess. Later, pauses
To read a book. Then sweeps with energy.

She strolls barefoot, my jacket on her shoulders.
Sings in the kitchen, mornings, who knows why.
Love? Never! What a notion! Don't believe it!
But if she left, I'd die.

1964

YEVGENY YEVTUSHENKO

"I'm of Siberian Stock"

I'm of Siberian stock.
Wild garlic I ate with my bread,
and as a boy
         I towed
the ferry just like a man.
The cables were steel: my hands
were on fire.
A muscular fellow,
               big-browed,
I was a riveter, and
with a shovel
         I dug
deep, where they told me to dig.
They didn't bawl me out,
didn't talk rot,
they put an axe in my hands,
like it or not, taught me to work.
And if they beat me when
the firewood I cut was no good,
they did as they should,
out of love, wishing me well.
I sweated blood,
bowed under a sack.
I worked with a scythe,
with chopper and pickaxe.
I fear nobody's lip;
there's no heartache I fear.
My hands are bruised,
my grip strong as a vise.

There's nothing in the world
that I don't dare. I grin
at an enemy,
because whatever it is, I'm fit,
I can handle it.

                              1954

"I Lie Upon Damp Earth"

I lie upon damp earth and hug
A spade, and let the minutes pass,
A blade of grass between my lips,
A rather sourish blade of grass.

In ground so devilishly hard
Spades break before they can strike deep;
And how I long to fall asleep,
But you are not allowed to sleep.

"You can't get on your legs at all,
Just look at the poor dear!" she hoots:
A girl in a blue sleeveless shirt,
Her overalls stuck in her boots.

As luck will have it, she strikes up
A song that lilts, a lilting song:
"I'll find my love, and when I do
Won't I torment him all day long! . . ."

Boldly she flashes her blue spade,
Jangles her earrings, for a stunt
Flings out a sudden word so raw
Even the boys look up and grunt.

They laugh, the lot!
                    "Eh, what a snake!
Well, Anka,
          how she hands it out!"
The currant bushes and the stars
May know, as I know without doubt

That, past the intoxicated bushes,
Pushing the towering grass aside,
She enters the night woods with me,
Moving as with a drunken stride,

And that she drops her swarthy arms,
Clumsy, as if her pulses failed,
And in the darkness speaks to me
Beautiful words, and veiled.

1956

"You Whispered"

You whispered as you asked again,
"And afterward, what then?
               What then?"
There stood, unmade, the tumbled bed,
Plainly you were discomfited.
But now you trip along in town,
Your chin held high, without a frown,
Your bangs, my dear with ginger hair,
Pert as the nailhead heels you wear,
And your eyes sparkle mockingly,
Commanding:
            don't confuse with me
that other one,
           that naked, weak
creature,
      like a victim, meek.
But this is poppycock. I say
you still belong to yesterday,
shamefaced
         and pitiful
             and shy,
and hot as fever where you lie.
Come, pray, what story will you weave
and how compel me to believe

another woman lay there, tender
and pitiful in her surrender,
whispering as she asked again,
"And afterward, what then?

                What then?"

                    1959

"To Me You Are as to a Ship"

To me you are as to a ship
Its very ribs and keel.
I love you to those breadths and heights
Where distances unreel.

I love you with the whole round earth,
And with the outer skies.
I catch you in each rustle's lisp,
And in all silences.

You have me, all of me. Henceforth
My nearest are just two,
Two who are one: my native town,
Zima, and, dearest, you.

You and the town: my family,
A home of no mean worth—
That was my birthplace, and in you
I also knew a birth.

"My Darling"

My darling will drive up, embrace me:
still holding me, all eyes and ears,
she'll notice all the trivial changes,
and understand my hidden fears.

From the black spurts of rain, the darkness,
letting the cab door swing, she'll tear
into the yard, all joy and longing,
and run up the ramshackle stair.

She'll run in, drenched, not knocking, take
my head between her hands; before
you know it, her blue coat will slide
happily from chair to floor.

In the Kashveti* Church

Aswarm with rowdy, disconcerting
$\qquad\qquad\qquad\qquad$ saints, angels,
that wall, I concede,
rears too huge an eyeful there before me
to squeeze into a rigid creed.
Hiding my wariness,
$\qquad\qquad$ a savage,
thickheaded, I know well enough
the great church doesn't frame the frescoes,
it's a detail:
$\qquad\qquad$ they're the big stuff.
The hand of Lado Gudiashvili,
having a space to occupy,
filled it with people who were sinners,
not with those hovering on high.
He's no mud-slinger, he's no scoffer,
he's tarred with the same brush, it seems,
perhaps a god,
$\qquad\qquad$ perhaps a sinner,
an angel, or
$\qquad\qquad$ perhaps a fiend!

* A district of Tbilisi (formerly Tiflis), capital of Soviet Georgia.

We artists,
            poets,
                    we creators
of covert change, we've certainly
crammed countless walls with our own frescoes
like this church of Kashveti.
We who are players—icon-painters,
diddled the masters, did 'em brown,
contriving to accept their orders,
then turn everything upside down.
No matter what we risked, how often,
or how we fought, against what odds,
we painted gods as human beings,
in human beings
            we saw
                    gods!

                                        1959

Talk with an American Writer

"They told me: 'You're a daring man!'
                                        Not true.
Daring I'm not.
            Simply, I could not stoop
To the behavior of that groveling group:
It is degrading to do what they do.

            I had no wish to be a man who made
            Foundations shake.
                        I laughed at falsity;
            I wrote—that's all!
                        I never blabbed; for me
            It was enough
                        to call a spade a spade.

Yes, I defended decent folk.
                        Then, too,
I branded the pretentious,
                    made short shrift

—But that's one's duty—
                    of those with no gift;
This is audacity in people's view.

    Those who come after us, how shamefully,
    As they uproot these horrors,
                                        they'll look back
    To the time,
                    the unbelievable,
                                the black
    Time, when plain candor
                            was called audacity."
                                        1960

A Knock at the Door

"Who's there?"
            "I'm old age.
                        Time I came to you, eh."
"Not now.
        I've got work.
                    I'm too busy today."
I wrote.
        Made some calls.
                        Took an omelette to stay
Me awhile. At the door
                    there was no one and nix.
Have my pals played a trick on me just for the kicks?
Was that the right name that I heard him say?
Not old age,
        but maturity came here, I lay,
Got fed up waiting,
                sighed, went away.

                                    1962

The Foreigner

In the seaport of Archangel,
foreign ships early and late,
foreign sorrow in that seaport,
foreign fate.

Like a rook, a young one, swarthy,
all the white night through, you lie
huddled beside Peter's statue,
small Greek seaman, and you cry.

Not in any foreign fashion,
on the dusty square you smear,
drunkenly, with dirty knuckles,
that dark face of yours with tears.

Did the skipper bawl you out, boy?
Someone in your family die?
Maybe you've had too much vodka?
Nothing's right, you don't know why?

What on earth has happened to you?
Greek, where is it you were hit?
What has happened is quite simple:
You are human—and that's it.

There's a sailor from a schooner,
Russian; liquored up, he slumps,
lurching, copper-faced, no question
but the fellow's in the dumps.

Down he sits beside the Greek now:
"How about a drink, chum, eh?"
And into his leather jacket
His huge rough hand makes its way.

Deft and serious, from the pocket
pulls a pint-interpreter,
bangs the bottle's neck against the
bench; the Greek does not demur.

Arm in arm, the two together
sit in silence there and booze,
as into the farther distance
stare Greek grief and Russian blues.

1965

YELENA AKSELROD

At Night

Nightfall was cold, the town felt so chilly
Night brought a blanket to answer its need,
Wrapped it in snow, spread so gently, so stilly,
Then herself brightened at such a good deed.

1962

RIMMA KAZAKOVA

"It Is Awkward"

It is awkward for horses, for how can they manage
A simple embrace: without arms they are lost;
Yet they understand the meaning of friendship,
And of separation, when it hurts most.

They stand there alone in the dew-drenched meadow,
In the wide, naked, speechless world, together,
And they are quiet, they ask no questions,
Leaning their big heads one on the other.

1963

NOVELLA MATVEYEVA

"That Shot"

That shot was the smart crack of a herder's whip.
The road through the woods is violet and holds warmth.
Above, the leaves, crisscross, are a black sieve
For the filtering of the sunset's gold.

It's growing dark. . . . The stump's rings melt away.
Like slag's warm rustle, the dry noise of the firs.
Between their trunks in a bath of rosy fire
Midges, like crumbs of darkness, driven, skirr.

And still I am living in the day that's gone;
The dance is over, I dance with my thoughts, now play
Is over, and chase the fire as it ebbs,
"Sun, listen, Sun, I beg of you, stay!"

But now—night, its breath hot as the promise
That tomorrow too will be fine. And I feel within
The darkness, somewhere, the pulse of the sun,
Hidden, like blood under the skin.

1962

Smoke

A thicket.
   Frost.
      The air coarse as a brush.
But light is tender, winterily shy.
The houses are withdrawn.
           Alone from the red chimneys gushes
Smoke that rolls freely, soaking in the sky.
Like memories of distant days,
        that slept for years,
In a hushed pause it scans itself, and then
Fades into twilight . . .
       but not before it draws
Upon the sky soft images of warmth . . .
           itself erasing them. . . .
I love the smoke at dusk, in frosty silence!
It gives a pleasure somehow cordial
       to just glance at the smoke,
         think of a fire—
And . . . to resist
    as comfort calls.

             1964

VLADIMIR TSYBIN

"You and I"

You and I stand
                almost
        face to face!
Silently
I shout into your eyes.
My shout tears past your pupils,
        passes a thousand landmarks—
have you left for a month?
Or forever?
How long have I been hallooing in vain?
I'm prepared to wade across years
as if they were a ford—
And I shall see
        in you, living there in darkness,
a hundred others—
none of them you!
You are their stepmother,
        ready to curse!
You are a foreign land
        where I am sure to die,
a land from which no one sends me a word.
Words—are twigs,
as soon as it rains: plop-plop.
They are a foreign land
whence a hundred eyes look—
        none of them you,
        a hundred words look,
        a hundred meetings
        and a hundred partings. . . .

A hundred partings,
like a hundred birches, grow there.
I want to descry you
        through the blue,
across a hundred yous I shout to you.
Halloo!

1964

ANDREY VOZNESENSKY

Fire in the Architectural Institute

Fire in the Institute!
It shoots through halls, through blueprints,
Like an amnesty sprinting through jails—
Fire! Fire!

Up the façade that's half asleep,
Shamelessly, rowdily,
Like a red-assed
                ape,
A roaring window soars.

We're primed for our diplomas,
Time we tackled our finals.
Sealed, in the closet,
My demerits crackle!

Sheets of drawing paper
Caper like a wounded fall of red leaves.
My stretchers burn, twisting, turning.
Cities are burning.

Same as a jar of kerosene:
Five summers, five winters gone up in flame. . . .
Karen, my joy,
Oy, we're burning!

Good-by, architecture!
Blaze sky-high,
Cow sheds with cupids and their bows,
District clubs, O so rococo!

O youth! Phoenix, silly filly,
Your diploma's flaming!
With a flirt of the short red skirt,
The tongue stuck out.

Good-by, outskirts—you've had your turn!
Life's a series of charred ruins.
We all burn out.
You live—you burn.
Tomorrow, scratching the finger suddenly,
The compass point will flash
Out of a handful of ashes and sting
Worse than a bee. . . .
It's all burnt to cinders,
All you hear is sighs.
Everything's—done for?
                    Goofy: everything's—begun!
Come on to the movies!

Anti-Worlds

The clerk Bukashkin is our neighbor.
His face is gray as blotting paper.
But like balloons of blue or red,
Bright Anti-Worlds
                    float over his head!
On them reposes, prestidigitous,
Ruling the cosmos, a demon-magician,
Anti-Bukashkin the Academician,
Lapped in the arms of Lollobrigidas.

But Anti-Bukashkin's dreams are the color
Of blotting paper and couldn't be duller.

Long live Anti-Worlds! They rebut
With dreams the rat race and the rut.
For some to be clever, some must be boring.
No deserts? No oases, then.
There are no women—
                    just anti-men.
In the forests, anti-machines are roaring.
There's the scum of the earth, as well as the salt.
If the earth broke down, the sun would halt.

Ah, my critics; how I love them.
Upon the neck of the keenest of them,
Fragrant and bald as fresh-baked bread,
There shines a perfect anti-head. . . .

. . . I sleep with windows open wide;
Somewhere a falling star invites,
And skyscrapers
                    like stalactites
Hang from the planet's underside.
There, upside down,
                    below me far,
Stuck like a fork into the earth,
Or perching like a carefree moth,
My little Anti-World,
                    there you are!

In the middle of the night, why is it
That Anti-Worlds are moved to visit?

Why do they sit together, gawking
At the television, and never talking?

Neither can understand a word.
How can they bear it? It's too absurd.

Neither can manage the least *bon ton.*
Oh, how they'll blush for it, later on!

Their ears are burning like a pair
Of crimson butterflies, hovering there. . . .

. . . A distinguished lecturer lately told me,
"Anti-Worlds are a total loss."
Still, my apartment-cell won't hold me.
I thrash in my sleep, I turn and toss.

And, radio-like, my cat lies curled
With his green eye tuned in to the world.

1961

The poem below, originally entitled "Evening Windows," and that immediately following it, are from a group sent by the author to a friend, N. Sukhanov, an architect. In the accompanying letter he said that these pieces were "connected not by subject, not by external similarity. They are fragments of a world that I have seen these last months. They are united by an internal musical theme. They were written at the same time. They are like the little towers of Basil the Blessed, all different, but, it seems to me, tied in an ensemble. Or like people whose faces are different but whose blood is the same. And the same rhythmical pulse."

Longjumeau is a suburb of Paris, where, in 1911, Lenin conducted classes for revolutionaries. Voznesensky gave the title "Longjumeau" to a sequence of poems about Lenin and his work there that he called an "epic."

"My Scarf, My Paris"

My scarf, my Paris,
silvery, with a cherry,
well, you've done plenty!

My scarf—the hairy Seine, how furry
the glitter of lights,

my Boulogne scarf, my shaggy fog,
headlights are racing on toward Monaco!

What are you whispering shrilly, hot one, scarf,
burning like the lit panel of a radio?

My scarf, Parisianly irreparable,
with a wild drop of blood?

That salesgirl with gray eyes,
what care she took to have you smartly tied,
the streets' reflection winking
upon her pinkie, as it tenderly grazed the carotid.

My scarf's electric: check!
I wear a stuffy city round my neck.

I'll tack it on the wall
as if it were a window at St. Cloud and Longjumeau,

beside it flaring brush strokes will declare
a slushy Moscow,
              dear Moscow.

                                        1963

"Lilac"

Lilac resembles Paris, burning
          with waspish windows—just to touch
the silver cluster of her mansions
          chilled to the marrow—that is much.

My beetling eyebrows buzz; ferocious
          with joy and longing, I devise
a way, like bees, to collect Paris
          in the pouches beneath my eyes.

                                        1963

"I'm Goya"

I'm Goya!
The enemy, gliding down upon naked fields,
          has pecked out my sockets: blindly the craters gaze.

I am grief.
I'm the groan
Of war, the embers of cities glowing
                    black on the snow of the year forty-one.

I'm hunger.
I'm the closed gullet
          of the woman who hangs there, her body a bell
                    tolling over the bare square.

I'm Goya!
O grapes
            of retribution! I soared like a shot going west,
                I, the ashes of an unbidden guest!

Into the memorial sky I hammered strong stars—
Like nails.
I'm Goya!

Siberian Bathhouses

Bathhouses! Bathhouses! The door bangs like a shot!
Women, no shift to the lot, jump into a drift.

From the heat, from the steam to the snow—
So, so!

Renoir would be crude
Trying to catch these Siberian nudes!

What madonnas! Those shoulders,
Those powerful rumps, molded
As if in cast iron
Blast furnaces spewed.

Breathless with running—
Here purity: snow's, fire's,
Is thee-and-thouing
Nakedness' purity.

A clean, frosty day.
We stand there, four fellows, steaming,
In sheepskins, blood and fire,
And make like stampeding those dames—what a game!

Oh, the scare!
Oh, into the hut
At full speed, like a cannon volley.
Ugh!

But golly! lingering, one, leaning against the jamb,
Will stoop
And with a laugh fling
A snowball at a boyfriend—bam!

Mountain Spring

The small heels clatter
like small hooves pattering
a girl
        runs down
to the spring to drink

and her waist gleams
more slithery than a snake flashing
and her little skirt splashes like spray
from a watering pot

the girl rocks with laughter
and wets her head
her purling forelock
and the water muttering daftly together

two lovely streams
who nestles near to whom?
and who here
            is the girl?
and who the spring?

Selling Watermelons

Moscow lies buried under watermelons.
Everywhere the surge of boundless freedom,
And the vendors' excitement smites the air
With an unbridled strength.

Stalls. Hubbub. The girls' kerchiefs.
Bursts of laughter. Wink and clink of coins.

Knives. Ace-shaped wedges.
Hey, uncle, look alive!

Who wants a watermelon?
It's about to burst!
All's juicy, luscious: the very bands
On the militia's caps and
The motorbikes that lean against the wall.

Fresh on the palate, the September air,
And as sonorous as a watermelon.

And just as gaily, in the same homely way
As the watermelons at the gate,
The earth is slewed around
In a shopping bag
Of latitudes and longitudes.

Bio-Bibliographical Notes

AKHMATOVA, ANNA (pseudonym of Anna Andreyevna Gorenko), was born in 1889 at a summer resort near Odessa. The daughter of a naval engineer, she spent most of her childhood and early youth at Tsarskoe Selo (now Pushkin), where she attended school, completing her secondary education in Kiev. She took university courses in law and in the humanities and traveled abroad. She was eighteen when her poems began to be published, her first book appearing in 1912, her sixth in 1923. In 1916 she moved to Petrograd (Leningrad), where she has lived ever since. Two years later she divorced her husband, the poet Nikolay Gumilyov, who was to be executed for alleged counterrevolutionary activities. While Akhmatova was out of sympathy with the Soviet regime, she did not expatriate herself.

At the height of the nightmarish period of purges, in 1937, two years after the arrest of her third husband (he died in 1942), her son was taken into custody. The young man was kept in prison for seventeen months before being confined to a concentration camp, and was not released until two years after Stalin's death. For three hundred hours his mother stood in the queues outside the Kresty prison in Leningrad to deliver food parcels for the prisoner and perhaps to catch a glimpse of him. Her experiences are recorded in "Requiem," a sequence of poems dedicated to the memory of the victims of the Red Terror. Composed between 1935 and 1943?, and provided with a brief foreword dated 1957, it was not published until 1963, and then under a Munich imprint. In 1940 a selection from her verse, including the poems written after the publication of her previous book, came out in Moscow, and three years later a similar work on a smaller scale was issued in Tashkent, to which she had been evacuated during the siege of Leningrad.

A Party edict dated August 14, 1946, condemned Akhmatova's poetry as decadent and likely to corrupt the youth, whereupon she was scurrilously denounced by a high-ranking Party functionary and expelled from the Writers' Union. She became a proscribed author, mentioned in print only as a horrible example. Since Stalin's death she has been an active contributor of lyrics to the monthlies. Two selections from her work were published under Soviet imprints in 1959 and 1961 respectively. On the occasion of her seventy-fifth birthday she was accorded public praise, and was allowed to travel to Sicily to receive the Etna–Taormina literary prize. More recently Oxford University has awarded her an honorary degree. She has joined the ranks of translators of verse from the languages of the Soviet minorities and "the people's democracies," and has also published a volume of renderings of ancient Korean poetry. Her own verse has been translated into many languages, including Japanese, and it is natural that some of her lyrics have been set to music.

AKSELROD, YELENA, born in 1934, studied at the Moscow Teachers' Institute. She began to publish verse in 1956 and brought out a book of poems in 1961.

ALIGER, MARGARITA IOSIFOVNA, was born in 1915 in Odessa. From 1934 to 1937 she attended the Maxim Gorky Literary Institute in Moscow. Her first book of verse appeared when she was twenty-three. It was followed by half a dozen other collections of lyrics. She has also written several long narratives in verse. One of them, about a Communist girl partisan hanged by the Germans, won her the Stalin Prize in 1943. The previous year she had joined the Party. During the war she was on the staff of the newspaper of the Soviet Air Force. The latest of several selections from her verse appeared in 1958. She has also translated poetry.

ANNENSKY, INNOKENTY FYODOROVICH, 1856–1909, a native of Siberia, was educated in the capital and became a high school teacher of Greek and Latin, eventually rising to the position of district school inspector. He was in his late forties when his first book of poems, *Quiet Songs*, made its appearance. *The Cypress Casket*, which contains his best work, was published posthumously, as was one more collection. He also wrote critical essays and translated all of Euripides' plays extant.

ASEYEV, NIKOLAY NIKOLAYEVICH, 1889–1963, was born into the family of an office worker. On completing his secondary education, he left his native provincial town for Moscow, where he wrote verse in the Futurist manner. After the Revolution he spent several years in the Far East. In 1922 he returned to the capital and became active in the "Left Front of the Arts," a group headed by his close friend, Mayakovsky. During the years of the New Economic Policy he was critical of the regime, but before long made peace with it, and the verse that he wrote for forty years or so is mainly of the approved political variety. In 1941 he was awarded the Stalin Prize for a poem about Mayakovsky. Several editions of his collected verse have appeared, the latest, in two volumes, dated 1959.

BAGRITZKY (Dzyubin), EDUARD GEORGIEVICH, 1895–1934, though the son of a poor Jewish tradesman, received a good general education in his native Odessa and studied to be a surveyor. At twenty he broke into print with some verse. He greeted the Revolution with enthusiasm and, since he was physically handicapped, fought for it chiefly with his pen. When his first book of verse appeared in 1928, he was already known as a poet and particularly as the author of a long dramatic poem posing the problem of allegiance to the Soviet regime against the background of the civil war in the South. In his few remaining years he brought out two more books of verse, wrote some rhymes for children, recast his dramatic poem as a libretto, and started a long narrative piece in his characteristic loose metre. He has to his credit a translation of Rimbaud's verse. A bedridden invalid, he went on working to the end. His collected poems were first published in 1938. Selections have been reprinted more than once.

BALMONT, KONSTANTIN DMITRIEVICH, 1867–1943, belonged to the landed gentry, his family claiming remote Scottish ancestry. He was expelled from the University of Moscow for participation in student disorders, and his first two books of verse, published respectively in 1890 and 1894, were in the tradition of civic poetry. A recrudescence of his youthful political ardor occurred during the upheaval of 1905–6. But those were just temporary deviations in a poetic career devoted to championing estheticism, individualism, and the other features of what went by the name of Modernism at the turn of the century. He traveled far and wide, his journeys carrying him to Egypt, Mexico, India, and the South Seas; exotic themes abound in his work. His stay abroad was somewhat of an exile, since certain revolutionary poems he had written in 1906 barred him from Russia. Returning home in 1913, he remained there through the World War and the Revolution, but in 1920 shook the dust of the Soviet Republic from his feet. He was a prolific poet and a translator from many languages, including English. He gave Russia a complete Shelley and a partial Whitman. The expatriate continued to turn out quantities of vacuous verse, not all of which, fortunately, was printed. He died in occupied France after years of insanity, a destitute and forgotten man.

BARATYNSKY, YEVGENY ABRAMOVICH, 1800–1844 (sometimes also transliterated as Boratynsky), was the scion of an aristocratic family with high court connections. At the age of sixteen he was expelled from the Corps of Pages, an exclusive military school, for having been party to a theft. The disgrace, which brought him to the verge of suicide, may have accentuated his gloomy temper, but the lapse itself seems to have been only the prank of an adolescent actually possessed of a keen moral sense. Disbarred from Government service other than that of a private, he entered the army in this capacity at the age of nineteen. The precocious youth was then already contributing poems to periodicals. Half a dozen years later he obtained his commission, whereupon he retired and settled in Moscow. He is the author of several long narratives in verse, but his reputation as a poet rests chiefly on his short lyrics. They were first collected in a volume that appeared in 1827. Two more such books came out during his lifetime. The circumstances of his mature life, including marriage and contacts with fellow writers, were paradoxically happy.

BAYEVA, ANTONINA, is the author of *The Road Ahead*, a book of poems published in 1961 in a Siberian town.

BEDNYI, DEMYAN (Demyan the Poor, pen name of Yefim Alexeyevich Pridvorov), 1883–1945, was the son of a railway porter. Wretched as were his early circumstances, he succeeded in getting a university education. He was thirty at the time of the appearance of his first book, a collection of political fables. A few of these had previously been printed in the organ of the Bolshevik faction of the Socialist Party, to which he belonged. When the Bolsheviks came to power, he fought for their cause as a member of the Red Army, but chiefly as a purveyor of numerous propaganda pieces, so that when in 1923 he received the Order of the Red Banner, it was as both soldier and poet of the Revolution. He went on steadily turning out reams of newspaper verse in which he championed the polices of the Soviet Government and attacked its enemies. On one occasion, failing to anticipate a twist in the Party line, he fell into official disfavor, but only for a short while. Indeed, he was practically the unacknowledged poet laureate of the regime. His lines mark the common grave of the revolutionary heroes on the Red Square. His work, which often verges on doggerel, is interesting chiefly as an almost day-to-day rhymed commentary on more than three decades of Soviet history. Its bulk may be judged from the fact that his collected output up to the year 1932 fills nineteen volumes. His collected works, in five volumes, came out under a Moscow imprint in 1953–54; a two-volume selection was published in 1959.

BELKIN, FYODOR PARFYONOVICH, of peasant stock, was born in 1911. Before attending the Literary Institute in Moscow he worked as a mason and carpenter. He is the author of several books of verse dealing chiefly with kolkhoz life, the earliest one dated 1947.

BELYI, ANDREY (pen name of Boris Nikolayevich Bugayev), 1880–1934, was reared in an academic atmosphere, a bone of contention between his worldly, neurotic mother and his father, a professor of mathematics at the University of Moscow. There the youth studied the natural sciences, while maintaining his interest in literature and philosophy. Between 1902 and 1908 he composed four "symphonies," collections of pieces of musically structured prose. During approximately the same period he brought out three books of poems, the last in 1909. He produced no more verse until after the Revolution, but wrote criticism, studies in style, and a body of remarkable, quasi-autobiographical fiction. Having for some time been attracted to theosophy, he and his wife lived for two years in Rudolf Steiner's anthroposophic colony at Dornach, Switzerland. Disappointed in the cult, they returned to Russia in 1916.

Belyi greeted the Revolution with frantic enthusiasm, and his poem "Christ Is Risen" (1918) was not unnaturally read as a pæan to it. In 1921, to escape the hardships of life under the new regime, he crossed the frontier, but after two years in Berlin the émigré returned to Soviet Russia, where he spent his last decade. During those years he wrote his memoirs, a valuable source for the cultural history of twentieth-century Russia up to the outbreak of the war. His obituary in *Pravda* had it that he died "a Soviet author." His verse was reprinted posthumously only once (1940).

BEZYMENSKY, ALEXANDER ILYICH, born in 1898, joined the Communist Party shortly after graduation from high school and took part in the revolutionary events of November 1917 in Petrograd. Later he was prominently associated with the Communist League of Youth. In 1920 he brought out his first collection of verse, and he was a charter member of the Moscow group of proletarian writers known as *October*. "Flesh of the revolution's flesh," as Trotsky called him, he has since written many lyrics and long poems dealing with the Revolution, the Party, and various aspects of Soviet life. He has also engaged in journalism. During the war he contributed to the front-line press and participated in the defense of Leningrad. A selection from his work appeared in 1958 in two volumes. In 1961 he published a narrative in verse directed against bureaucrats.

BLOK, ALEXANDER ALEXANDROVICH, 1880–1921, saw little of his eccentric father, a professor of public law with a gift for music, since shortly after the child's birth the parents separated. He was deeply devoted to his mother, who doted on him. A cultivated woman, interested in poetry, she was the daughter of the rector of Petersburg University, and it was in the home of this eminent, and opulent, scientist that the sensitive boy spent his childhood, breathing a hothouse air. He began writing verse almost as early as he remembered himself, but his first book of poems did not appear until he was twenty-four. He was then a graduate student of the humanities and a married man, his wife being the daughter of the celebrated chemist Mendeleyev. His contacts were mainly with fellow poets, especially Andrey Belyi, with whom he was to quarrel violently later. As the author of several lyrical dramas, he also moved in theatrical circles. The circumstances of the couple—the two were not to stay together long—at first moderate, were soon improved by legacies, and Blok was able to travel and give himself wholly to literary work. He composed lyrics chiefly, their number running into many hundreds; he wrote essays, mostly on literature and the theater, and also translated verse from several languages, including Armenian and Finnish. An edition of his collected poems in three volumes appeared in 1910–12. During his last decade he was busy, on and off, with a long, quasi-autobiographical narrative in verse, which remained unfinished.

By the time the World War broke out, his position as the foremost Russian poet of his generation was firmly established. He was drafted and went to the front, but he saw no action. On the fall of the monarchy, in February 1917, he served on a commission appointed by the Provisional Government. When, in October, the Bolsheviks seized power, he neither joined the Communist Party nor did he, like many of his fellows, expatriate himself. The Revolution presented itself to him as the inevitable catastrophe out of which the good society would arise. It was in this frame of mind, with the crashing of the old world in his ears, as he put it, that in January 1918 he composed "The Twelve," a long narrative poem, the first and perhaps the most significant evocation of the Revolution. He set it down in a burst of creative energy that occupied two or three days, at the end of which he wrote in his diary: "Today I am a genius." "The Scythians," a shorter and more overtly political piece, written at about the same time, was virtually his last poem. Thereafter he wrote several essays, delivered a few public addresses, did some editorial work, headed the board of the Bolshoi Theater, all the while deeply distressed by the course that the Revolution was taking.

Except for Bryusov, a Party member, Blok is the only Symbolist poet whose work is prized in the Soviet Union. His writings are issued in large popular editions and subjected to painstaking study. An edition of his collected works in ten volumes appeared under a Moscow imprint in 1932–36.

BOKOV, VIKTOR FYODOROVICH, was born in 1914 into a peasant family. He worked as a livestock expert and lathe operator before entering the Moscow Literary Institute, from which he graduated at the age of twenty-four. He saw action in the Second World War. In 1950 he published an anthology of *chastushki* (humorous quatrains or couplets, popular rather than literary, often nonsense verse, sometimes topical jingles). Two books of his verse came out eight years later. Some of his poems have been set to music.

BORATYNSKY. See BARATYNSKY.

BRYUSOV, VALERY YAKOVLEVICH, 1873–1924, born into a wealthy merchant family of Moscow, received a thorough training in the humanities. He was only thirteen when he felt himself, he wrote, "truly a poet." In his early twenties he broke into print with translations and imitations of French verse of the period, contributed to a miscellany entitled *Russian Symbolists*, which was edited and published by himself. At about the same time he brought out a collection of his own poems. Other books followed, some under the imprint of the publishing house that he established for the promotion of "the new poetry." The leader of the Moscow Symbolists, he edited the *avant garde* monthly V*esy* (*The Balance*) throughout the years of its existence: 1905–09. He was a prolific writer, producing tales, novels, plays, critical essays, literary mono-graphs, in addition to poems, many of them translations. The edition of his collected works, which began to appear when he was forty, was planned to comprise twenty-five volumes. One was to be a rendering of Poe's verse, four more were to consist of other trans-lations, chiefly from the French.

When the Bolshevik Revolution occurred, Bryusov hailed the Soviet regime, and in 1920 sealed his new allegiance by joining the Communist Party. He died in harness, having been steadily busy editing, translating, turning out essays, reviews, studies in prosody, lecturing at the University of Moscow and the Higher Institute of Arts and Letters that he had founded—and also writing quantities of verse inspired by his new credo.

BUNIN, IVAN ALEXEYEVICH, 1870–1953, was a descendant of an old line of nobles that had earlier given Russia the poet Zhukovsky. He spent his boyhood in the feudal atmosphere of a manor, but it was a shabby one. So straitened were the family's circumstances that his schooling was cut short and he had to go to work at an early age. His first book, a collection of poems issued from a provincial press in 1891, passed unnoticed. His short stories attracted more attention, and indeed his wide reputation rests chiefly on his fiction, much of which is available in English trans-lation. Yet he continued to write verse until his middle fifties. He produced admirable translations of English verse, making poetry out of Longfellow's *Song of Hiawatha*.

The exotic strain in his poems is due to the fact that he was something of a globe-trotter. As soon as his circumstances per-mitted, he began to travel, particularly in the Near East. He kept aloof from literary cliques, but was generally identified with the group of naturalistic writers headed by Maxim Gorky. Not that he shared the latter's radicalism. In the civil war precipitated by the Revolution he found himself on the side of the Whites, and in 1920 he expatriated himself, settling in France. To the end, he maintained an intransigently anti-Soviet stand. The émigré's powers as a novelist were undiminished, but they were employed to produce nostalgic works about a vanished world. In 1933 he received the Nobel Prize, the first Russian author to be so honored. Not long after Stalin's death he was posthumously repatriated, as it were. In 1956 an edition of his collected works in five volumes, provided with a generously appreciative preface, appeared under a Moscow imprint.

CHULKOV, GEORGY IVANOVICH, 1879–1939, the son of a civil servant, was expelled from medical school as a political offender and deported to Siberia. On his release he settled in Petersburg, established contact with the *avant garde* poets there, and in 1904 published his first book of verse. He continued to write modernist lyrics, as well as stories, plays, and critical essays, including a piece entitled *On Mystical Anarchism* (1906), which exalted the individual's unlimited freedom. Five years after the Revolution he brought out a book of poems that differed from his earlier work only in having stronger religious overtones. Thereafter he gave up imaginative writing, confining himself to works of literary scholarship.

DERZHAVIN, GAVRIIL ROMANOVICH, 1743–1816, born into the lower gentry, was early acquainted with poverty. Though practically a self-taught man, he had a fairly good grounding in the humanities. Despite his contrariness and independence of spirit, he made a brilliant career in an age of favoritism, rising from the lowest rank in the army to the highest post in the bureaucratic hierarchy under Catherine the Great and her successors. He believed it to be the poet's duty to promote the common good by telling the truth—with a smile—to those in power. His numerous writings, most of them in verse, were the by-product of the busy life of a courtier and high-ranking administrator. Only during his last years, when as a retired statesman he moved out of his sixty-room house in the capital and lived in Horatian ease on his estate, was he able to devote himself wholly to literature.

DOLMATOVSKY, YEVGENY ARONOVICH, born in 1915, is the son of a lawyer. His first two collections of poems came out when he was nineteen and twenty, respectively. In 1914 he joined the Party. During the Russo–Finnish hostilities and the Second World War he sent dispatches to *Izvestia* from the front; at the same time he wrote enough poems to make up four volumes. A book of verse published in 1949 won him the Stalin Prize. The same year he wrote the text for an oratorio by Shostakovich. At the call of the Communist League of Youth he had, as a young man, volunteered for work on the construction of the subway in his native Moscow, and in 1956 he brought out a novel in verse tracing the fortunes of several subway volunteers he had known. The latest selection of his work was published in 1959.

FET (FOETH), AFANASY AFANASYEVICH, 1820–1892, was brought up as the son of Afanasy Shenshin, a well-to-do landed gentleman. He may actually have been fathered by Johann Foeth, of Darmstadt, to whom the poet's mother, also German, had been married before she threw in her lot with Shenshin and went to live with him in Russia. Since her marriage to Shenshin had not been performed by an Orthodox priest, her son was deprived of the right to bear the Shenshin name and to inherit from his "father." The stigma of illegitimacy weighed heavily upon him, and it was only in advanced middle age that he succeeded in removing it by dint of litigation.

Meanwhile he had achieved fame under the name that his mother had once borne. His first book of verse appeared in 1840, but it was the next two volumes, published respectively in 1850 and 1856, that established his reputation as a poet. Then for over a quarter of a century he remained silent. In 1858 he retired from the army and settled down to the life of a gentleman farmer. As the poet of ethereal moods was a practical and tight-fisted husband-man, he waxed fat and prosperous with the years. He did not give up his literary friendships with such men as Turgenev and Tolstoy, but unlike them he was a black reactionary, fearful of revolution and believing that art flourished at the foot of the throne.

In his seventh decade the poet came to life again in the sybaritic country gentleman, producing four volumes of verse, appropriately entitled *Evening Fires* (1883–91). It has been truly said of Fet that, like the nightingale, he sang only at dawn and at sunset. In his last years he devoted himself to translating the Latin poets.

FYODOROV, VASILY DMITRIEVICH, born in 1918, the son of a mason, is a native of Siberia. He worked in airplane factories before graduating, at thirty-two, from the Gorky Literary Institute in Moscow. He is the author of several books of verse, one of them entitled *Not Left of the Heart* (Moscow, 1960). A second edition of his collected verse narratives was issued in 1961 under a Moscow imprint.

GUMILYOV, NIKOLAY STEPANOVICH, 1886–1921, the son of a navy doctor, studied at the University of Petersburg and at the Sorbonne. In 1910 he married the poet Anna Akhmatova (who was to divorce him), and made an extensive trip abroad. Three years later he took part in an expedition organized by the Russian

Academy of Sciences to study East African tribes. His interest in distant lands is reflected in his verse, the first volume of which appeared in 1905. Both he and his wife were leading members of the Acmeist group and of the Guild of Poets, 1911–1914. He fought in the World War as a volunteer and was back in Petrograd in 1918, writing poems, translating, editing, lecturing. He had always been a monarchist and a loyal son of the Orthodox Church. In August 1921 he was arrested and shot for alleged participation in an anti-Soviet conspiracy. In addition to a dozen little books of original verse, he left behind various translations, including a rendering of Théophile Gautier's *Emaux et Camées* and of "The Rime of the Ancient Mariner."

HOFMAN, VIKTOR VIKTOROVICH, 1884–1911 has to his credit some short stories and two books of intimate lyrics, the second of which appeared the year before his suicide in Paris.

IVANOV, VYACHESLAV IVANOVICH, 1866–1949, the son of a minor government official, received a religious education. He attended the university of his native Moscow and that of Berlin, supplementing his academic studies of classical antiquity with travel and years of residence in Italy. He wrote a thesis in Latin on Roman tax farming, but over many years his researches were devoted mainly to the cult of Dionysos, which, he held, was tributary to Christianity. Modern thought interested him as well, his mentors including Nietzsche and Dostoevsky. He underwent long and arduous preparation for his work as a writer. His first book of poems, *Pilot Stars*, appeared in 1903. Two years later he settled in the northern capital, where for half a dozen years his "Wednesdays" in the "Tower," as his apartment was known, were symposia on poetics and religion. Several further volumes of esoteric verse and of abstruse essays confirmed his position as the High Priest of Symbolism.

After the Revolution he remained in Russia for some time. In 1921 he accepted the post of professor of Greek at the University of Azerbaijan in Baku, and for a while he acted as Vice-Commissar of Education in that Soviet Republic. In 1924 he expatriated himself, settling in his beloved Italy, where he forsook the Orthodox for the Catholic Church. Shortly before World War II a long, rather vacuous poem of his and a group of "Roman Sonnets" were brought out in Paris. He died in Rome. *Vecherny svet* (*Evening Light*), a posthumous collection of his verse, appeared in 1962 under the Oxford imprint in the original Russian.

KAZAKOVA, RIMMA FYODOROVNA, was born in 1932, presumably in the Soviet Far East, since her first book of verse was published, in 1958, under a Khabarovsk imprint. Three more little collections of her lyrics came out in Moscow, the most recent in 1964.

KAZIN, VASILY VASILYEVICH, was born in 1898 into a working-man's family. A high school graduate, he was an alumnus of the literary studio of the Moscow Proletcult and a charter member of the *Smithy* group. As a poet he was productive chiefly during the first decade of the Soviet period. Since 1921 he has occupied himself with editorial work, but of late he resumed the writing of poems. An edition of his collected verse came out in 1957, and another in 1964.

KHLEBNIKOV, VELIMIR (Viktor Vladimirovich), 1885–1922, was the son of a provincial schoolteacher. In his middle twenties he lost interest in his studies; he had majored in mathematics at the University of Kazan and subsequently shifted from biology to Slavic philology at the University of Petersburg. He remained in the capital and devoted himself to writing. His initial efforts appeared in the earliest miscellanies of the Futurists, and he was soon a prominent figure in their ranks. In addition to turning out much verse and prose of sorts, he was busy formulating numerical laws, which, he believed, govern both past and future events. Numbers were an obsession with him. He was also occupied with various plans of a madly chimerical nature. When the World War was in its second year, he founded "The Society of Presidents of the Globe," alias "The Society of 317" (that number had a special significance for him). It was to be made up of the élite of the earth—including himself and some of his friends—who were to replace the existing governments. These he also designated as governments of Space, in contradistinction to governments of Time, headed by the Presidents of the Globe. One of these eventually resigned on the ground that Khlebnikov was willing to admit "practically anybody, even Kerensky and Woodrow Wilson."

One reason why he welcomed the Revolution was that it enabled him to return to civilian life, after bleak months of military service as a private. Some of the civil war years he spent in the south, half-starved and ailing. He managed to write a good deal, but most of his work remained in manuscript on pages of a large ledger or on scraps of paper stuffed into a pillowcase that he toted around. He wrote some propaganda pieces and was attached to an army unit dispatched to Iran in 1921 to foment a Communist uprising. Returning to Moscow the following year and suffering from the effects of chronic malnutrition, he was being taken to the country to recuperate, but died on the way. Inscribed on his coffin were the words: "President of the Globe."

Most of Khlebnikov's writings have been published post-humously. His collected works in four volumes appeared under a

Leningrad imprint (1928–33), and a supplementary volume (1940) came out in Moscow.

KHODASEVICH, VLADISLAV FELITZIANOVICH, 1886–1939, published his first book of poems in 1908. He also managed to bring out two volumes of verse in the early years of the Soviet regime, during which he suffered severe hardships. In 1922 he expatriated himself. The émigré wrote criticism and engaged in journalism. His last book, published in Brussels the year of his death, is a volume of literary reminiscences. His collected works were issued in Munich in 1961.

KIRSANOV, SEMYON ISAAKOVICH, born in 1906 into the family of an impecunious tailor, managed nonetheless to get a university education. His first book of verse came out when he was twenty. A disciple of Mayakovsky in his youth, he clung to an unconventional style, combining verbal dexterity with a turn for the whimsical. During the Second World War he was with the Red Army as a correspondent, and he produced propaganda in the shape of songs and lyrics. He wrote a number of verse narratives, one of them, for which he received the Stalin Prize in 1951, about a master steel-maker put to death by the Germans. A selection from his work, in two volumes, appeared in 1961, and his collected lyrics the following year. *One Day Tomorrow*, published in 1964, is the odd title of a book of his latest poems.

KLYUYEV, NIKOLAY ALEXEYEVICH, 1887–1937, a native of a remote northern village, was of peasant stock. He was proud of his Old Believer ancestry—zealots, some of whom burned themselves alive rather than accept the innovations in ritual and liturgy introduced by a seventeenth-century patriarch. At an early age Klyuyev became known for his verses in the vein of the canticles of the schismatic Church. Four collections of his poems were published under the old regime, and in 1918 another collection came out under the imprint of the Petrograd Soviet. He expected the Revolution to result in a peasant paradise, and so won a hearing for several other books of verse. Before long, however, he turned against the new order. He particularly abhorred the forcible collectivization of the farms. A selection from his prerevolutionary verse, published in 1928, was his last work to appear under a Soviet imprint, although he continued to write verse that circulated in manuscript. In 1933 he was deported to Siberia for "kulak propaganda." There he went on writing, but his manuscripts have been lost. He is believed to have been at work on a long poem, writing the stophes on scraps of wrapping paper that he destroyed as soon as he learned the lines by heart. He died aboard a train that was taking him to Moscow, after he had served his time. His collected works, in two volumes, were published in 1954 in the original under a New York imprint.

KOCHETKOV, VIKTOR. A slim collection of his poems was published in 1960.

KOLTZOV, ALEXEY VASILYEVICH, 1809–1842, was the son of a fairly prosperous cattle dealer from the steppe region who was still much of a peasant. He received an extremely scanty schooling, his father having taken him into the business at an early age. The youth, unhappy in the sordid atmosphere of his home in Voronezh, during his few leisure hours turned to reading books and writing verse in the style of folksongs. On a business trip to Moscow he ran into several literati, who took an interest in him and encouraged him to write. In 1835 his new friends brought out a little book of his poems, the only one to appear in his lifetime. Thereafter Koltzov made other trips to the two capitals, where he met the eminent literary figures of the day, including Pushkin, and, like another Burns, dinnered wi' lairds. After he returned from a stay in Moscow or Petersburg he felt even more wretched at home, where his literary ambitions were jeered at. Moreover, his intercourse with the intellectuals led him to lamentable attempts at philosophical poetry. His life, embittered by the increased hostility of his family and wrecked by a disastrous connection with a prostitute, came to an untimely end.

Not many years after his death, Koltzov attained the status of a minor classic, his poems finding their way into school readers and anthologies. Of the 150 pieces he wrote, nearly two thirds have been set to music.

KOMAROV, PYOTR STEPANOVICH, 1911–1949, of peasant stock, lived in the Soviet Far East and worked there as a journalist. In 1945 he was in Manchuria with the occupation troops. He has to his credit three books of verse published at Khabarovsk. In 1950 he was posthumously awarded the Stalin Prize.

KOROSTYLEV, VADIM, is the author of a verse narrative for children (Moscow, 1960) and of several plays.

KUZMIN, MIKHAIL ALEXEYEVICH, 1875–1936, counted a French émigré among his ancestors. He studied at the Petersburg (Leningrad) Conservatory under Rimsky-Korsakov, and until the age of thirty confined himself to writing librettos for his own operettas. In 1905 he contributed a group of sonnets to a review and in the next two decades brought out a dozen books of poems. The Revolution did not affect his work. While he remained in the Soviet Union, he was not of it. Exactly when and under what circumstances he died is uncertain.

LERMONTOV, MIKHAIL YURYEVICH, 1814–1841, was descended from George Learmont, a Scottish mercenary in the Polish service, who, taken prisoner by the Russians in 1613, settled in Muscovy. The Scotsman's grandsons traced their lineage to the Learmont who fought with Malcolm against Macbeth. The poet would have been even prouder of his Scottish origins had he known that the same surname was borne by Thomas the Rhymer, the thirteenth-century bard who is said to have received his poetic and prophetic gifts from the Fairy Queen.

His mother, who had been deserted by her husband, died when the boy, the sole offspring of the unhappy marriage, was two years old, and he became a cause of discord between his father, a country squire in moderate circumstances, and his wealthy, highborn, and overbearing maternal grandmother. It was she who brought him up and did everything to spoil him. His early education was of the usual imported variety, and it was not until, at the age of fourteen, he entered the Boarding School for Nobles attached to the University of Moscow that he became acquainted with Russian poetry. He was extraordinarily precocious in love as in literature. Between the ages of fourteen and eighteen he wrote three hundred lyrics, fifteen long narrative poems, three dramas, and one prose tale. He first fell in love at eleven and, in spite of an unprepossessing exterior, excelled in breaking hearts.

At twenty he graduated from a military school and received his commission, having previously attended the University of Moscow. Thereafter the young hussar plunged into a life of pleasure, one element of which was what he had earlier called "poetry drowned in champagne." His verse began to appear in the magazines, but it was his angry elegy on Pushkin's death, which circulated in manuscript, that brought him fame, and also transfer to a line regiment engaged in border warfare in the Caucasus, by way of punishment for a piece of writing judged subversive. Indeed, he was hospitable to ideas of political liberty.

He stayed less than a year in the Caucasus, but in 1840 was again banished there for having fought a duel. That romantic land deeply impressed itself on his imagination. It is the locale of his remarkable *A Hero of Our Time*, a work of prose, as well as of his major poems, "The Novice" and "The Demon." A few months after his second departure for the Caucasus a collection of his poems appeared, the only book of his verse to be issued during his lifetime. Much of his work was published posthumously.

When not in exile, Lermontov lived in the capital, moving in the *beau monde*, which he both sought after and despised, and generally avoiding literary circles. Morbidly sensitive and hungry for affection, he chose to hide his real feelings under a frivolous and arrogant exterior. During his last sojourn in the Caucasus, he saw action in the fighting against the natives. Spared by their bullets, the young poet was killed in a duel with a fellow officer who had been the butt of his merciless gibes.

LOMONOSOV, MIKHAIL VASILYEVICH, 1711–1765, was the son of a White Sea fisherman, prosperous if illiterate. At first self-taught, the youth attended secondary school in his twenties, and in 1736 was sent by the Government to Germany to study chemistry and metallurgy, as well as philosophy. He was thirty-one when he was appointed lifetime professor at the Petersburg Academy of Sciences, later becoming virtually its head. A fabulously gifted "universal man," he made outstanding contributions to science and technology, devised fireworks for court occasions, made mosaics, and in his leisure hours wrote on history and economics. Further, he broke fresh ground as grammarian and rhetorician, and distinguished himself as a man of letters.

LVOV, MIKHAIL DAVYDOVICH, a native of the Ural region and the son of a schoolteacher, was born in 1917. He attended the Pedagogical Institute at Ufa and in 1941 graduated from the Literary Institute in Moscow. The previous year his first book of verse appeared in Chelyabinsk. During the war he served in a volunteer tank corps and was decorated with the Order of the Patriotic War and the Badge of Honor. The latest of his five books of poems was published in 1964.

MAIKOV, APOLLON NIKOLAYEVICH, 1821–1897, was brought up by a mother with literary leanings and an aristocratic father who gave up a military career for that of a painter. He himself studied painting early but turned to literature, publishing his first volume of verse in 1842. The book brought him instant renown and a Government stipend, and was followed at rather long intervals by other collections of poems. Much of his work has to do with antiquity—he had a thorough classical education—some of his best known pieces being in the manner of the Greek anthology. He also wrote idyls, patriotic lyrics, and poems on historical subjects. The conflict of early Christianity with imperial Rome is the theme of three of his long dramatic poems, including his major work, *Two Worlds* (1881). An epicurean and an esthete, Maikov was, not surprisingly, a man of conservative views. For nearly half a century he faithfully served his monarch as a censor.

MANDELSHTAM, OSIP EMILIEVICH, 1891–1938, was born in Warsaw into a middle-class Jewish family, which removed to Petersburg (Leningrad) when he was small. He attended one of the better secondary schools there, took a course in Old French at the University of Heidelberg and studied Western languages and literatures at the University of Petersburg. Like Pasternak, he fully assimilated the elements of Russian culture, including Christianity.

He was nineteen when several of his earliest poems were printed in a review. A slim book of his verse appeared in 1913, a second, enlarged edition coming out in 1916. During the civil war he spent some time in the south, but by 1920 he was back in his beloved Petrograd. It was there that his second collection of poems came out in 1923. A sheaf of his verse for children was also brought out under the same imprint. His collected verse was issued in 1928. Two years later he visited Armenia and recorded his impressions in a cycle of poems. Until 1933 a gradually diminishing number of his poems found their way into the periodicals. The author of literary essays and of an autobiographical tale, he worked also as a translator and as an editor.

His verse and his prose alike failed to meet the demands made on literature by the Party, and since in the second decade of the Soviet era official intolerance was on the increase, Mandelshtam became a marked man. One night in May of 1934 the police searched the flat in which he lived with his wife and small daughter, and arrested him. He was sentenced to three years of banishment, apparently on the charge of having composed a piece in which the henchmen of the "Kremlin mountaineer" were described as a gang of "half-humans" and himself as taking pleasure in every execution that he nonchalantly ordered. The poet was deported to a small town in the Ural region. There, in a fit of mental derangement he threw himself out of a hospital window and suffered a broken arm. He was then removed to the city of Voronezh, in the southwest. Exactly a year after he had served his term of banishment he was rearrested, sentenced to five years in a labor camp for "counter-revolutionary activities," and shipped off to the Far East. In October 1938 he reached Vladivostok and was lodged in a prison for convicts waiting to be assigned to their respective places of exile or confinement. He was spared the lot of a concentration camp inmate by death, which came to him shortly before the end of the year. The persistent reports that he was of unsound mind in his last months are seemingly without foundation.

In 1959 a Soviet edition of a selection of Mandelshtam's verse was announced, but it has not materialized. He remains among the victims of Stalinist terror who have not been posthumously rehabilitated. The Russian text of his verse, including pieces unpublished in the Soviet Union, appeared in 1964 under a Washington, D. C. imprint as Volume I of Mandelshtam's collected works, admirably edited by Professor G. P. Struve and B. A. Filipoff. This supersedes their one-volume edition of his verse and prose in the original, issued in New York in 1955.

MARIENHOF, ANATOLY BORISOVICH, 1897–1962, began to write in the early years of the Soviet era. He called himself an Imagist and wrote *outré* verse. In 1928 he published a novel, translated into English under the title *The Cynics*, about his friend Yesenin. More recently he has written several plays. Announcement has been made of the publication of his memoirs in a Moscow monthly.

MARKOV, ALEXEY YAKOVLEVICH, was born in 1920 into the family of a field hand who had settled in the Caucasus. After his father's death the boy lived in various children's homes. He attended normal school and was on the staff of a local newspaper when, at the outbreak of the Second World War, he went into the service. Upon demobilization he studied at the Literary Institute in Moscow, and in 1954 published his first book, a tale in verse. A collection of poems followed, and thereafter a narrative poem on Lomonosov.

MARTYNOV, LEONID NIKOLAYEVICH, a native of Omsk, Siberia, was born in 1905. His schooling was scanty. He has been writing for newspapers and periodicals since his early youth. The first book of his poems was published at Omsk in 1939. It was followed by five other collections of verse, the latest dated 1962. He has also translated verse from the languages of the Soviet minorities and the satellite countries.

MATUSOVSKY, MIKHAIL LVOVICH, born in 1915, worked as a construction technician before graduating from the Literary Institute in Moscow at the age of twenty-four. He took courses at the Institute of Philosophy, History, and Literature in the capital until the country was attacked by Germany. During the war he was at the front in the capacity of a newspaper correspondent. He is the author of several books of verse, the earliest of which is dated 1940.

MATVEYEVA, NOVELLA NIKOLAYEVNA, one of the younger women writing verse. Her first sheaf of lyrics came out in 1961, her third, and latest, in 1964. The range of her themes is wide, the workmanship trim, the mood usually intimate yet bespeaking strength.

MAYAKOVSKY, VLADIMIR VLADIMIROVICH, 1893–1930, a Great Russian by birth, opened his eyes at Bagdadi (renamed Mayakovsky), a village in what was to become the Georgian Soviet Republic. He was thirteen when, upon his father's death, the family moved to Moscow, exchanging comfort for poverty. Two years later he joined the Bolshevik faction of the Socialist Party and left high school rather than incur the disabilities attached to expulsion. The youthful agitator was arrested and served several short prison terms. About this time he started writing verse. On his release he went to an art school, but was expelled for publications and public appearances that smacked of scandal. He continued to flabbergast people with sartorial extravagances and Futurist poetry.

At a meeting which took place shortly after the October Revolution he summoned writers and artists to hail the Soviet power. He soon developed enormous activity in the service of the new regime. From 1919 to 1921 he was employed by Rosta (Russian Telegraphic Agency), the Soviet publicity bureau. He headed the Moscow Association of Futurists and later edited two periodicals speaking for the Left Front in the Arts. His few plays were not successful, but his poems enjoyed great popularity. Traveling all over the country, he recited his verse before audiences made up of soldiers, workers, students, children. Between 1922 and 1929 he also made frequent trips abroad. In 1925 he visited Mexico and spent three months in the United States, the spectacle of this seat of capitalism moving him to indignant if unimpressive utterance. He ended his stormy career by shooting himself.

Mayakovsky's collected works appeared in Moscow (1956–61) in thirteen volumes, edited with the scholarly care accorded a classic.

NEKRASOV, NIKOLAY ALEXEYEVICH, 1821–January 8, 1878 (December 27, 1877, Old Style), in his early years observed the worst excesses of serfdom, since his father was a brutal, dissolute country squire who, after retiring from the army, had become a rural police officer. From his frail, gentle mother he may have derived the ideal of womanhood to which he held all his life. After attending a secondary school for a few years, at seventeen he was sent to Petersburg to enter a military school. He defied his father's will by enrolling in the university as an auditor—he had failed to pass the entrance examinations—and therewith was thrown on his own resources.

For several years he was a starving hack, yet in 1840 he managed to bring out at his own expense a little volume of verse, a deserved fiasco. Before long he made a successful entrance into the publishing field. At twenty-five the hard-headed, wide-awake young man was the co-owner and moving spirit of a monthly and, incidentally, the lover of his partner's wife. Under his guidance the magazine grew in importance and during the stormy sixties was the organ of the democratic intelligentsia. When, in 1866, it was suppressed, Nekrasov acquired another magazine. The flower of Russian prose appeared in the pages of the two periodicals, along with Nekrasov's own poems. These were first collected in a volume in 1856, and as new pieces came from his pen, the book was reissued in successive augmented editions. From the first its success was enormous. His poems, with their libertarian and Populist message, were the Bible of the radical youth. Those that were barred by censorship were circulated in manuscript or appeared in the underground press. Some of his verse joined the body of popular balladry. Not a little of his verse is in the vein of folk poetry. As a successful author and publisher, Nekrasov lived extravagantly, in spite of ethical scruples that dictated poems of self-scorn.

He was particularly productive in the last decade of his life, during which he wrote his major works, conceived on an epic scale, *Russian Women* and *Who Lives Happily in Russia?* He completed these amidst the cruel sufferings of his last illness. To the end he continued to write verse. On his deathbed he married a woman of the people who had shared his life in his last years. At the time of his death, he was considered by many the greatest Russian poet, not excluding Pushkin. His posthumous reputation, after suffering an eclipse at the turn of the century, has more recently regained its luster.

ORLOV, SERGEY SERGEYEVICH, son of a schoolteacher, was born in 1921. His university studies were interrupted by the war, in which he fought as a tank man. At thirty he graduated from the Literary Institute in Moscow. He is the author of half a dozen books of verse.

PANCHENKO, NIKOLAY. A book of his poems, entitled *Warm Weather*, appeared in 1958 under a Moscow imprint.

PASTERNAK, BORIS LEONIDOVICH, 1890–1960, was born in Moscow. His mother was an accomplished pianist, his father a noted painter, who, unlike his son, derived some of his subject matter from his Jewish background. The child's nurse was responsible for his having been baptized, and "Christian thought," as he put it later, was of decisive moment in his formative years. In his teens, under the spell of Scriabin, a friend of the family, he trained himself to become a composer, but gave up music for philosophy. He studied it at the University of Moscow and, briefly, at that of Marburg, Germany. Exempted from military service because of an injured leg, he spent the first year of World War I with a wealthy family as a tutor, and during the next two years was employed in a factory in the Urals. All the while he was developing a passion for literature. When the Revolution began, he returned to Moscow. For a time he was on the staff of the library of the Commissariat of Education. Thereafter he lived by his pen. He made his home in the capital, and from 1937 to the end of his days, in a suburb of it. In 1921 his parents and two sisters, unlike his brother, expatriated themselves.

His first two books of verse, *A Twin in the Clouds* and *Above the Barriers*, appeared in 1914 and 1917, respectively. The dawn of the Soviet era was the period of his greatest productivity. The poems making up *My Sister—Life* and *Themes and Variations*, which came out in 1922 and 1923, respectively, and were reprinted four years later, had been written earlier. In addition to lyrics, these volumes include four narratives in verse. Another book of his poems was brought out in 1932, shortly after the publication of *Safe Conduct*, an autobiographical fragment dedicated to the memory of Rainer Maria Rilke, and couched, like several previously published stories, in a most unconventional prose. The following year his verse was collected in one moderately sized volume, which was reprinted, with a few additional pieces, in 1936. He had at this time a considerable following, in spite of the esoteric quality of his work, but the Party hacks strongly disapproved of it, and he was under a cloud. During his lifetime none of his other original verse appeared in book form under a Soviet imprint, except for two small groups of poems, published during the Second World War. He supported himself and his family—he was married twice, and had children by both wives—by translating Georgian, English, and German poetry, including Shakespeare's plays and Goethe's *Faust*. And he worked on a long prose narrative, which was to become world-famous. After Stalin's death he composed a number of lyrics, but only a few of them were printed in Soviet periodicals before the appearance abroad, in translation, of his novel *Doctor Zhivago*, which had been refused publication at home. This, and his acceptance of the Nobel Prize in the autumn of 1958, made him a proscribed author, publicly vilified and threatened with loss of citizenship and expulsion from the country. He withdrew his acceptance of the Nobel Prize and made a public apology for his "errors." Death released him from a situation that he had described nine months before the end, in a private letter, as "unbearable" beyond words.

Several selections from his verse were published in Moscow during his lifetime, and one posthumously, in 1961. A nearly complete, carefully edited collection, prefaced by a laudatory essay on his poetry, appeared under a Soviet imprint in 1965. Excluded are a number of pieces, nearly all of them on religious themes, from among the poems supplementing *Doctor Zhivago*. Those reprinted from that work, which is still on the Soviet Index, are listed evasively as "from the novel." No other reference to it is made anywhere in the book. The several remaining omissions belong to Pasternak's last poems. Among them is, of course, the outspoken piece entitled "The Nobel Prize." His collected works in the original were published by The University of Michigan Press, 1958–1961, four volumes. His writings have been widely translated.

PUSHKIN, ALEXANDER SERGEYEVICH, 1799–1837, was descended on his father's side from an old, patrician, though by no means opulent, family; his maternal great-grandfather was a Negro, or, according to one account, "an African Moor from Abyssinia." The poet liked to allude to his exotic origins and made his black ancestor the hero of his first, unfinished, novel.

Instructed as a child by French tutors, he graduated at the age of eighteen from a boarding school for the scions of the nobility, an indifferent scholar, but already looked upon in *avant garde* circles as a poet of the highest promise. For three years he remained in Petersburg (Leningrad), holding a clerkship at the Ministry of Foreign Affairs, but chiefly engaged in versifying and in sowing wild oats. Because he composed some poems in praise of liberty and a few barbed epigrams against highly stationed personages, he found himself, in the spring of 1820, transferred to a minor post in a remote southern section of the empire. Several months later his first book, a fairy tale in verse, appeared in the capital.

The banished poet spent two years in Bessarabia, traveled in the Crimea and the Caucasus, and made a stay in Odessa. During those years he wrote not only lyrics but also long narrative poems, which established his reputation as "the Byron of Russia." He also started his major work, *Eugene Onegin*, a novel in verse, which was not printed in full until 1833.

"Exile" did not have the sobering effect on Pushkin that the authorities had counted on and, as a result, in the summer of 1824 he was dismissed from the service and confined to his family estate. There he composed many short lyrics, some derived from such diverse sources as Russian folklore and the Koran; he also wrote an historical play in blank verse, *Boris Godunov*. In September 1826 his banishment finally came to an end. In fact, he became a protégé of the Czar, the latter undertaking to censor his writings in person. The situation had its drawbacks, and in any event the poet remained a political suspect, kept under police surveillance and forbidden to travel abroad.

Back in the capital, Pushkin resumed the giddy, undisciplined life to which he was accustomed, but he managed to turn out much verse, including "Poltava," a narrative poem about Peter the Great and Mazeppa, and he also composed a group of short stories, as well as several dramatic sketches and delightful adaptations of folk tales in verse. At the age of thirty-one he married a society girl who, he said, was his 113th love. She was beautiful, but empty-headed and coldhearted. Although his frivolous young wife's social ambitions interfered with his work, he was now writing some of his finest lyrics and his best prose. He also produced "The Bronze Horseman," a narrative poem, and a work of history, and started editing a review, which offered his novel, *The Captain's Daughter*.

In his last years Pushkin was beset by many harassments. His income was insufficient to meet the needs of his growing family and, in spite of a subvention from the Czar, his debts kept mounting. A court appointment, which he had accepted for his wife's sake, was another source of vexation. And then he suspected her of infidelity. In an access of jealousy he provoked an admirer of hers, who had recently become her brother-in-law, into offering him a challenge. In the duel the poet was fatally wounded, dying on February 10 (New Style).

RYLENKOV, NIKOLAY IVANOVICH, born in 1909 into a peasant family, taught school, and during the period of rural collectivization was chairman of a village soviet. Later he engaged in journalism. He saw action in the Second World War, and by the time it ended he had published half a dozen books of verse. His collected poems came out in 1956 and in 1964.

RYLEYEV, KONERATY FYODOROVICH, 1795–1826, like not a few of his fellow officers, was infected with liberalism while campaigning against Napoleon in western Europe. Retiring from the army in his early twenties, he settled in the capital, married, and took a post, first in the judiciary and then in the administration of the Russian-American Company, which traded in Alaska. In 1823 he joined a secret society pledged to bring about the downfall of the autocracy and the establishment of representative government in Russia. For some time he had been contributing poems to reviews and miscellanies, and in 1825 he published two slim books: a long poem and a collection of historical ballads. They carried a protest against despotism, as did his imitations of folksongs. In the days that followed the death of Alexander I, he took a leading part in organizing the military insurrection of December 14 (26), 1825. When this proved a miserable fiasco, he was seized and, with four other Decembrists, hanged. Some of his poems were circulated in manuscript and in clandestine editions.

SELVINSKY, ILYA LVOVICH, born in 1899 in the Crimea, is the son of a fur merchant. He saw action with the Reds in the civil war. At twenty-four he graduated from the University of Moscow. In 1933–34 he took part in an Arctic expedition as a correspondent of *Pravda*. He fought in the Second World War, receiving the Order of the Red Star. His first collection of verse came out in 1926; his tragedies were published in 1952, and a two-volume selection from his work in 1956. For years he has been teaching at the Literary Institute in Moscow.

SEREBROVSKAYA, YELENA, is the author of two novels, published in the 1950s.

SHCHIPACHEV, STEPAN PETROVICH, born in 1899 into a peasant family, in his teens worked as a farm hand and a store clerk. At twenty he joined the Communist Party and enlisted in the Red Army. Copies of his poems—he had been writing verse for some time—were dropped into the trenches of the Whites. When the civil war was over he taught in military schools. Later he edited an army journal and attended the Institute of Red Professors. During the Second World War he worked on a trench newspaper. In the last thirty years he has published numerous poems, for which he was awarded the Stalin Prize several times. A work of his that received this mark of official approval was a verse narrative which appeared in 1950. It is based on one of the tragedies caused by the brutal expropriation of the well-to-do peasants in the early 1930s. The hero of the poem is a fourteen-year-old peasant boy—there is a statue of him in a Moscow park—who was murdered for having informed against the saboteur kulaks of his village and against their secret accomplice, his own father. The edition of his collected poems, issued in 1957, was followed in 1960 and in 1962, respectively, by two books of new verse.

SIMONOV, KONSTANTIN MIKHAILOVICH, born in 1915, worked as a turner before enrolling at the Literary Institute in Moscow, from which he was graduated in 1938. That year he brought out his first book of poems. He achieved great popularity during the war with his dispatches from the front in the Red Army newspaper, his patriotic lyrics, and a novel about the siege of Stalingrad. In 1946 he toured the United States and wrote a play which inaugurated the anti-American campaign in the Soviet press. A staunch supporter of the Party line in letters, and a prolific and versatile writer, he was awarded the Stalin Prize for literature six times and given other tokens of official recognition. It was only after the deceased leader had been officially if discreetly pulled down from his pedestal that Simonov was emboldened to join in attacking what is euphemistically called "the cult of personality." His collected poems were published in 1964.

SKORODUMOV, YURY. No information available.

SLUTZKY, BORIS ABRAMOVICH, born in 1919, attended the Literary Institute in Moscow and saw action in the war. For several years he was on the staff of the All-Union Radio Network. His first book of poems appeared in Moscow in 1957. Two other collections appeared: *Today and Yesterday* (1963) and *Work* (1964). He also edited an anthology of Israeli verse in Russian translation.

SMELYAKOV, YAROSLAV VASILYEVICH, born in 1913, was the son of a railroad weigher. A trained printer, with limited schooling, the young man was employed as a typesetter, and at various times also worked as stoker, coal miner, ditch-diggers' foreman, lumberjack, reporter. His first book, published under a Moscow imprint in 1932, was followed by other collections of verse. Much of this grew out of his experiences as a wage earner. While interned in a concentration camp, he wrote a poem that Yevgeny Yevtushenko described as "full of courage and faith in the ideals of the Revolution."

SOLOGUB (Teternikov), FYODOR KUZMICH, 1863–1927, was the son of a tailor and grew up in a house where his widowed mother was a servant. For ten years after his graduation at the age of nineteen from a normal school, he taught in the provinces, learning to know the Main Streets of Russia, which were to furnish the stuff of his fiction. In 1892 he moved to the capital, where his uncanny verse and short stories soon gave him entrée to the circle of Modernist poets, his first book of poems appearing four years later. Thus, unlike the other Symbolists, he came to literature as a mature man. He continued to teach until 1907, meanwhile producing much verse and prose, as well as some closet plays, so that his collected works, brought out just before the outbreak of the World War, comprised twenty volumes, of which five contained verse.

After the Revolution he continued to write without attempting to adjust himself to the new conditions, and several of his books appeared under Russian imprints, as well as in Sofia, Tallinn, Berlin. His sixtieth birthday was the occasion of a public celebration by the thin ranks of the old guard. He had always been a stay-at-home, but so completely was he out of sympathy with Bolshevism that he was eager to leave the country. When the necessary papers had at last been obtained, his wife committed suicide and he became too apathetic to make use of them. He was thus spared death in exile.

His work has been neglected in Soviet Russia, apparently only one volume of selections from his poems having been issued posthumously (in 1939) and only one of his novels having been reprinted.

SOLOVYOV, VLADIMIR SERGEYEVICH, 1853–1900, the grandson of a priest and the son of an eminent historian, was himself Russia's foremost lay theologian, and also a mystic and a visionary. After receiving his degree from the University of Moscow he traveled abroad, and on his return became a university instructor. But his academic career ended abruptly when, shortly after the assassination of Alexander II, he delivered a public lecture in which he urged the new Czar to forbear punishing his father's assassins in a spirit of Christian forgiveness. Thenceforth he devoted himself to studies in religious philosophy. He also wrote a good deal on literature and on public affairs. One of his cardinal concepts was the Eternal Feminine, which he identified with Sophia: Divine Wisdom. He claimed to have beheld her with his own eyes on three occasions. He first glimpsed her in Moscow when he was nine. He next saw her thirteen years later, while poring over abstruse mystical writings in the reading room of the British Museum. She bade him follow her to Egypt. Arriving in Cairo, he went on foot into the desert and there beheld his beatific vision for the last time. These experiences are the subject of a poem which he composed, after another trip to Egypt, two years before his death. From time to time in the last twenty-five years of his short life, he composed verse in a comic vein as well as lyrics of high seriousness. In 1891 his poems were collected in a volume, two enlarged editions of which were published within his lifetime, some of his lyrics appearing only posthumously.

TARKOVSKY, ARSENY ALEXANDROVICH, born in 1907, is a native of Kirovograd in the Ukraine. Since the age of sixteen he has lived in Moscow, where he took courses in writing and engaged in journalism. During the war, from which he returned minus a leg, he was an army correspondent. *Before the Snow*, his first book of poems, came out in 1962; *To the Earth the Earthy*, his second collection, is in the press. He has translated verse from the Turkic languages of the Soviet Union.

TATYANICHEVA, LYUDMILA KONSTANTINOVNA, born in 1915, hails from the Ural region. A graduate of the Correspondence Department of the Literary Institute in Moscow, she worked on a Magnitogorsk newspaper and subsequently directed a Ural publishing house. She is the author of half a dozen books of verse, the first of which appeared in 1944.

TIKHONOV, NIKOLAY SEMYONOVICH, born in 1896, came from a poor home and received a scanty education, attending a commercial high school. He fought in the World War, and having enlisted in the Red Army, took part in the defense of Petrograd against White troops. A restless spirit, he traveled a great deal in the outlying parts of the Soviet Union and tried several occupations—acting, among them—before he turned to literature. In his youth he belonged to a confraternity of writers who, in defiance of the prevailing trend, championed apolitical art. Eventually he underwent a change of heart and became a staunch proponent of Communist literary policy. Indeed, from 1944 to the purge of 1946 he held the important post of chairman of the board of the Writers' Union. His first book of poems appeared in 1922. He continued to write lyrics and narratives in verse, in addition to fiction, more recently using his pen as a weapon in the cold war. Besides several decorations, he was twice awarded the Stalin Prize for his writings. The first two volumes of his collected work (Moscow, 1958–59, six volumes) contain verse, including translations. A selection from his lyrics appeared in 1964.

TOLSTOY, COUNT ALEXEY KONSTANTINOVICH, 1817–1875, came of the same old aristocratic line that was to give the world Leo Tolstoy. He sat on Goethe's knees and was a playmate of Emperor Alexander II. A fairly good education enhanced by foreign travel, a great fortune and the highest court connections held out the promise of a brilliant bureaucratic career, but he was jealous of his independence and preferred to concentrate on his writing. Among his friends he counted Gogol, Nekrasov, Turgenev. In the score of years that he filled with literary activity, he produced a considerable amount of verse—publishing a group of poems in his late thirties—as well as an historical novel and a trilogy of plays which testify to his dramatic talent and an ability to evoke his country's past. The volume of his poems which came out in 1867 was the only one to appear during his lifetime, not a little of his work having been collected only posthumously. In addition to long narrative pieces, he wrote ballads in the folk manner and satires poking fun at both the radicals and officialdom.

An aristocrat by conviction as well as by birth, he abhorred the materialism of his time and regarded the doctrine of equality as "the foolish invention of 1793," but he also despised the parasitic bureaucrats ruling in the name of an irresponsible autocrat. There was a strong comic streak in his make-up: with the aid of two other writers, his cousins, he perpetrated an elaborate hoax on the public, inventing an author by the name of Kozma Prutkov and providing him with a biography and works. These consisted of aphorisms, skits, parodies, and other facetiae. Tolstoy's reputation as a poet rests chiefly on his lyrics and ballads. Many of them have been set to music by eminent Russian composers.

TSVETAYEVA, MARINA IVANOVNA, 1892–1941, studied at the University of Moscow, where her father had been a professor, and at the Sorbonne. Over half a dozen little books of her verse were published between 1910 and 1922, when she emigrated to join her husband, a former White officer, who had crossed the border earlier. She took with her a sheaf of poems honoring the lost cause of the armed resistance to the Bolshevik regime. This was published in Munich posthumously. It is reported that in the thirties her husband became a Soviet agent and was later shot. *After Russia*, the last collection of her verse to appear in her lifetime, came out in Paris in 1928. The expatriate's writings continued to reflect a sharp anti-Soviet stand, but in 1939 she returned to the Soviet Union with her son. Less than two years later she hanged herself, apparently after her son was killed at the front.

The original text of her essays, in book form, was printed in New York in 1953. A Soviet edition of a selection from her verse appeared in 1961.

TSYBIN, VLADIMIR DMITRIEVICH, born in 1932, found his first employment in a mine. He had had no more than secondary schooling when he entered the Moscow Literary Institute, from which he graduated in 1958. Thereafter he published four collections of verse, the latest entitled *The Insomnia of the Age*. He is also the author of an epic that offers a flattering survey of the history of Russia as a land of heroes.

TUSHNOVA, VERONICA MIKHAILOVNA, born in 1915, is the daughter of a biologist and is herself a practicing physician. Four collections of her poems appeared between 1945 and 1963.

TVARDOVSKY, ALEXANDER TRIFONOVICH, the son of a village blacksmith who worked a farm that he owned, was born in 1910. The boy began to versify before he learned to read and write. Until the age of eighteen he stayed at home, doing chores and helping in the smithy. Then he tried his hand at journalism in Smolensk, where he attended a teachers' college. A verse narrative on farm collectivization, which made him widely known, appeared in 1936. A little later he published a book of poems about the rural scene. Thereupon he settled in the capital, continuing to write verse and taking university courses in the humanities. In 1938 he joined the Communist Party. He served as a correspondent attached to the troops that invaded East Poland and those who fought the Finns. During the Second World War he produced a tale in verse, *Vasily Tyorkin, a Book About the Soldier*, and soon after the end of the war he brought out another one relating the fate of a peasant woman who is a soldier's wife. These works greatly enhanced his popularity and won him two Stalin prizes. He continued to write shorter poems, too. In 1960 and 1963, respectively, he published two major verse narratives with which he had busied himself for a decade. He is also the author of stories and prose sketches. The Soviet presses have turned out millions of copies of his writings in a score of languages. Since 1950, except for the interval of 1954–58, he has been editing *Novy Mir* (*The New World*), the leading and most liberal Moscow monthly.

TYUTCHEV, FYODOR IVANOVICH, 1803–1873, came of an old line of noblemen said to have been founded by a Venetian who, after accompanying Marco Polo on his travels, had settled in Russia. A member of a precocious generation, he graduated from the University of Moscow at eighteen and was shortly thereafter appointed to the staff of the Russian embassy at Munich. For over a score of years he remained abroad, where he married in succession two aristocratic Bavarian widows, to whom he was devoted if not faithful. On returning to Russia, he continued in the diplomatic service, but did not advance far, partly because of an open extramarital union (with his daughter's governess) of long duration, which he erroneously called his last love. During the final two decades of his life he held the post of censor, not inappropriate to a man of conservative convictions. In 1848, when thrones were shaking all over Europe, he wrote an essay in which he predicted that Orthodox Russia, at the head of the united Slavs, would be the sacred ark riding the waves of the Western revolutionary deluge.

Tyutchev had not been long abroad when poems from his pen began to appear in the miscellanies and magazines. During the forties his name practically vanished from the public prints, but the revolutionary upheaval with which the decade closed in western Europe moved him to write a series of political poems. In 1850 his verse was enthusiastically commented upon in the leading monthly, but it was four years later, when about a hundred of his lyrics were issued separately, owing to the efforts of his friend Turgenev, that he achieved a standing with the general public. Only one other more inclusive collection of his verse appeared during the poet's lifetime (in 1868). After his death his reputation, based on a slight but distinguished body of work, continued to grow steadily, particularly after the turn of the century, when the Symbolists rediscovered him and hailed him as a great forerunner.

VENEVITINOV, DMITRY VLADIMIROVICH, 1805–1827, was of gentle birth. He received a good education and was a student of the Romantic German philosophy of his time. Like Pushkin, to whom he was related, he sympathized with the aims of the Decembrists, but did not participate in their conspiracy against the autocracy. He left behind some forty original poems and a few translations and essays, dying (by his own hand) before he could fulfill his brilliant promise. His work was published between covers only posthumously.

VINOKUROV, YEVGENY MINHAILOVICH, born in 1925, is the son of a professional soldier. At the age of eighteen, fresh from a military college, he found himself at the front in command of an artillery squad. Upon being demobilized, he was admitted to the Moscow Literary Institute, graduating in 1951. That year marked the appearance of his first book of verse, which was to be followed by half a dozen such volumes. A selection from his work was published in 1962, another in 1964.

VOLOSHIN, MAXIMILIAN ALEXANDROVICH, 1877–1932, a native of Kiev, was of mixed Cossack and German stock. His earliest impressions were associated with the Crimea, and in Koktebel, on the eastern littoral of the peninsula, he eventually found a home to which he became passionately attached. He was expelled from the University of Moscow for participation in student disorders and deported to Tashkent. On being released, he traveled in Italy and Greece. Then came Paris and French poetry, which, he said, taught him rhythm and form. In his middle twenties he took up painting, and at the same time began to contribute verse to *avant garde* periodicals, but the first collection of his poems did not come out until 1910.

The Revolution put an end to his complete aloofness from the contemporary scene. A note of mystic patriotism came into his lyrics and he wrote poems about the Red Terror which no Soviet censor could have passed and which appeared abroad. He did not expatriate himself, yet remained remarkably free from official molestation on political grounds. In his last years he published nothing. Clad in the classical Greek garb he affected, he led the life of a hermit in his beloved Koktebel and became a legend long before he died there, an exile in his own country, if ever there was one.

VOZNESENSKY, ANDREY ANDREYEVICH, the son of a scientist, was born in 1933. A native of Moscow, he attended the Architectural Institute in that city, graduating at the age of twenty-four. He did not, however, follow his profession, but turned to literature. He began to publish verse in 1958, and before long was one of the most popular young poets, enthusiastically applauded at public readings of verse. Two collections of his poems, *Parabola* and *Mosaic*, came out in 1960. A third book, *The Triangular Pear*, appeared two years later. The November 1963 issue of the Moscow monthly *Znamya* (*Banner*) contains a group of his lyrics, opening a sequence dedicated to the students who attended the courses given in 1911 by Lenin at Longjumeau (near Paris). A selection from his work, entitled *Anti-Worlds*, was brought out in 1964. In 1965 he published a long verse narrative on a romantic theme. He has traveled abroad and has recorded his impressions in lyrics. His poems have been translated into several languages.

VYAZEMSKY, PYOTR ANDREYEVICH, 1792–1873, Irish on his mother's side (she was an O'Reilly), was, on his father's, a scion of an old princely family and heir to a large fortune. He made a brilliant bureaucratic career. A close friend of Pushkin's, in his youth he was a liberal, like the other young aristocrats who dominated Russian letters at the time. He wrote light verse, lyrical and satirical, in the French manner, but his critical essays spoke for classicism. Gloom pervaded the poems of his old age, when he had become an embittered reactionary. His collected works were published posthumously in twelve volumes (1878–96).

YEGOROV, NIKOLAY, is a member of the younger generation of writers of verse. A book of his poems appeared under a provincial imprint in 1960.

YESENIN, SERGEY ALEXANDROVICH, 1895–1925, was brought up by his grandparents, fairly well-to-do peasants who were devout Old Believers. At the age of seventeen he left his native village in the province of Ryazan for Moscow. There he worked in a printing shop and attended courses in a people's university. Two years later, already a budding poet, he found himself in the capital, where his first book of verse appeared in 1916. That year he was drafted into the army, but deserted when the Revolution broke out. He greeted it with enthusiasm. Following the Soviet Government to Moscow, he became a familiar figure in the literary cafés there, breaking away occasionally to go off on trips to outlying sections of the country. His brief, tempestuous marriage to Isadora Duncan (1922–23) gave him a chance to make the grand tour, which included the United States. He had long had a weakness for drink, but now he was rarely sober. His loss of faith in the Revolution may have contributed to his growing rowdyism and bohemian bravado. When, in 1923, he returned to Russia, he did a good deal of writing, but his work clearly showed mental deterioration due to drink and cocaine. Under the influence of alcohol he was given to fits of violence which necessitated the intervention of the police. In the winter of 1925, after some weeks in a mental hospital, he hanged himself with a strap from his suitcase. The previous day he had complained to a friend that he could find no ink in the wretched hotel where he was stopping and handed him a poem written in his own blood.

For so short and disordered a life, Yesenin's output was not inconsiderable. In addition to lyrics, he composed several long poems and a drama in verse. To judge by the rapidity with which the huge 1956 edition of his work was exhausted, his popularity is very great. His collected works, in five volumes, were reprinted in 1961–62. The seventieth anniversary of his birth was celebrated by numerous articles in the Soviet press and by many memorial meetings.

YEVTUSHENKO, YEVGENY ALEXANDROVICH, was born in 1933 at Zima Junction, a town near Lake Baikal. His father was a geologist of Latvian origin whose family was settled in Russia; his mother was the granddaughter of a Ukrainian villager who had been deported to Siberia for having set fire to his landlord's house, and the daughter of a peasant who fought with the Bolsheviks in the civil war, eventually becoming a brigade commander. The Revolution was the family's religion, and Stalin the object of adoration, in spite of the fact that both grandfathers perished in the purges of the late thirties.

The boy spent his early childhood in Moscow and the war years at Zima Junction, returning to Moscow at the age of eleven. His parents were divorced, Yevgeny staying with his mother, later adopting her maiden name. The teen-ager wrote quantities of verse at the expense of his school work and was duly expelled. Soon after, he ran off to Kazakhstan to join his father, who headed a geological expedition there. Yevgeny, wanting no privileges, joined the staff as a laborer.

He was back in Moscow before long, and was sixteen when his verse began to appear in a sports journal there. Three years later his first book of poems came out, and on the strength of it the precocious youth was admitted to the Literary Institute and to the Union of Writers. He was expelled from the Union and from the League of Communist Youth because of a long verse narrative that he contributed to a monthly in 1956, as well as for his defense of a novel considered subversive. Soon, however, he was reinstated in both organizations and he continued to write much verse, which won him enormous popularity, especially with the ebullient, recalcitrant youth. He was able to travel widely both at home and abroad. A selection from his work appeared in 1959 and a more ample one in 1962. That year, while in Paris, he arranged for the publication, in French, of his *Precocious Autobiography,* which has not been issued in the Soviet Union (an English version appeared the following year). As a result, on his return home, he found himself under a cloud, but only temporarily. A major work of his was published in 1965—a poem, executed on an epic scale, dealing with the hydroelectric station at Bratsk, Siberia.

ZABOLOTZKY, NIKOLAY ALEXEYEVICH, 1903–1958, was the son of an agronomist. In his teens he decided to become a writer, and to prepare himself for this profession, he took courses in language and literature at the Leningrad Pedagogical Institute. He began by contributing verse and prose to the juvenile press. At the same time he was composing poems not meant for the young. These made up his first two books of verse, published in 1929 and 1937, respectively. There was much about certain inclusions that failed to meet with official approval. In 1937 Zabolotzky disappeared from the scene. His autobiography, appended to the posthumous selection from his verse, ends abruptly with that year. In his supplementary note the editor of the book writes with something less than candor: "From 1938 on, Zabolotzky was in the Far East and the Altai region, in Karaganda [a coal-mining center in Kazakhstan]." It is believed that during those years the poet was confined to concentration camps. In 1946 he returned to Moscow and literature. Some of the poems dating from that year and the one following appear to echo his camp experiences. Far from suggesting even a shadow of resentment, they breathe enthusiasm for the mighty construction efforts promoted by the Government. To the end he was writing lyrics—which were to appear in a selection published in 1960—and working on a translation of classical Georgian poetry, which was published in 1958 and won him the Order of the Red Banner of Labor. He lived in the capital, except for his last two years, which he spent at Tarusa, a small town not far from Moscow, which for nearly a century has been the Russian Barbizon, haunted not only by painters but also by scholars and writers.

ZENKEVICH, MIKHAIL ALEKSANDROVICH, born in 1891 into a schoolteacher's family, received a university education. He began to publish verse at an early age, his first collection of poems appearing when he was twenty-one. A member of the Acmeist group, he adjusted himself to Soviet conditions without giving up his distinctive style, but for the last thirty years or so he has been active chiefly as an editor and as a translator of verse. In 1947 he brought out an anthology of American poems translated into Russian.

ZHUKOVSKY, VASILY ANDREYEVICH, 1783–1852, was the illegitimate son of an aged country squire and a Turkish woman taken captive by one of his serfs and presented to him as a war trophy. Adopted by his godfather, the boy attended a school for the nobility, and afterward continued to enlarge his knowledge of history and especially of the Western languages and literatures. When Napoleon invaded Russia, he joined the army as a volunteer, but soon retired from the service. He was then already famous as the author of sentimental ballads and patriotic poems and as a translator of German and English verse. For nearly a quarter of a century he was a tutor to royalty, and he took advantage of his high connections to intercede in behalf of erring men of letters, such as Pushkin, and to alleviate the lot of political prisoners. He continued to turn out many translations and adaptations, and a little original verse. At the age of fifty-eight he married an eighteen-year-old German girl and went to live in Germany. In his last years he produced, among other translations, an admirable version, at second hand—he had no Greek—of the entire *Odyssey* and of a part of *The Iliad*.

INDEX OF AUTHORS

INDEX OF TITLES

AVRAHM YARMOLINSKY was born in Russia in 1890 and went to school in Kishinyov. He was further educated at the University of Neuchâtel, Switzerland, and in 1913 came to this country, where he received his A.B. from the College of the City of New York (1916) and his Ph.D. from Columbia University (1921). From 1918 to 1955 he was Chief of the Slavonic Division of the New York Public Library. Mr. Yarmolinsky has written many books on all phases of Russian literature and civilization and has prepared American editions of almost all the great Russian writers. His most recent works are RUSSIANS THEN AND NOW *(1962) and* A RUSSIAN'S AMERICAN DREAM *(1965).*

BABETTE DEUTSCH, a native New Yorker, is the author of nine collections of poems, as well as works of criticism, and other books. She is known on both sides of the ocean as the translator of Rilke's BOOK OF HOURS *and of Pushkin's* EUGENE ONEGIN. *She is a member of the National Institute of Arts and Letters, and lectures on poetry at Columbia University. Her most recent books are* POETRY IN OUR TIME, THE POETRY HANDBOOK, *and* COLLECTED POEMS, 1919-1962.